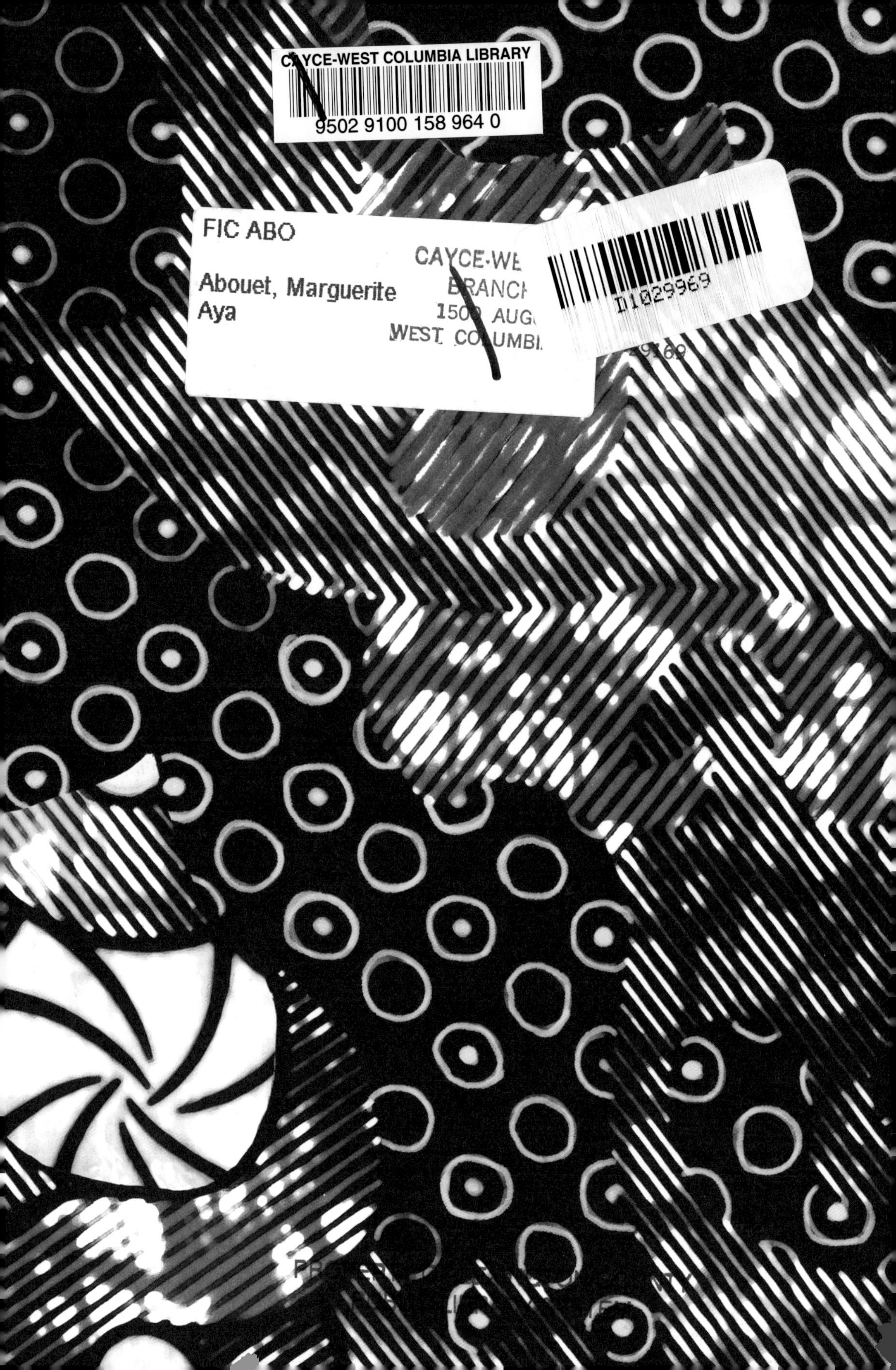

MARGUERITE ABOUET   CLÉMENT OUBRERIE

AYA

The Secrets Come Out

DRAWN & QUARTERLY
MONTREAL

The first two volumes of this series are also available:
AYA (ISBN 978-1-894937-90-0)
AYA OF YOP CITY (ISBN 978-1-897299-41-8)

A big thank you goes to Agathe Faucompré for her invaluable help.

*Thanks also to all of our friends for their wonderful photos and/or general help:
Nina and Patricia N'Gbandjui, Nicolas Merki, Reynold Leclerq, Christian Ronget,
Antoine Delesvaux and Olivier Vitrat.*

Marguerite Abouet and Clément Oubrerie

Translation by Helge Dascher.
Translation assistance by Dag Dascher. Once again, thank you to Herman Koutouan for sharing his knowledge of Ivorian culture.
Lettering font by Rich Tomasso and John Kuramoto, based on hand-lettered text by Tom Devlin in AYA volume 1.

Previously published in French by Gallimard Jeunesse (ISBN 9782070615438) as part of the Joann Sfar edited Bayou collection.

Library and Archives Canada Cataloguing in Publication
Abouet, Marguerite, 1971–
Aya : The Secrets Come Out / Marguerite Abouet, Clément Oubrerie ; [translated by] Helge Dascher.
Sequel to: Aya of Yop City.
ISBN 978-1-897299-79-1
1. Teenage girls--Côte d'Ivoire--Comic books, strips, etc.
2. Côte d'Ivoire--Comic books, strips, etc.
I. Oubrerie, Clément II. Dascher, Helge, 1965- III. Title.
PN6790.I93A26 2009 741.5'96668 C2009-901575-7

Drawn & Quarterly, Post Office Box 48056, Montreal, Quebec, Canada H2V 4S8
www.drawnandquarterly.com

First hardcover edition: August 2009.
Printed in Singapore.
10 9 8 7 6 5 4 3 2 1

Distributed in the USA by:
Farrar, Straus and Giroux
18 West 18th Street, New York, NY 10011
Orders: 888.330.8477

Distributed in Canada by:
Raincoast Books
9050 Shaughnessy Street, Vancouver, BC V6P 6E5
Orders: 800.663.5714

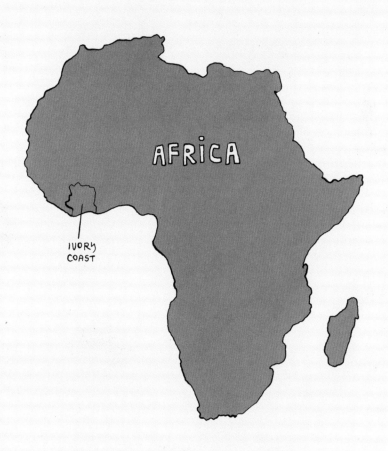

AFRICA

IVORY
COAST

The characters

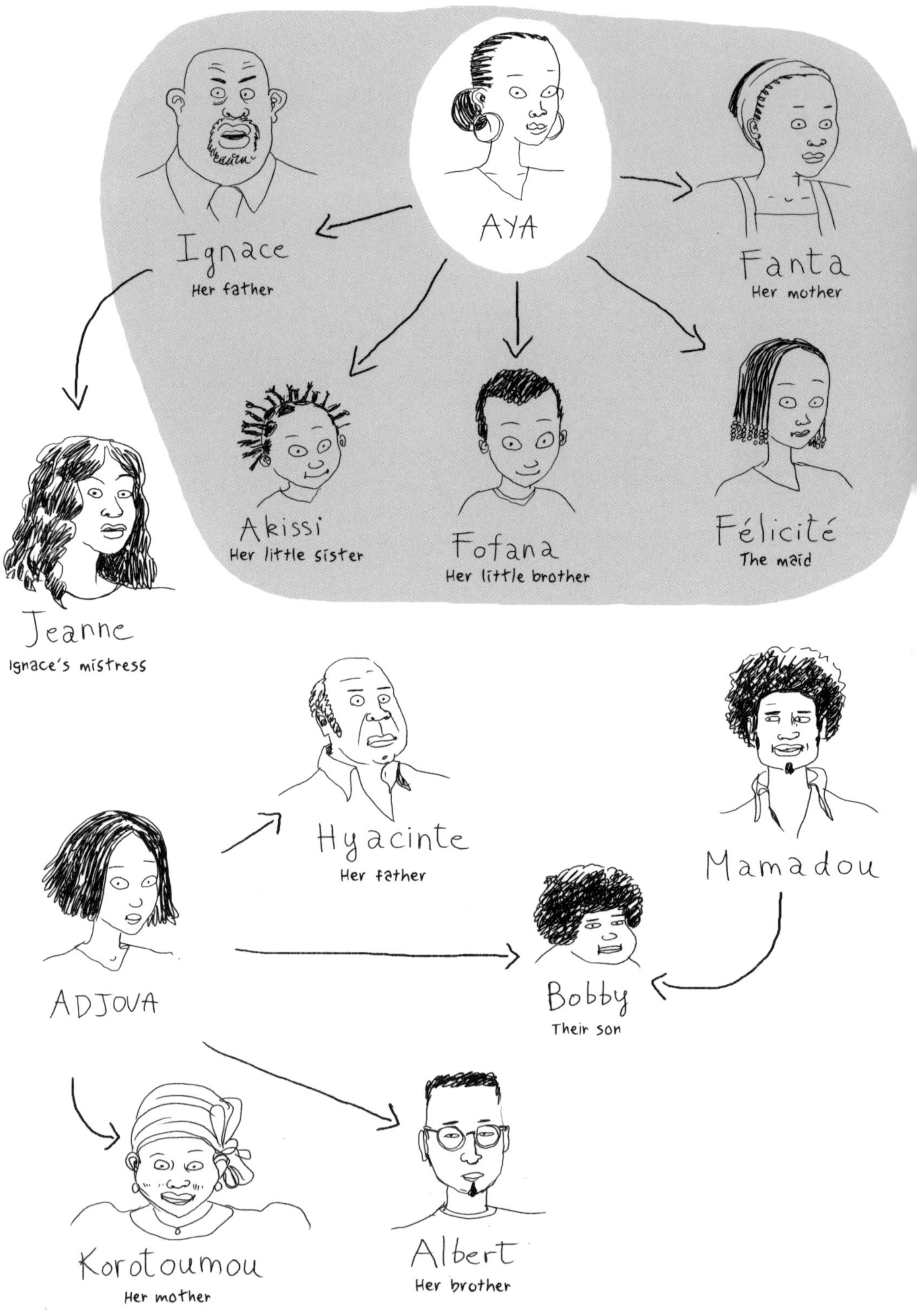
AYA
Ignace
Her father
Fanta
Her mother
Akissi
Her little sister
Fofana
Her little brother
Félicité
The maid
Jeanne
Ignace's mistress
Hyacinte
Her father
Mamadou
ADJOVA
Bobby
Their son
Korotoumou
Her mother
Albert
Her brother

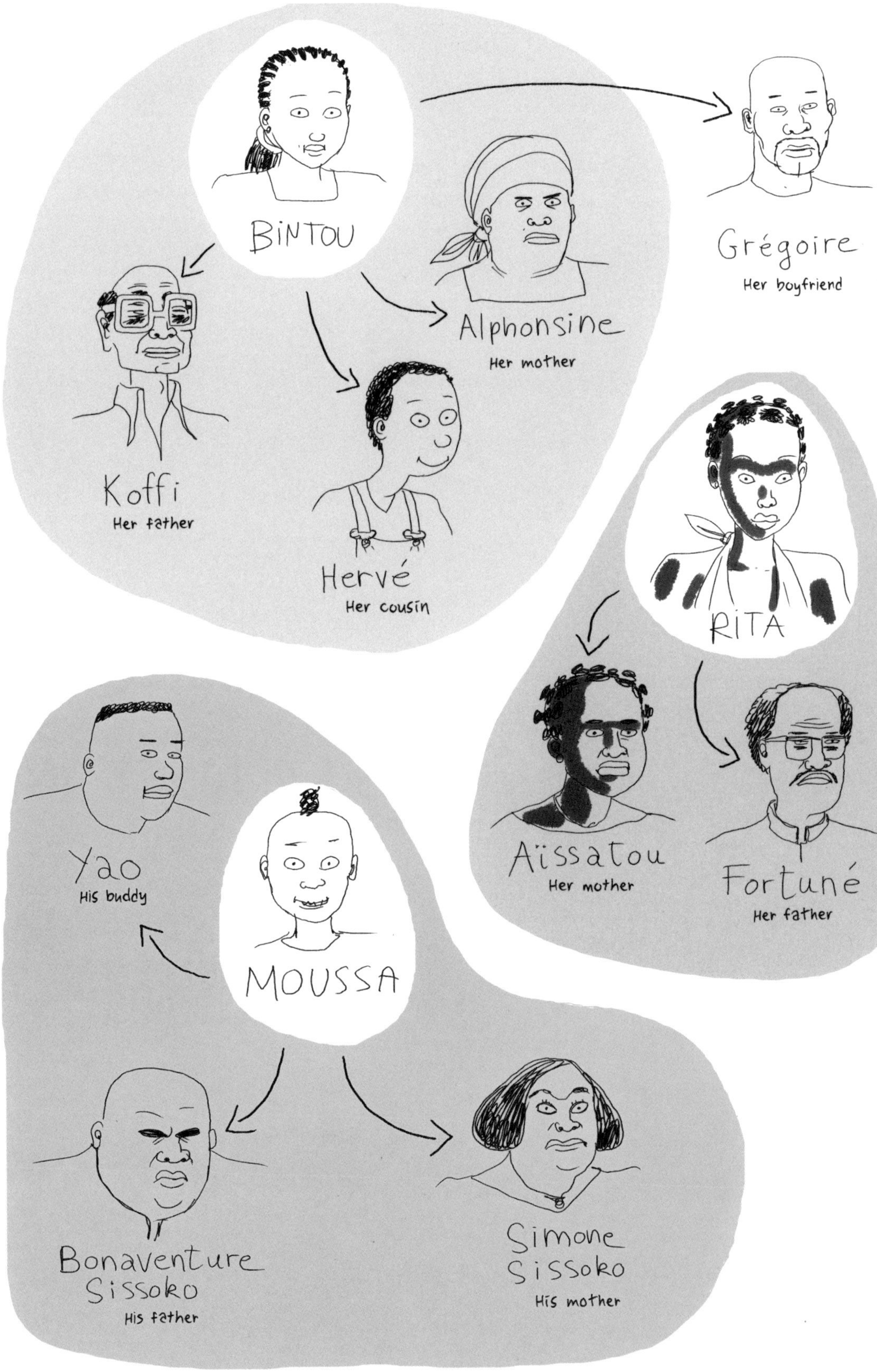
BINTOU
Grégoire
Her boyfriend
Alphonsine
Her mother
Koffi
Her father
Hervé
Her cousin
RITA
Aïssatou
Her mother
Fortuné
Her father
MOUSSA
Yao
His buddy
Bonaventure Sissoko
His father
Simone Sissoko
His mother

For Jules

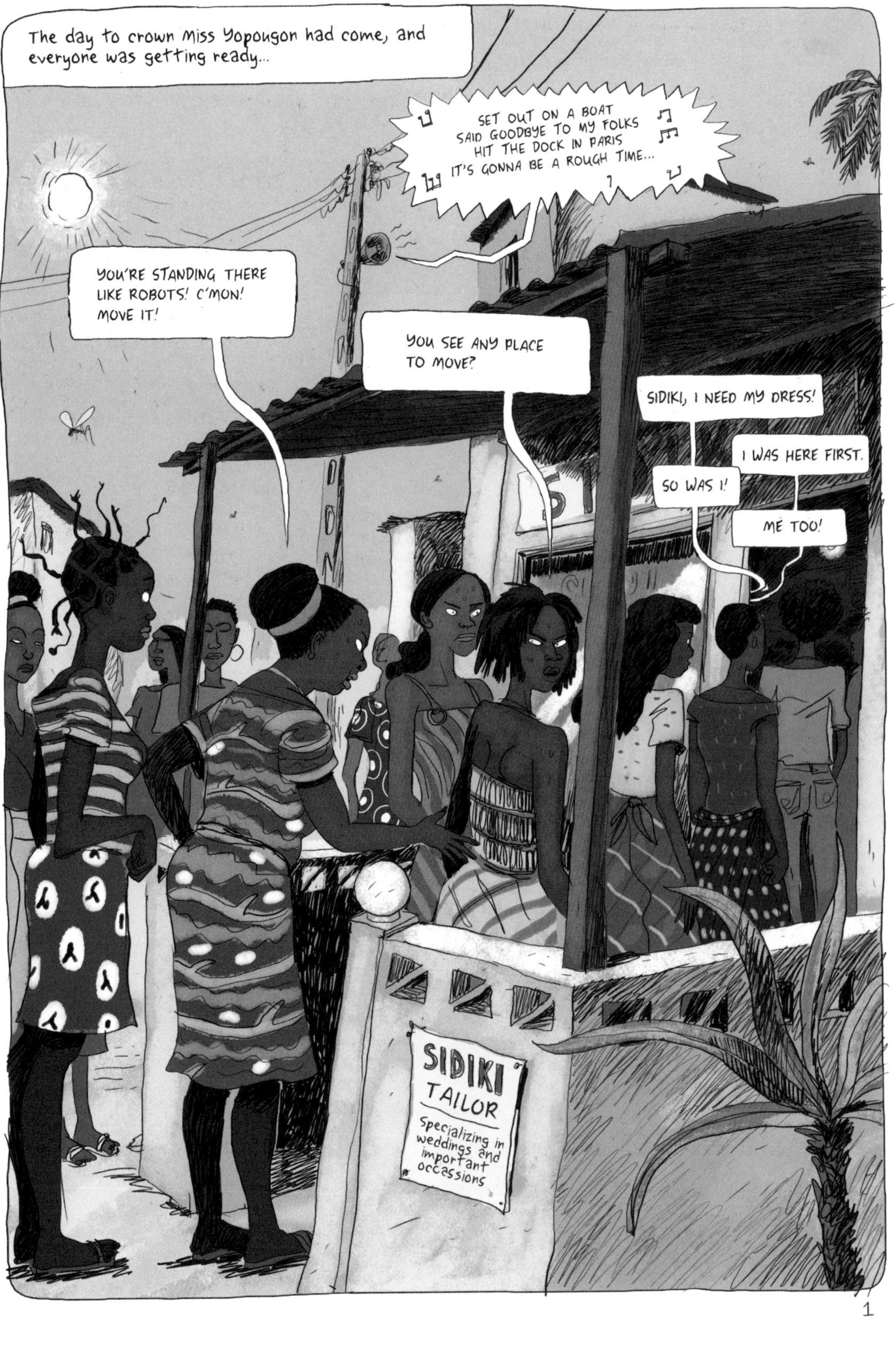
The day to crown Miss Yopougon had come, and everyone was getting ready...
SET OUT ON A BOAT
SAID GOODBYE TO MY FOLKS
HIT THE DOCK IN PARIS
IT'S GONNA BE A ROUGH TIME...
YOU'RE STANDING THERE LIKE ROBOTS! C'MON! MOVE IT!
YOU SEE ANY PLACE TO MOVE?
SIDIKI, I NEED MY DRESS!
I WAS HERE FIRST.
SO WAS I!
ME TOO!
SIDIKI
TAILOR
Specializing in weddings and important occasions

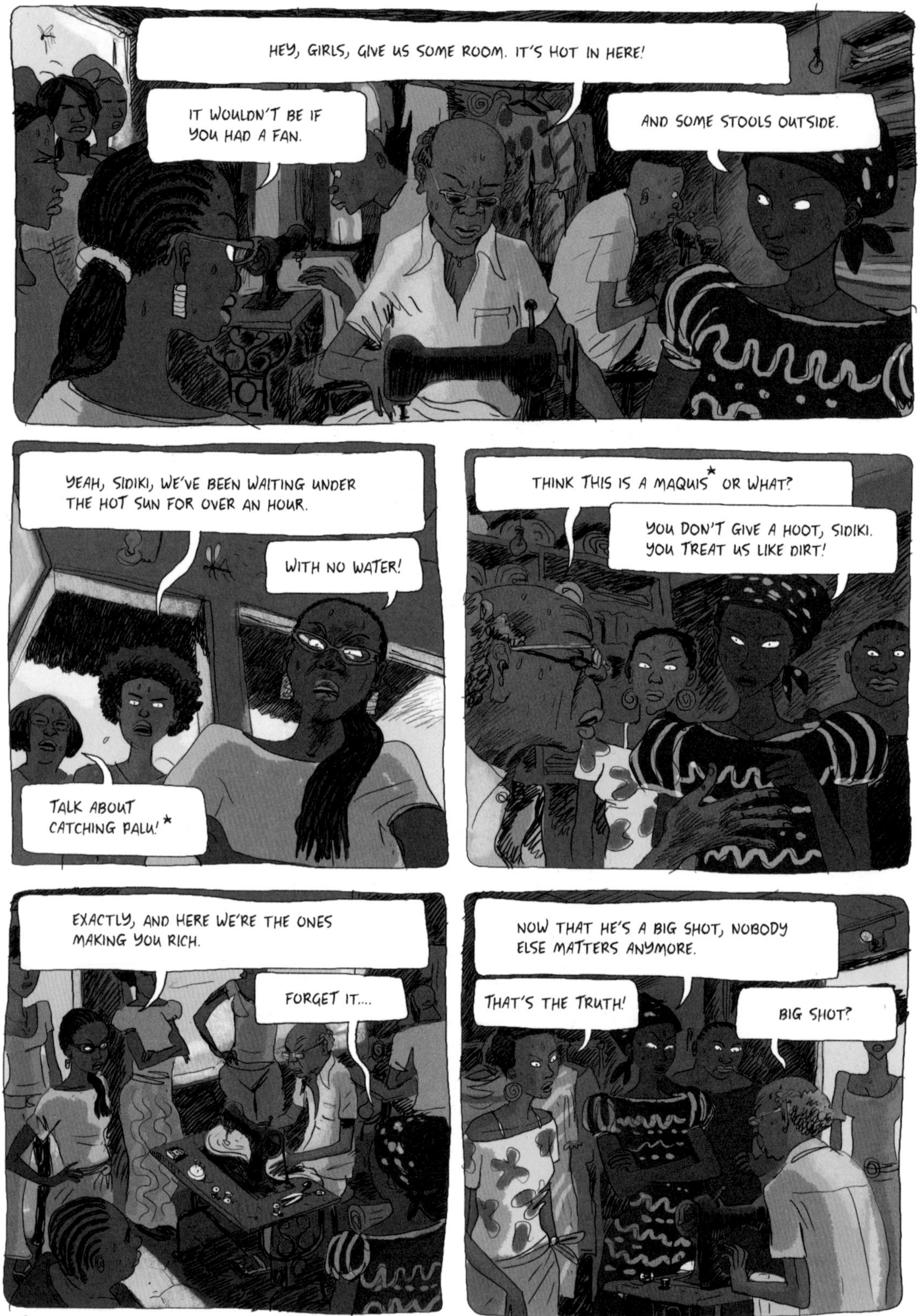
HEY, GIRLS, GIVE US SOME ROOM. IT'S HOT IN HERE!
IT WOULDN'T BE IF YOU HAD A FAN.
AND SOME STOOLS OUTSIDE.
YEAH, SIDIKI, WE'VE BEEN WAITING UNDER THE HOT SUN FOR OVER AN HOUR.
WITH NO WATER!
TALK ABOUT CATCHING PALU!*
THINK THIS IS A MAQUIS* OR WHAT?
YOU DON'T GIVE A HOOT, SIDIKI. YOU TREAT US LIKE DIRT!
EXACTLY, AND HERE WE'RE THE ONES MAKING YOU RICH.
FORGET IT....
NOW THAT HE'S A BIG SHOT, NOBODY ELSE MATTERS ANYMORE.
THAT'S THE TRUTH!
BIG SHOT?

* Friends, check out the glossary at the back of the book for definitions of words we use in the Ivory Coast.

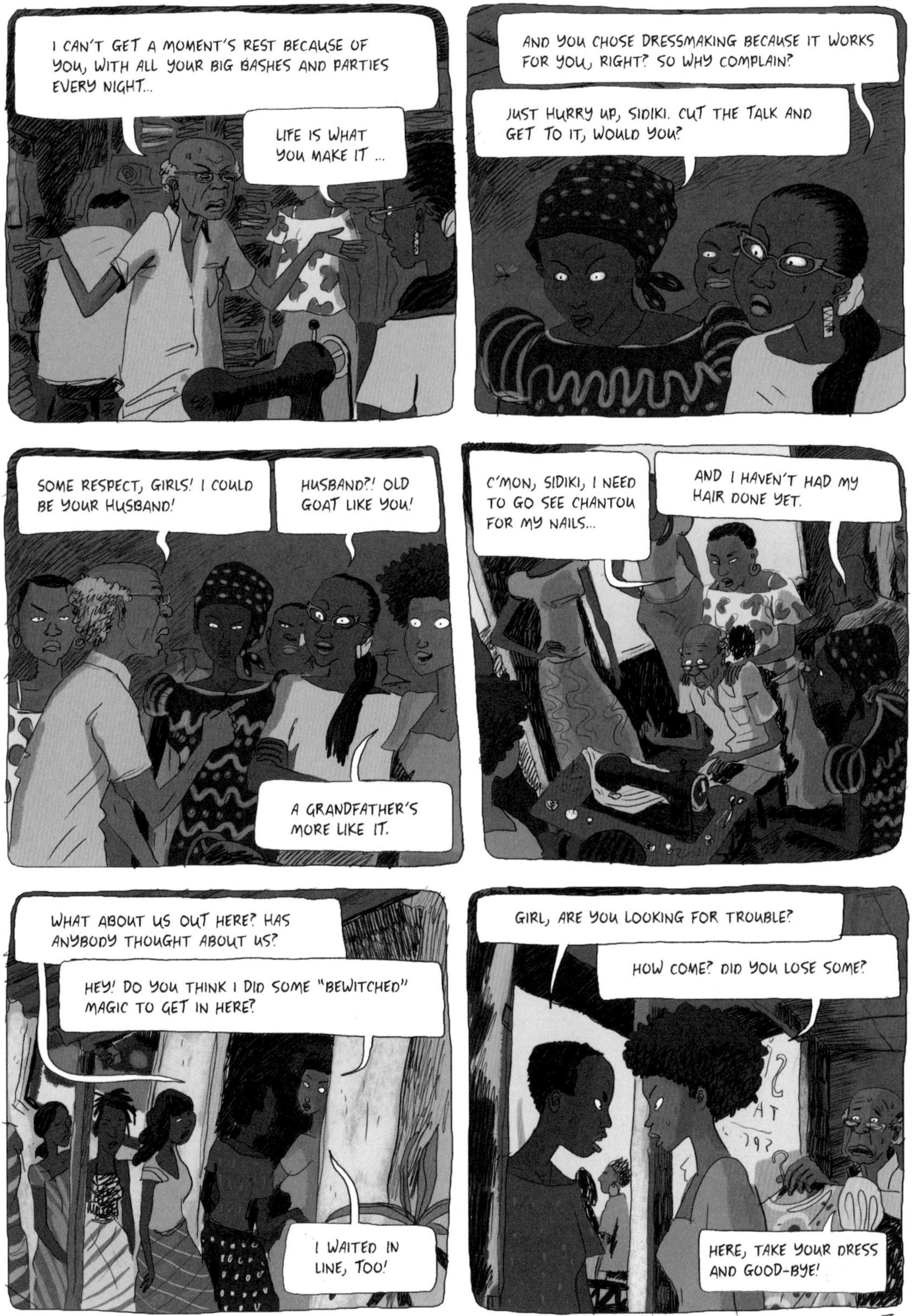
I CAN'T GET A MOMENT'S REST BECAUSE OF YOU, WITH ALL YOUR BIG BASHES AND PARTIES EVERY NIGHT...
LIFE IS WHAT YOU MAKE IT ...
AND YOU CHOSE DRESSMAKING BECAUSE IT WORKS FOR YOU, RIGHT? SO WHY COMPLAIN?
JUST HURRY UP, SIDIKI. CUT THE TALK AND GET TO IT, WOULD YOU?
SOME RESPECT, GIRLS! I COULD BE YOUR HUSBAND!
HUSBAND?! OLD GOAT LIKE YOU!
A GRANDFATHER'S MORE LIKE IT.
C'MON, SIDIKI, I NEED TO GO SEE CHANTOU FOR MY NAILS...
AND I HAVEN'T HAD MY HAIR DONE YET.
WHAT ABOUT US OUT HERE? HAS ANYBODY THOUGHT ABOUT US?
HEY! DO YOU THINK I DID SOME "BEWITCHED" MAGIC TO GET IN HERE?
I WAITED IN LINE, TOO!
GIRL, ARE YOU LOOKING FOR TROUBLE?
HOW COME? DID YOU LOSE SOME?
HERE, TAKE YOUR DRESS AND GOOD-BYE!

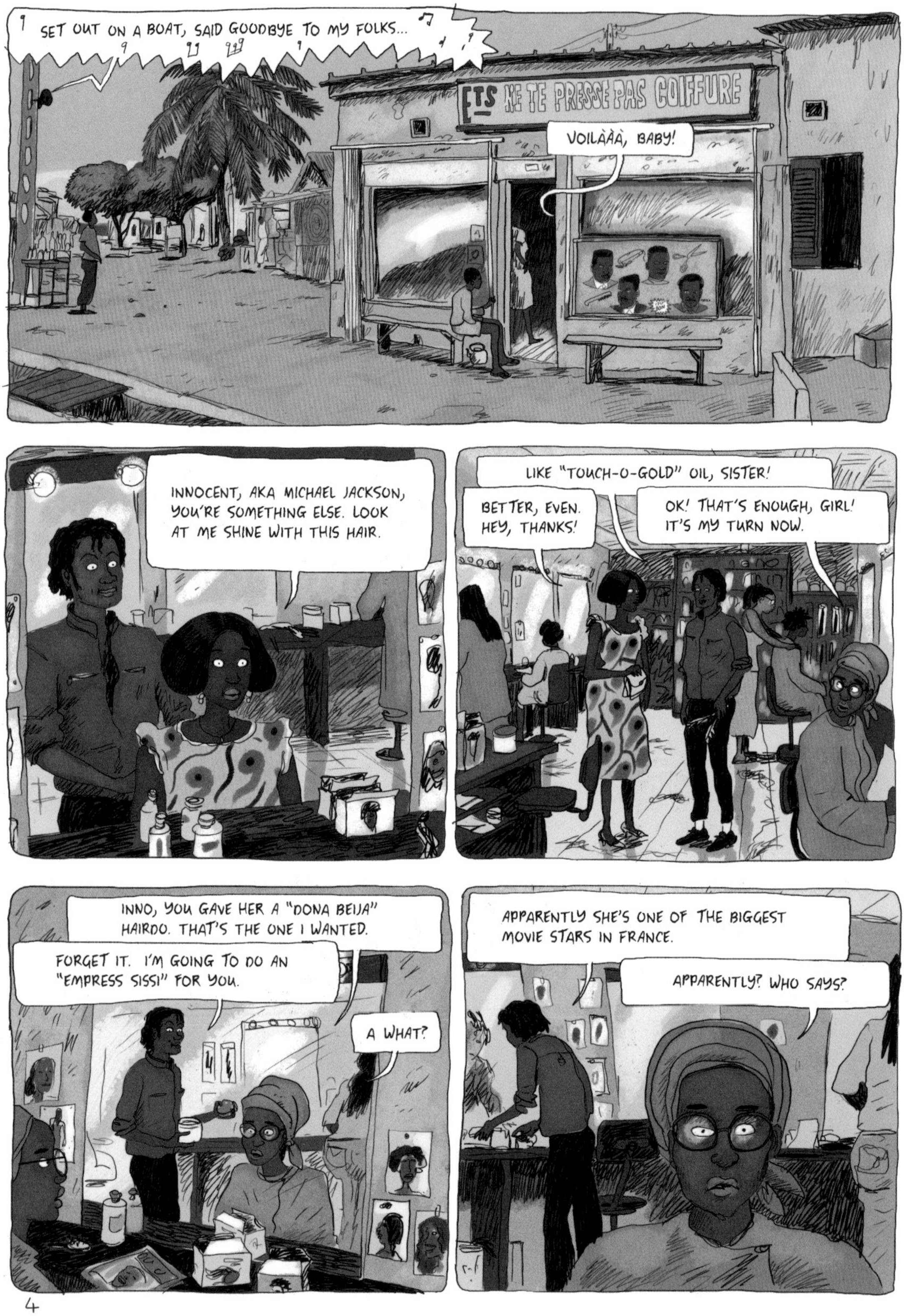
SET OUT ON A BOAT, SAID GOODBYE TO MY FOLKS...
ETS NE TE PRESSE PAS COIFFURE
VOILÀÀÀ, BABY!
INNOCENT, AKA MICHAEL JACKSON, YOU'RE SOMETHING ELSE. LOOK AT ME SHINE WITH THIS HAIR.
LIKE "TOUCH-O-GOLD" OIL, SISTER!
BETTER, EVEN. HEY, THANKS!
OK! THAT'S ENOUGH, GIRL! IT'S MY TURN NOW.
INNO, YOU GAVE HER A "DONA BEIJA" HAIRDO. THAT'S THE ONE I WANTED.
FORGET IT. I'M GOING TO DO AN "EMPRESS SISSI" FOR YOU.
A WHAT?
APPARENTLY SHE'S ONE OF THE BIGGEST MOVIE STARS IN FRANCE.
APPARENTLY? WHO SAYS?

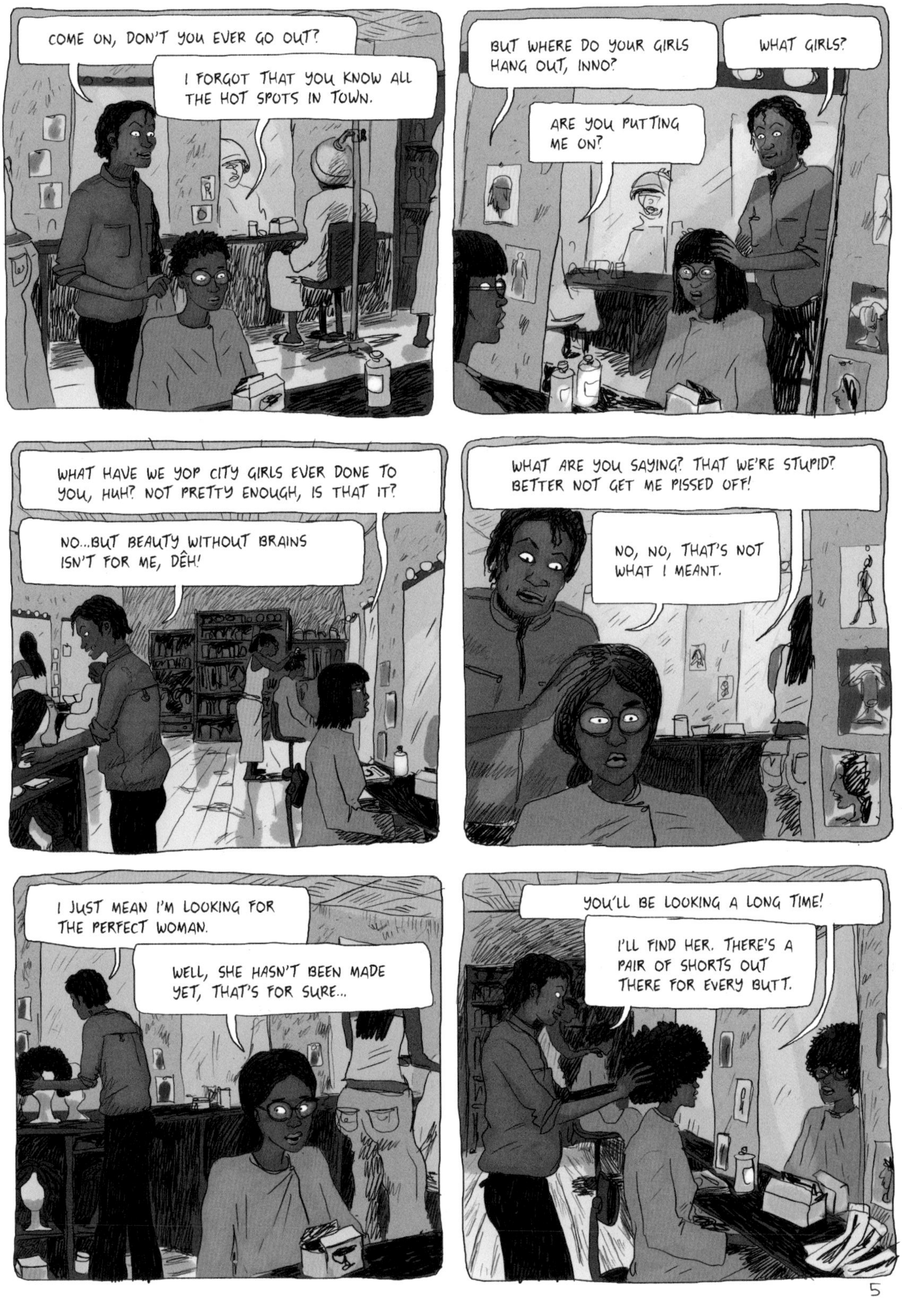
COME ON, DON'T YOU EVER GO OUT?
I FORGOT THAT YOU KNOW ALL THE HOT SPOTS IN TOWN.
BUT WHERE DO YOUR GIRLS HANG OUT, INNO?
WHAT GIRLS?
ARE YOU PUTTING ME ON?
WHAT HAVE WE YOP CITY GIRLS EVER DONE TO YOU, HUH? NOT PRETTY ENOUGH, IS THAT IT?
NO...BUT BEAUTY WITHOUT BRAINS ISN'T FOR ME, DÊH!
WHAT ARE YOU SAYING? THAT WE'RE STUPID? BETTER NOT GET ME PISSED OFF!
NO, NO, THAT'S NOT WHAT I MEANT.
I JUST MEAN I'M LOOKING FOR THE PERFECT WOMAN.
WELL, SHE HASN'T BEEN MADE YET, THAT'S FOR SURE...
YOU'LL BE LOOKING A LONG TIME!
I'LL FIND HER. THERE'S A PAIR OF SHORTS OUT THERE FOR EVERY BUTT.

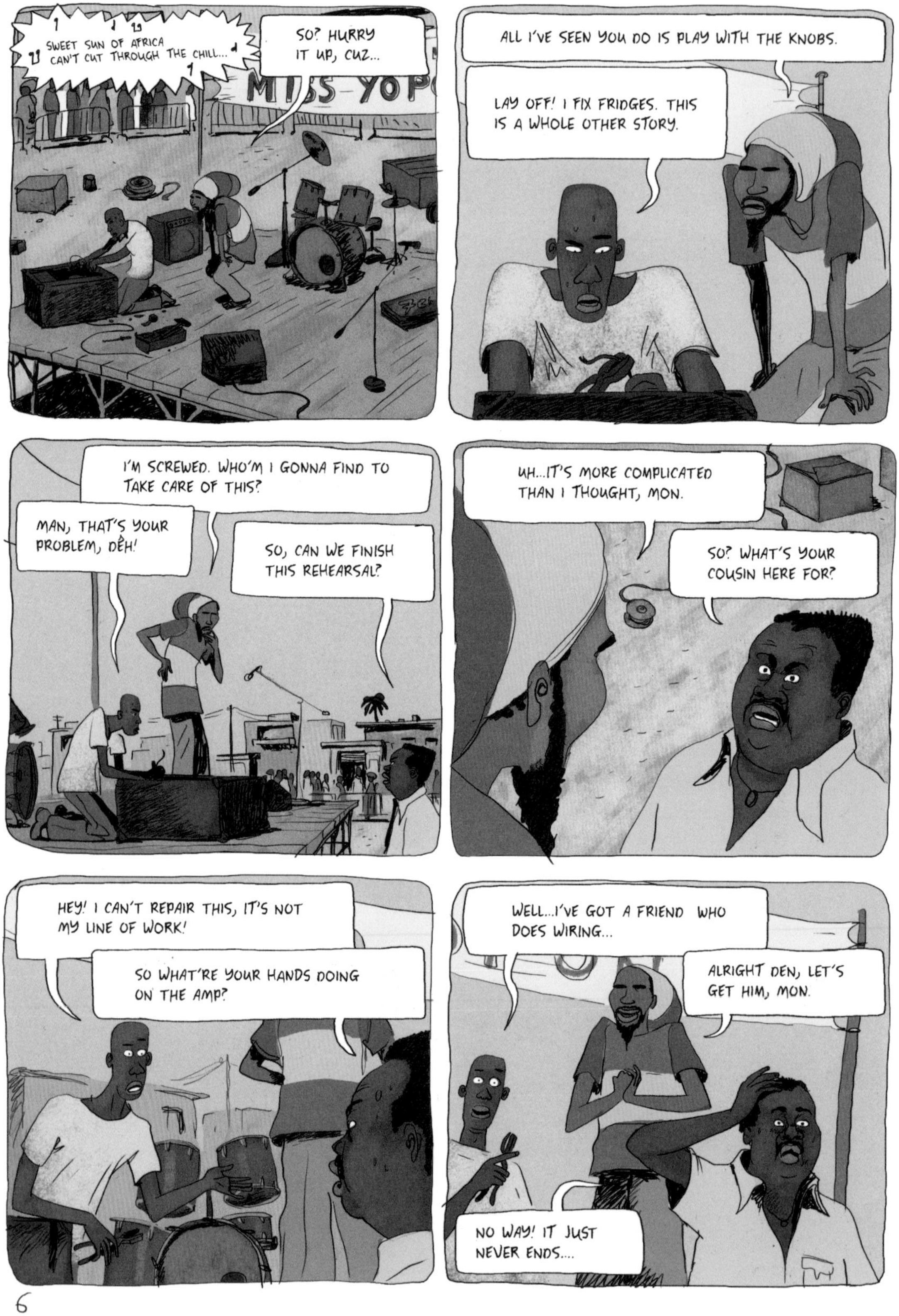
SWEET SUN OF AFRICA
CAN'T CUT THROUGH THE CHILL...
SO? HURRY IT UP, CUZ...
MISS YOPO
ALL I'VE SEEN YOU DO IS PLAY WITH THE KNOBS.
LAY OFF! I FIX FRIDGES. THIS IS A WHOLE OTHER STORY.
I'M SCREWED. WHO'M I GONNA FIND TO TAKE CARE OF THIS?
MAN, THAT'S YOUR PROBLEM, DÊH!
SO, CAN WE FINISH THIS REHEARSAL?
UH...IT'S MORE COMPLICATED THAN I THOUGHT, MON.
SO? WHAT'S YOUR COUSIN HERE FOR?
HEY! I CAN'T REPAIR THIS, IT'S NOT MY LINE OF WORK!
SO WHAT'RE YOUR HANDS DOING ON THE AMP?
WELL...I'VE GOT A FRIEND WHO DOES WIRING...
ALRIGHT DEN, LET'S GET HIM, MON.
NO WAY! IT JUST NEVER ENDS....

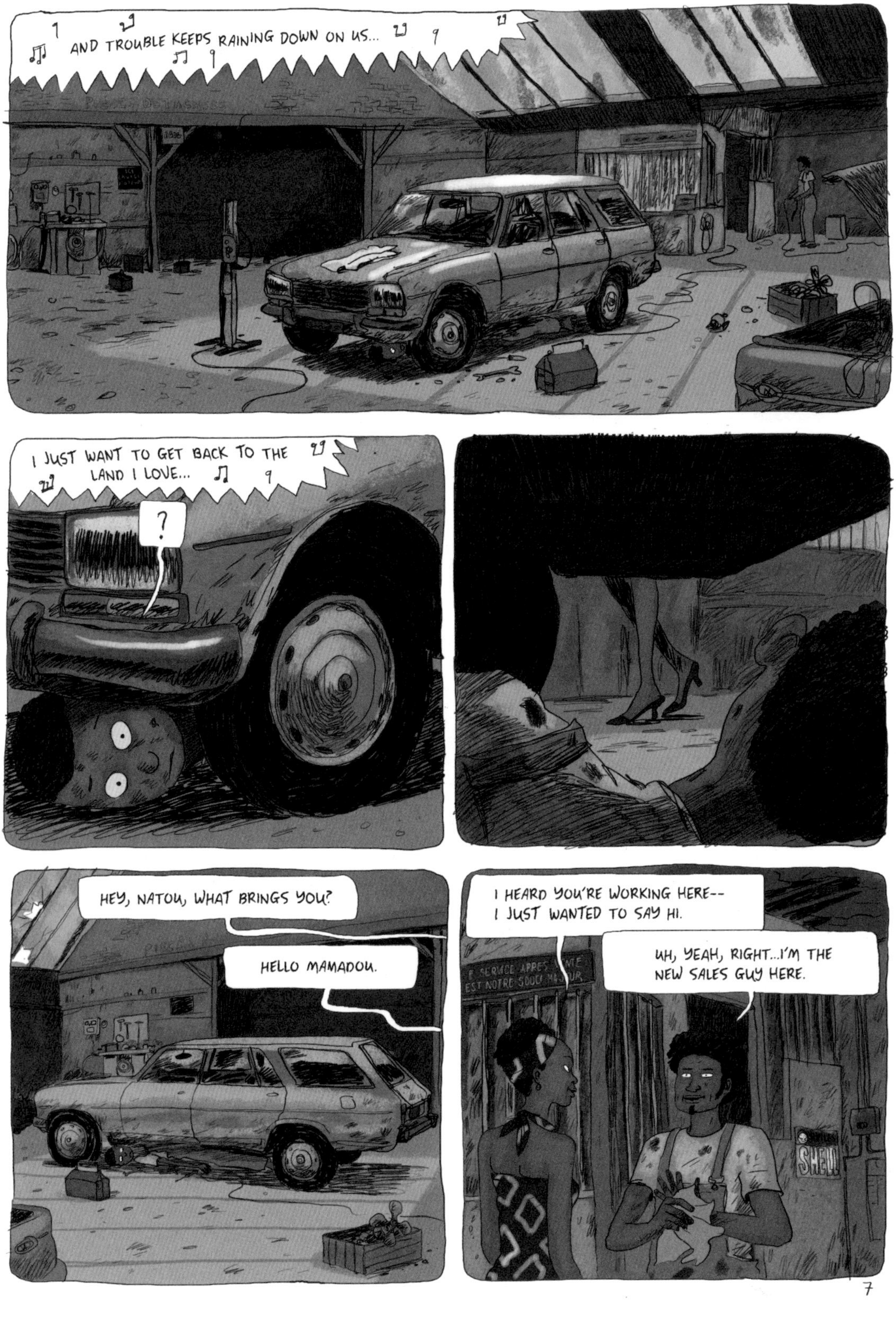
AND TROUBLE KEEPS RAINING DOWN ON US...
I JUST WANT TO GET BACK TO THE LAND I LOVE...
?
HEY, NATOU, WHAT BRINGS YOU?
HELLO MAMADOU.
I HEARD YOU'RE WORKING HERE-- I JUST WANTED TO SAY HI.
UH, YEAH, RIGHT...I'M THE NEW SALES GUY HERE.
SHELL

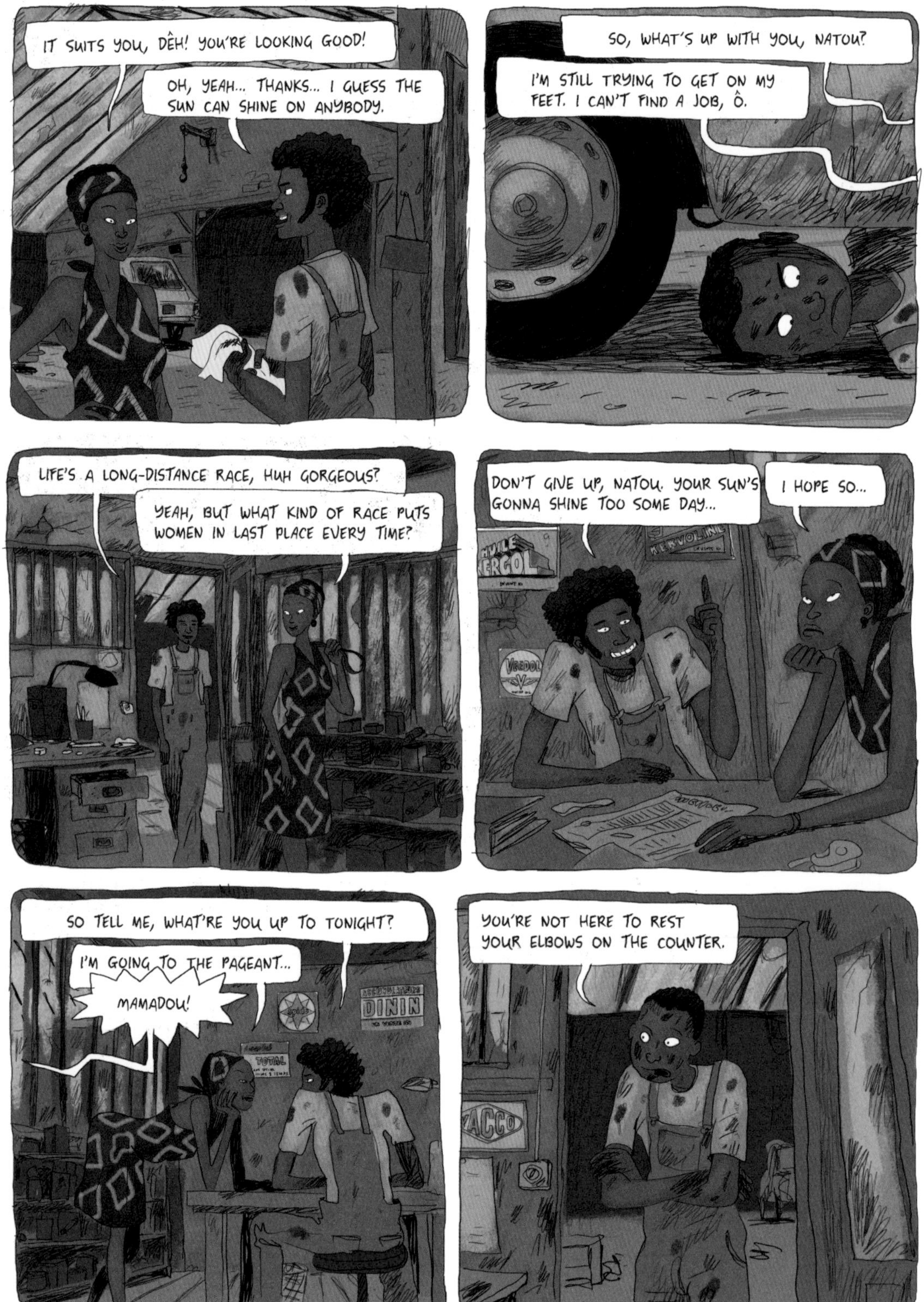
IT SUITS YOU, DÊH! YOU'RE LOOKING GOOD!
OH, YEAH... THANKS... I GUESS THE SUN CAN SHINE ON ANYBODY.
SO, WHAT'S UP WITH YOU, NATOU?
I'M STILL TRYING TO GET ON MY FEET. I CAN'T FIND A JOB, Ô.
LIFE'S A LONG-DISTANCE RACE, HUH GORGEOUS?
YEAH, BUT WHAT KIND OF RACE PUTS WOMEN IN LAST PLACE EVERY TIME?
DON'T GIVE UP, NATOU. YOUR SUN'S GONNA SHINE TOO SOME DAY...
I HOPE SO...
VEEDOL
SO TELL ME, WHAT'RE YOU UP TO TONIGHT?
I'M GOING TO THE PAGEANT...
MAMADOU!
DININ
TOTAL
YOU'RE NOT HERE TO REST YOUR ELBOWS ON THE COUNTER.

9

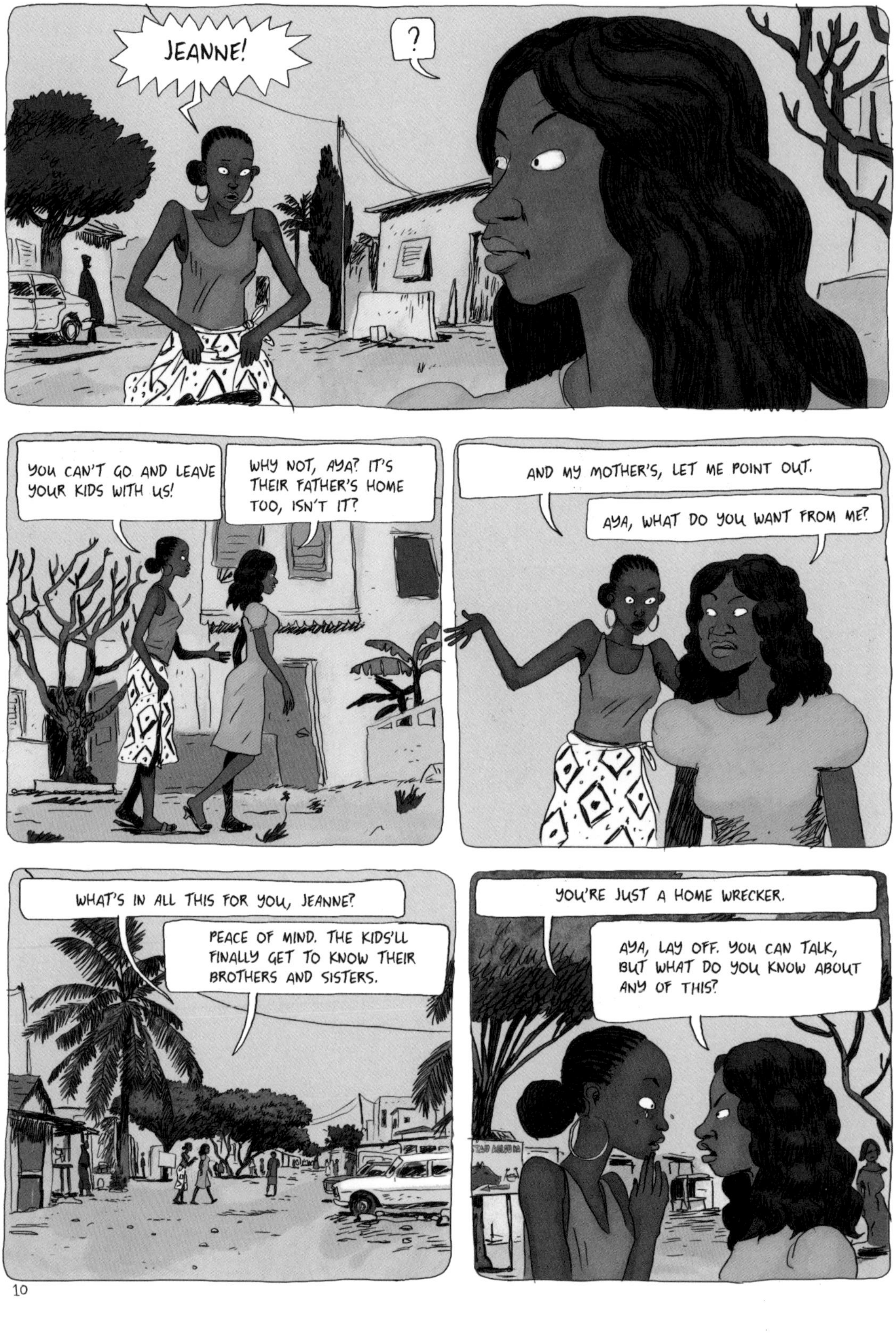
JEANNE!
?
YOU CAN'T GO AND LEAVE YOUR KIDS WITH US!
WHY NOT, AYA? IT'S THEIR FATHER'S HOME TOO, ISN'T IT?
AND MY MOTHER'S, LET ME POINT OUT.
AYA, WHAT DO YOU WANT FROM ME?
WHAT'S IN ALL THIS FOR YOU, JEANNE?
PEACE OF MIND. THE KIDS'LL FINALLY GET TO KNOW THEIR BROTHERS AND SISTERS.
YOU'RE JUST A HOME WRECKER.
AYA, LAY OFF. YOU CAN TALK, BUT WHAT DO YOU KNOW ABOUT ANY OF THIS?

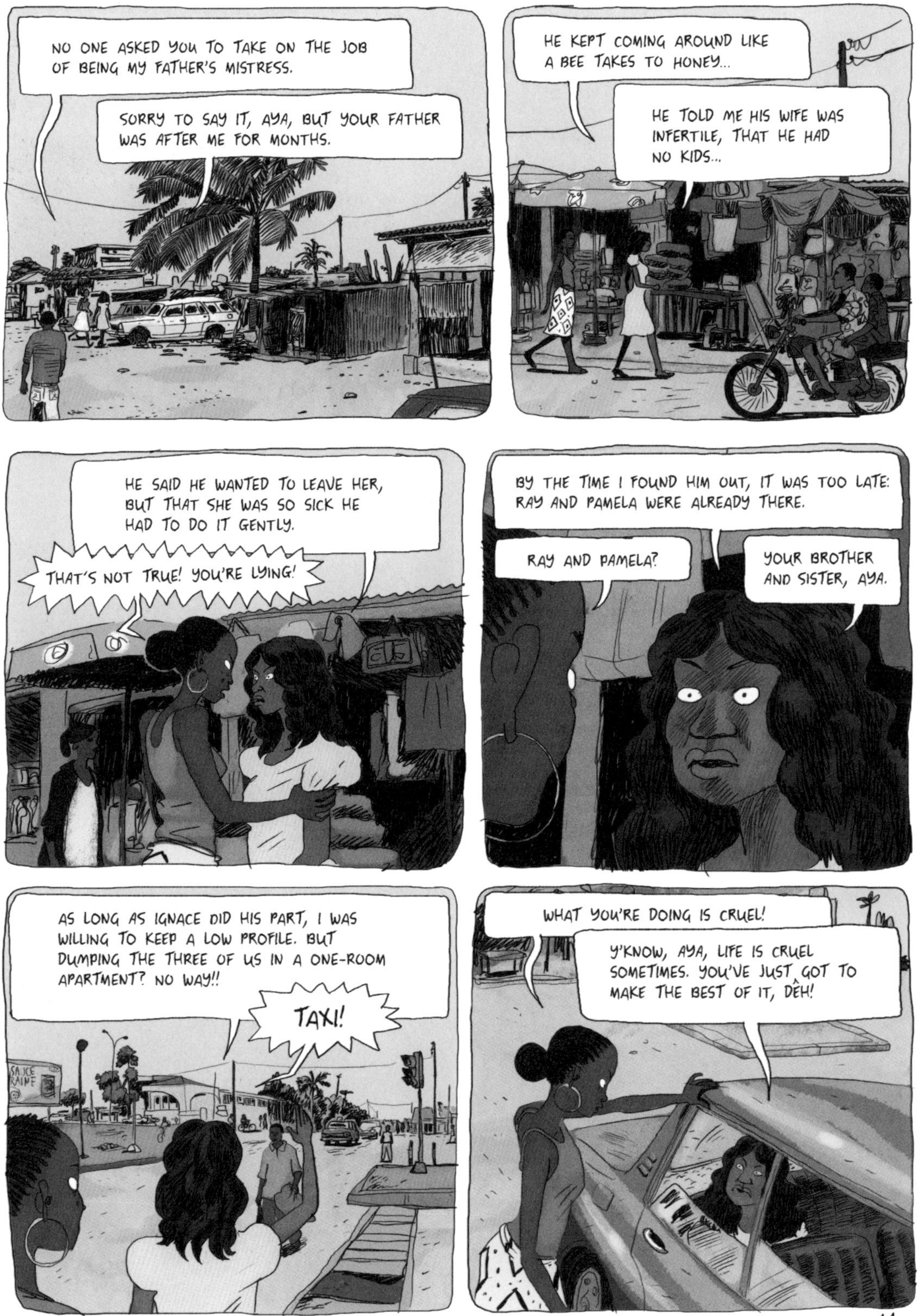
NO ONE ASKED YOU TO TAKE ON THE JOB OF BEING MY FATHER'S MISTRESS.
SORRY TO SAY IT, AYA, BUT YOUR FATHER WAS AFTER ME FOR MONTHS.
HE KEPT COMING AROUND LIKE A BEE TAKES TO HONEY...
HE TOLD ME HIS WIFE WAS INFERTILE, THAT HE HAD NO KIDS...
HE SAID HE WANTED TO LEAVE HER, BUT THAT SHE WAS SO SICK HE HAD TO DO IT GENTLY.
THAT'S NOT TRUE! YOU'RE LYING!
BY THE TIME I FOUND HIM OUT, IT WAS TOO LATE: RAY AND PAMELA WERE ALREADY THERE.
RAY AND PAMELA?
YOUR BROTHER AND SISTER, AYA.
AS LONG AS IGNACE DID HIS PART, I WAS WILLING TO KEEP A LOW PROFILE. BUT DUMPING THE THREE OF US IN A ONE-ROOM APARTMENT? NO WAY!!
TAXI!
WHAT YOU'RE DOING IS CRUEL!
Y'KNOW, AYA, LIFE IS CRUEL SOMETIMES. YOU'VE JUST GOT TO MAKE THE BEST OF IT, DÊH!

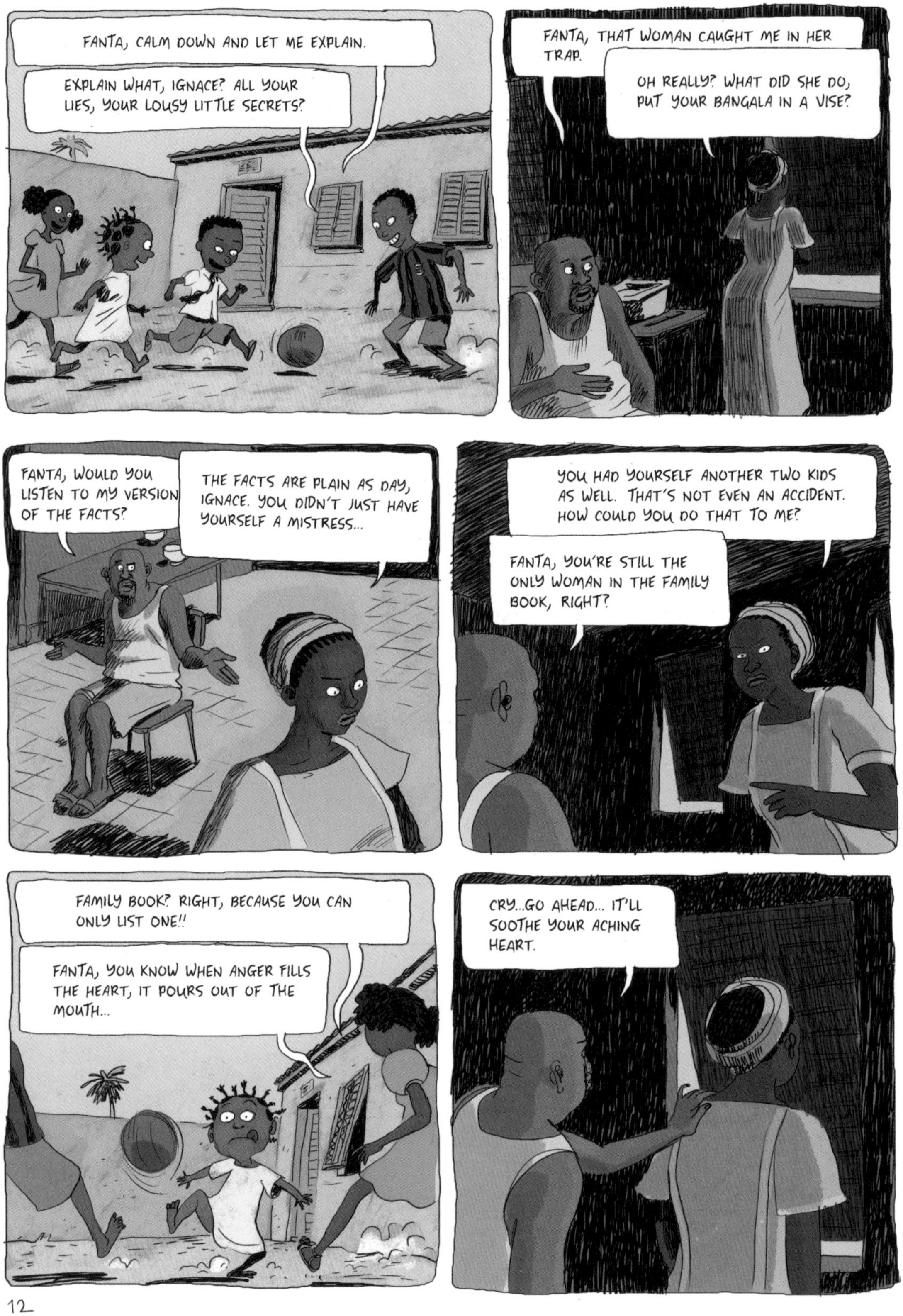
FANTA, CALM DOWN AND LET ME EXPLAIN.
EXPLAIN WHAT, IGNACE? ALL YOUR LIES, YOUR LOUSY LITTLE SECRETS?
FANTA, THAT WOMAN CAUGHT ME IN HER TRAP.
OH REALLY? WHAT DID SHE DO, PUT YOUR BANGALA IN A VISE?
FANTA, WOULD YOU LISTEN TO MY VERSION OF THE FACTS?
THE FACTS ARE PLAIN AS DAY, IGNACE. YOU DIDN'T JUST HAVE YOURSELF A MISTRESS...
YOU HAD YOURSELF ANOTHER TWO KIDS AS WELL. THAT'S NOT EVEN AN ACCIDENT. HOW COULD YOU DO THAT TO ME?
FANTA, YOU'RE STILL THE ONLY WOMAN IN THE FAMILY BOOK, RIGHT?
FAMILY BOOK? RIGHT, BECAUSE YOU CAN ONLY LIST ONE!!
FANTA, YOU KNOW WHEN ANGER FILLS THE HEART, IT POURS OUT OF THE MOUTH...
CRY...GO AHEAD... IT'LL SOOTHE YOUR ACHING HEART.

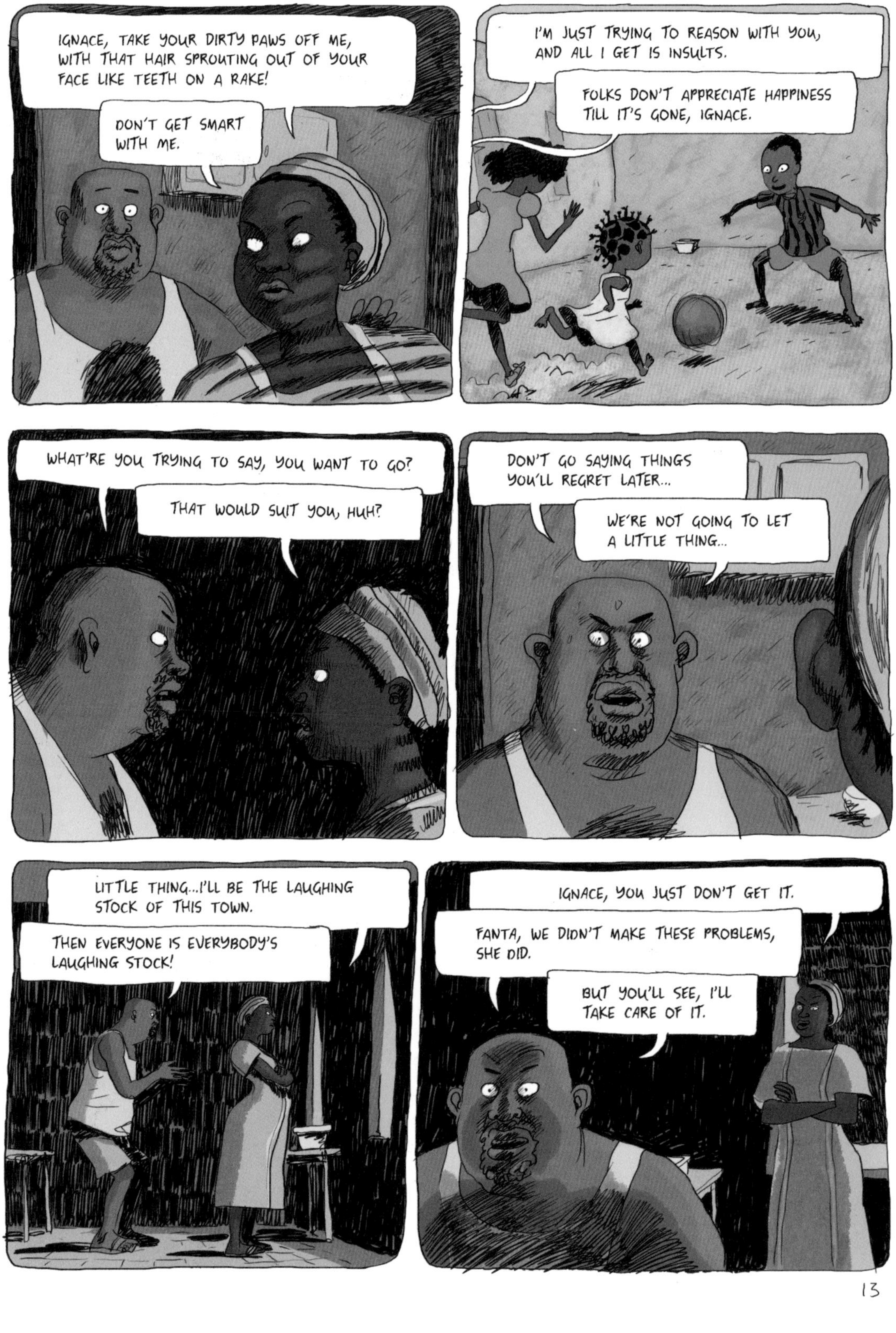
IGNACE, TAKE YOUR DIRTY PAWS OFF ME, WITH THAT HAIR SPROUTING OUT OF YOUR FACE LIKE TEETH ON A RAKE!
DON'T GET SMART WITH ME.
I'M JUST TRYING TO REASON WITH YOU, AND ALL I GET IS INSULTS.
FOLKS DON'T APPRECIATE HAPPINESS TILL IT'S GONE, IGNACE.
WHAT'RE YOU TRYING TO SAY, YOU WANT TO GO?
THAT WOULD SUIT YOU, HUH?
DON'T GO SAYING THINGS YOU'LL REGRET LATER...
WE'RE NOT GOING TO LET A LITTLE THING...
LITTLE THING...I'LL BE THE LAUGHING STOCK OF THIS TOWN.
THEN EVERYONE IS EVERYBODY'S LAUGHING STOCK!
IGNACE, YOU JUST DON'T GET IT.
FANTA, WE DIDN'T MAKE THESE PROBLEMS, SHE DID.
BUT YOU'LL SEE, I'LL TAKE CARE OF IT.

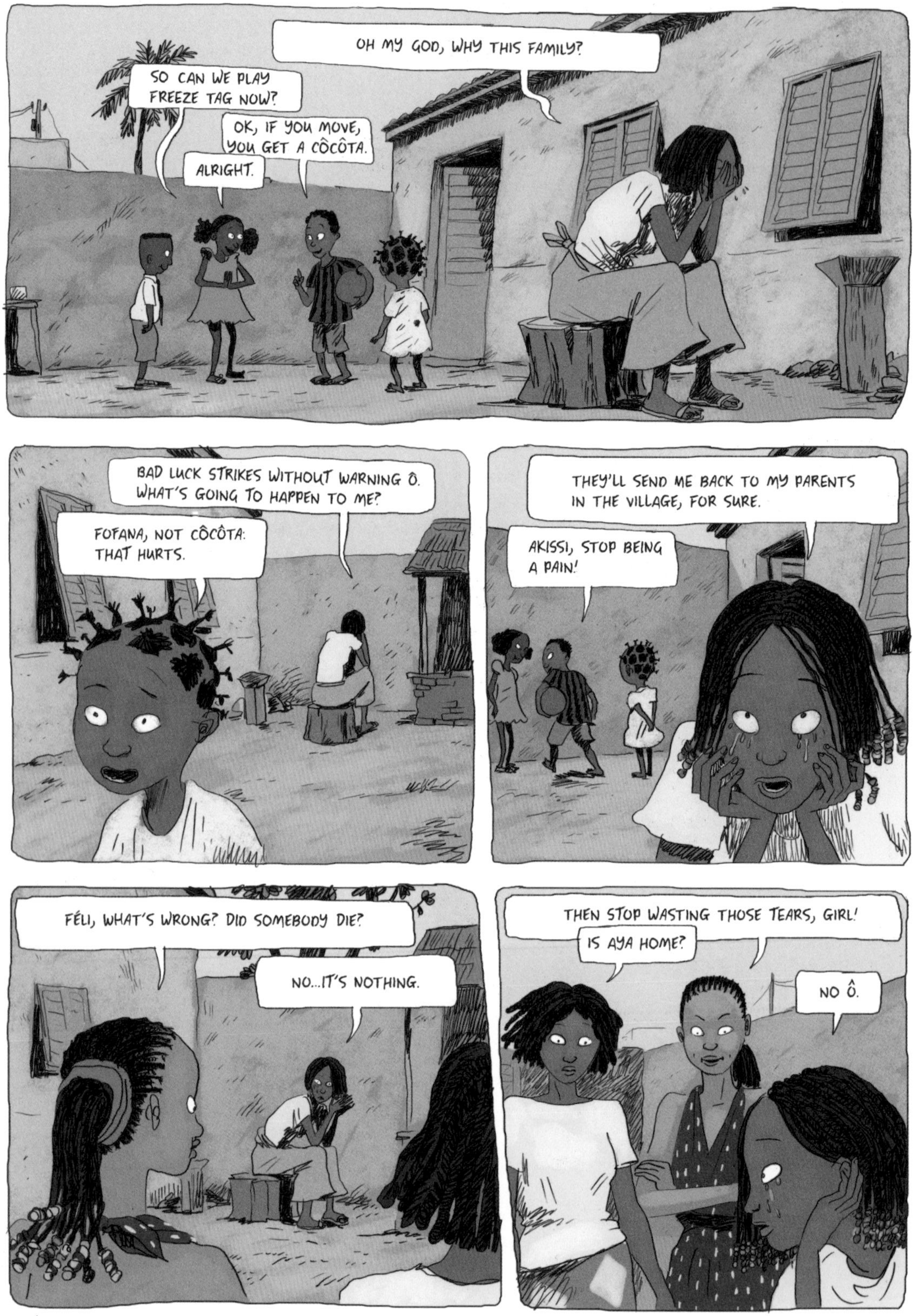
OH MY GOD, WHY THIS FAMILY?
SO CAN WE PLAY FREEZE TAG NOW?
OK, IF YOU MOVE, YOU GET A CÔCÔTA.
ALRIGHT.
BAD LUCK STRIKES WITHOUT WARNING Ô. WHAT'S GOING TO HAPPEN TO ME?
FOFANA, NOT CÔCÔTA: THAT HURTS.
THEY'LL SEND ME BACK TO MY PARENTS IN THE VILLAGE, FOR SURE.
AKISSI, STOP BEING A PAIN!
FÉLI, WHAT'S WRONG? DID SOMEBODY DIE?
NO...IT'S NOTHING.
THEN STOP WASTING THOSE TEARS, GIRL!
IS AYA HOME?
NO Ô.

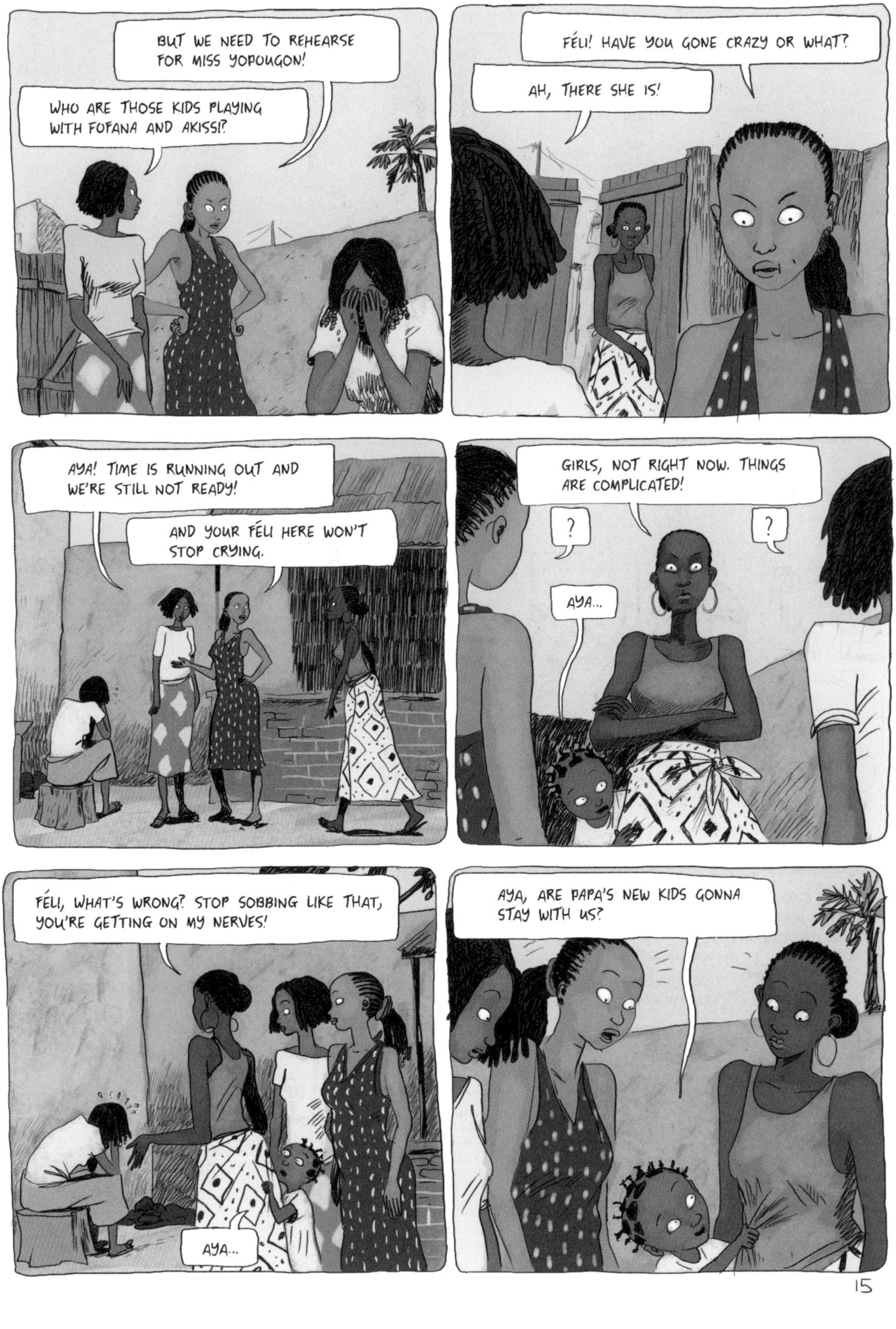
BUT WE NEED TO REHEARSE FOR MISS YOPOUGON!
WHO ARE THOSE KIDS PLAYING WITH FOFANA AND AKISSI?
FÉLI! HAVE YOU GONE CRAZY OR WHAT?
AH, THERE SHE IS!
AYA! TIME IS RUNNING OUT AND WE'RE STILL NOT READY!
AND YOUR FÉLI HERE WON'T STOP CRYING.
GIRLS, NOT RIGHT NOW. THINGS ARE COMPLICATED!
?
?
AYA...
FÉLI, WHAT'S WRONG? STOP SOBBING LIKE THAT, YOU'RE GETTING ON MY NERVES!
AYA...
AYA, ARE PAPA'S NEW KIDS GONNA STAY WITH US?

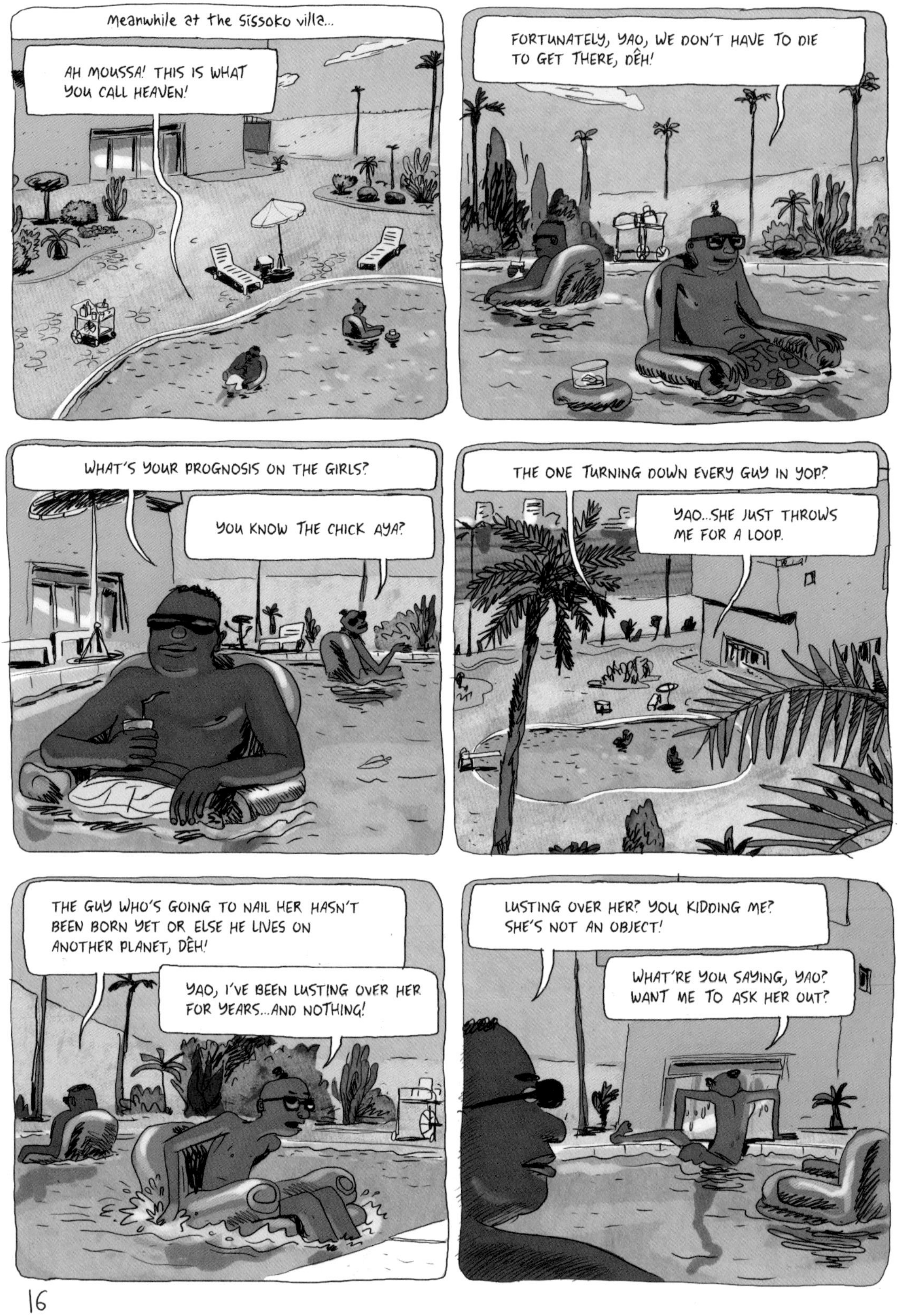
Meanwhile at the Sissoko villa...
AH MOUSSA! THIS IS WHAT YOU CALL HEAVEN!
FORTUNATELY, YAO, WE DON'T HAVE TO DIE TO GET THERE, DÊH!
WHAT'S YOUR PROGNOSIS ON THE GIRLS?
YOU KNOW THE CHICK AYA?
THE ONE TURNING DOWN EVERY GUY IN YOP?
YAO...SHE JUST THROWS ME FOR A LOOP.
THE GUY WHO'S GOING TO NAIL HER HASN'T BEEN BORN YET OR ELSE HE LIVES ON ANOTHER PLANET, DÊH!
YAO, I'VE BEEN LUSTING OVER HER FOR YEARS...AND NOTHING!
LUSTING OVER HER? YOU KIDDING ME? SHE'S NOT AN OBJECT!
WHAT'RE YOU SAYING, YAO? WANT ME TO ASK HER OUT?

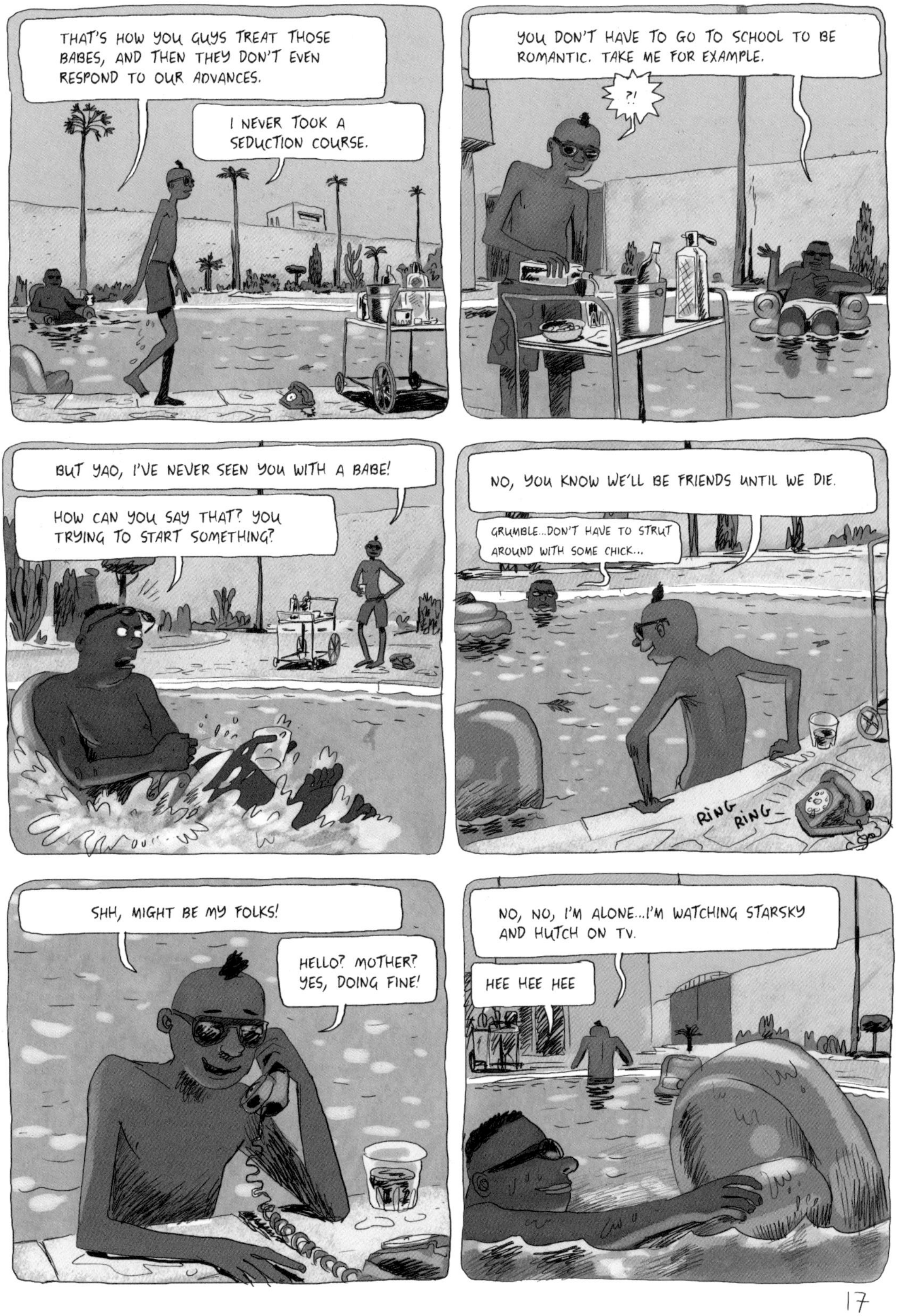
THAT'S HOW YOU GUYS TREAT THOSE BABES, AND THEN THEY DON'T EVEN RESPOND TO OUR ADVANCES.
I NEVER TOOK A SEDUCTION COURSE.
YOU DON'T HAVE TO GO TO SCHOOL TO BE ROMANTIC. TAKE ME FOR EXAMPLE.
?!
BUT YAO, I'VE NEVER SEEN YOU WITH A BABE!
HOW CAN YOU SAY THAT? YOU TRYING TO START SOMETHING?
NO, YOU KNOW WE'LL BE FRIENDS UNTIL WE DIE.
GRUMBLE...DON'T HAVE TO STRUT AROUND WITH SOME CHICK...
RING RING
SHH, MIGHT BE MY FOLKS!
HELLO? MOTHER? YES, DOING FINE!
NO, NO, I'M ALONE...I'M WATCHING STARSKY AND HUTCH ON TV.
HEE HEE HEE

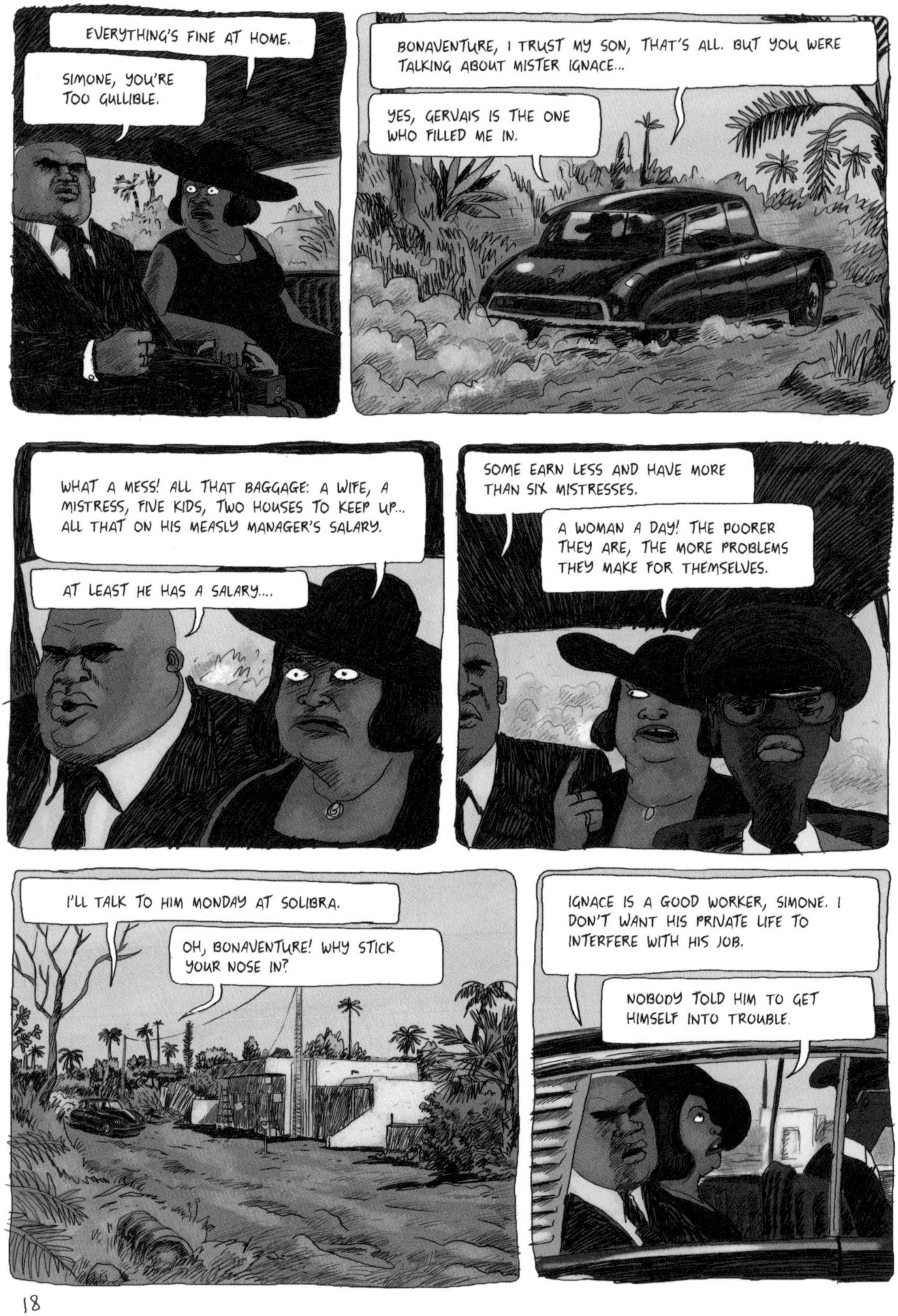
EVERYTHING'S FINE AT HOME.
SIMONE, YOU'RE TOO GULLIBLE.
BONAVENTURE, I TRUST MY SON, THAT'S ALL. BUT YOU WERE TALKING ABOUT MISTER IGNACE...
YES, GERVAIS IS THE ONE WHO FILLED ME IN.
WHAT A MESS! ALL THAT BAGGAGE: A WIFE, A MISTRESS, FIVE KIDS, TWO HOUSES TO KEEP UP... ALL THAT ON HIS MEASLY MANAGER'S SALARY.
AT LEAST HE HAS A SALARY....
SOME EARN LESS AND HAVE MORE THAN SIX MISTRESSES.
A WOMAN A DAY! THE POORER THEY ARE, THE MORE PROBLEMS THEY MAKE FOR THEMSELVES.
I'LL TALK TO HIM MONDAY AT SOLIBRA.
OH, BONAVENTURE! WHY STICK YOUR NOSE IN?
IGNACE IS A GOOD WORKER, SIMONE. I DON'T WANT HIS PRIVATE LIFE TO INTERFERE WITH HIS JOB.
NOBODY TOLD HIM TO GET HIMSELF INTO TROUBLE.

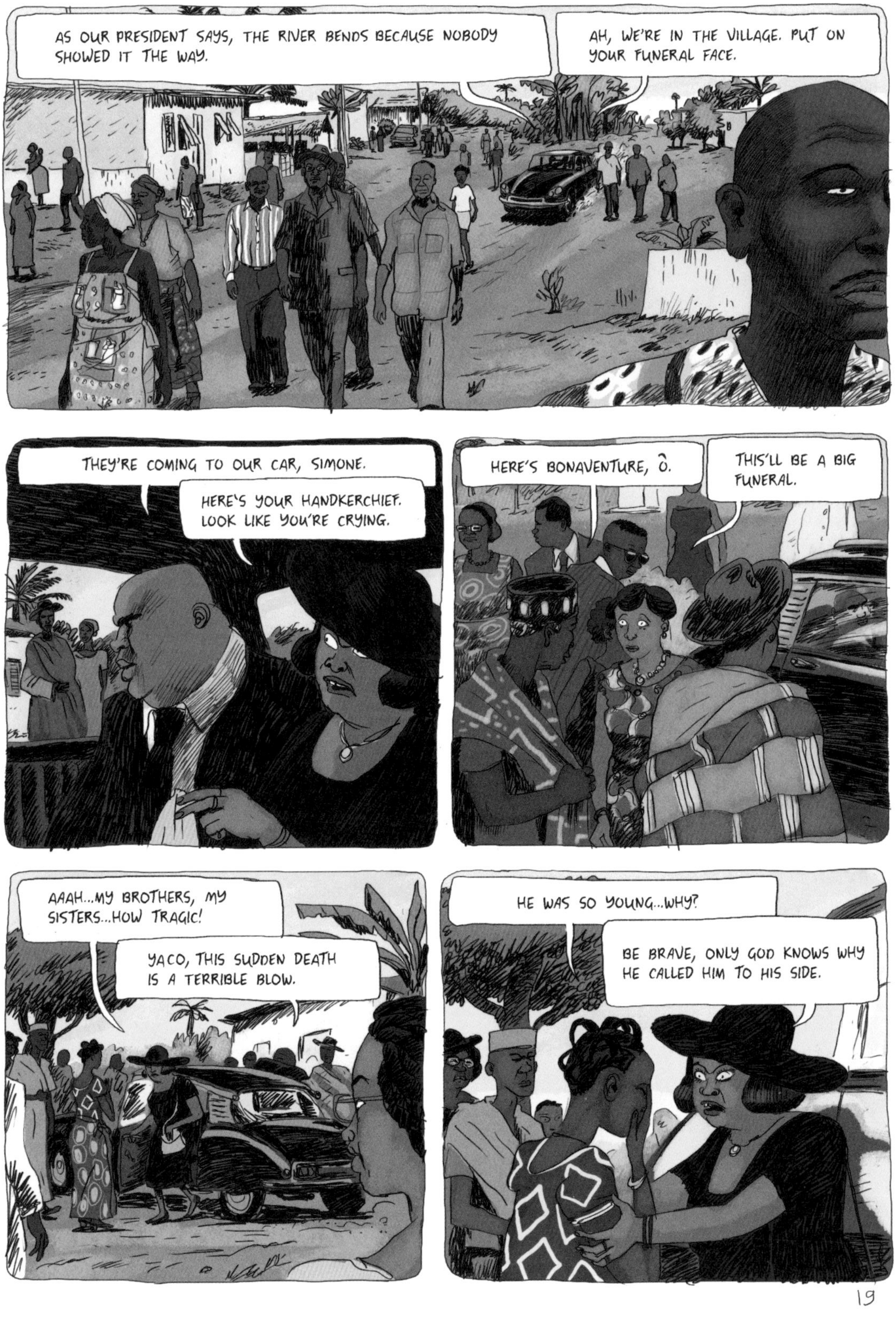
AS OUR PRESIDENT SAYS, THE RIVER BENDS BECAUSE NOBODY SHOWED IT THE WAY.
AH, WE'RE IN THE VILLAGE. PUT ON YOUR FUNERAL FACE.
THEY'RE COMING TO OUR CAR, SIMONE.
HERE'S YOUR HANDKERCHIEF. LOOK LIKE YOU'RE CRYING.
HERE'S BONAVENTURE, Ô.
THIS'LL BE A BIG FUNERAL.
AAAH...MY BROTHERS, MY SISTERS...HOW TRAGIC!
YACO, THIS SUDDEN DEATH IS A TERRIBLE BLOW.
HE WAS SO YOUNG...WHY?
BE BRAVE, ONLY GOD KNOWS WHY HE CALLED HIM TO HIS SIDE.

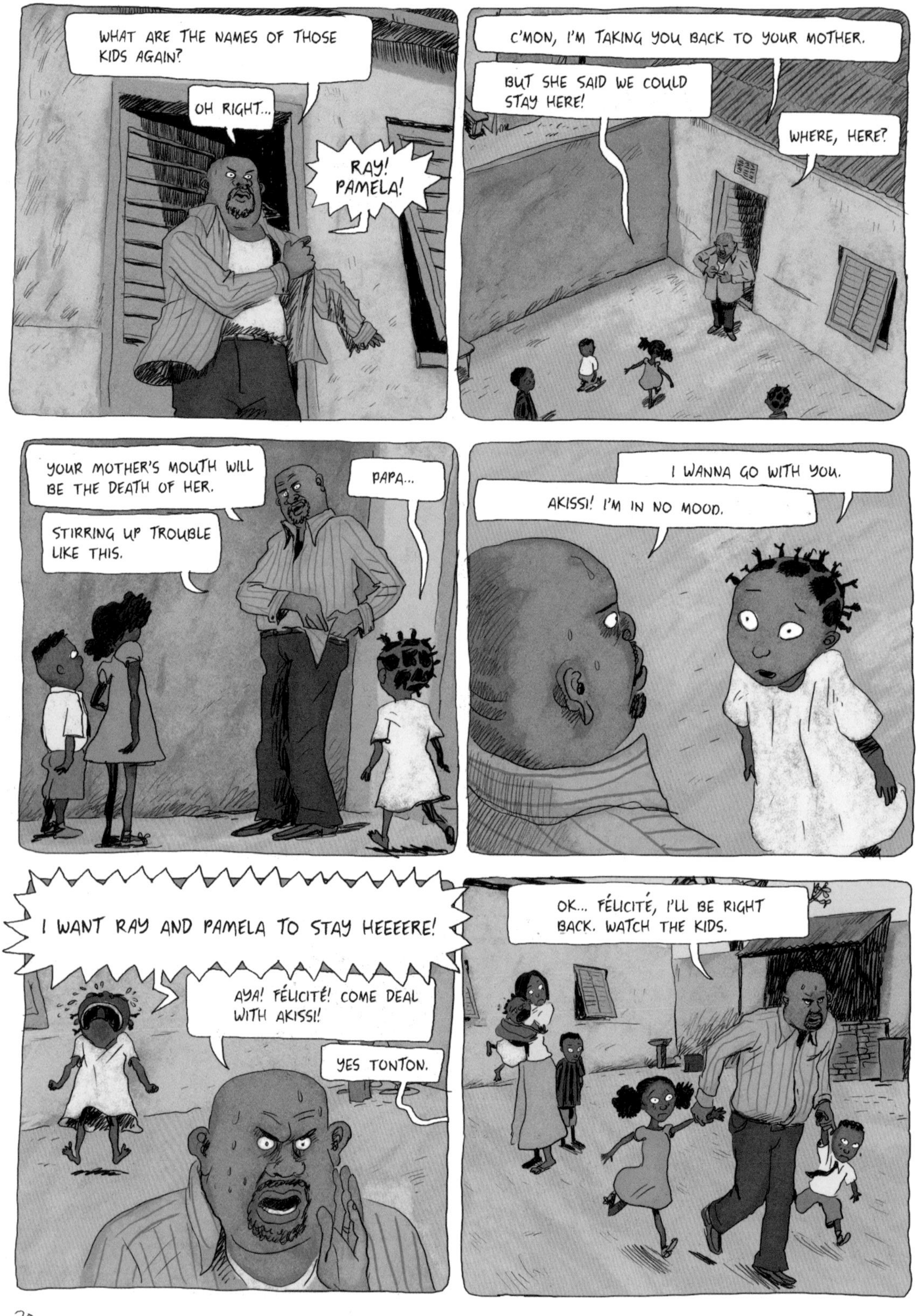
WHAT ARE THE NAMES OF THOSE KIDS AGAIN?
OH RIGHT...
RAY! PAMELA!
C'MON, I'M TAKING YOU BACK TO YOUR MOTHER.
BUT SHE SAID WE COULD STAY HERE!
WHERE, HERE?
YOUR MOTHER'S MOUTH WILL BE THE DEATH OF HER.
STIRRING UP TROUBLE LIKE THIS.
PAPA...
I WANNA GO WITH YOU.
AKISSI! I'M IN NO MOOD.
I WANT RAY AND PAMELA TO STAY HEEEERE!
AYA! FÉLICITÉ! COME DEAL WITH AKISSI!
YES TONTON.
OK... FÉLICITÉ, I'LL BE RIGHT BACK. WATCH THE KIDS.

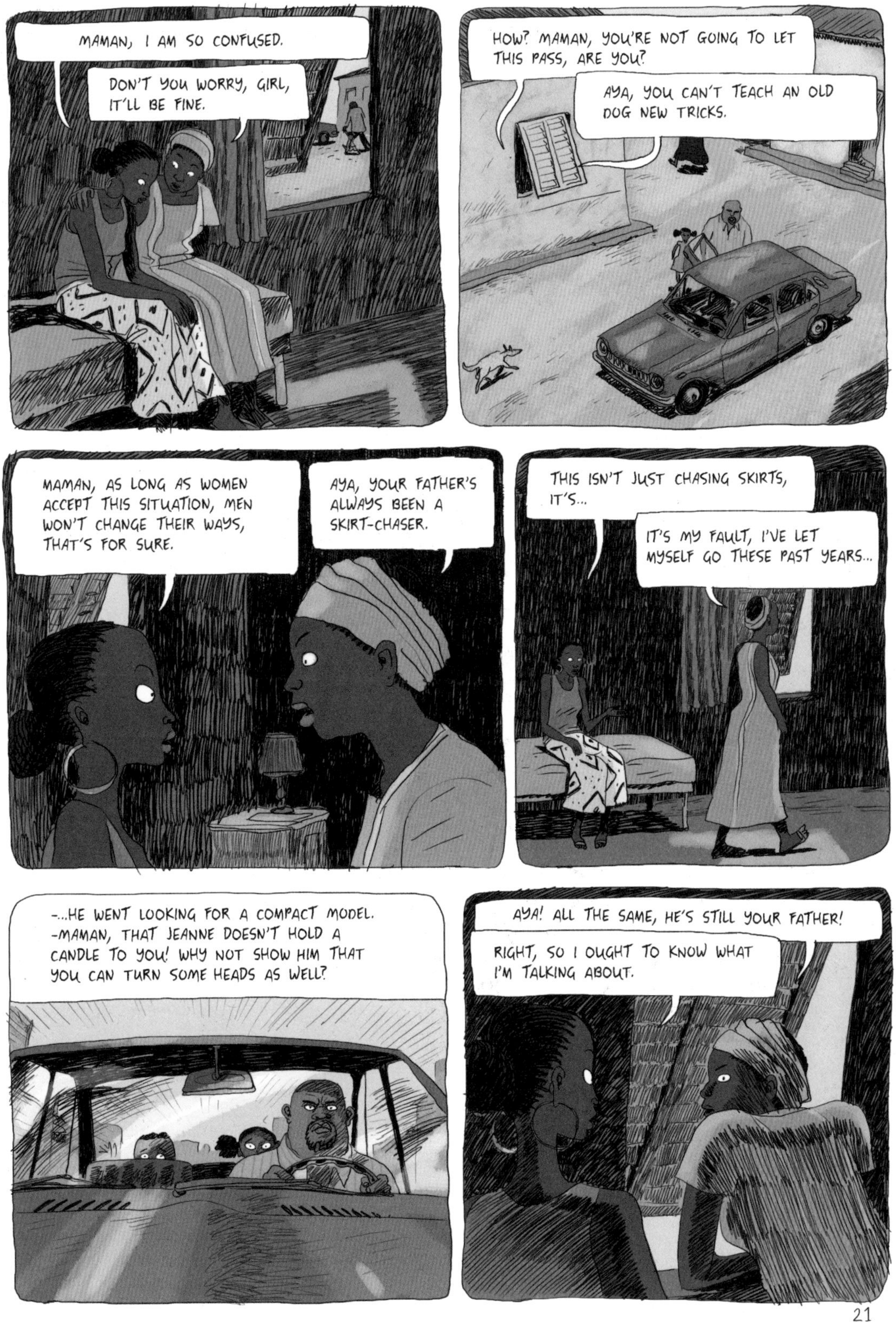
MAMAN, I AM SO CONFUSED.
DON'T YOU WORRY, GIRL, IT'LL BE FINE.
HOW? MAMAN, YOU'RE NOT GOING TO LET THIS PASS, ARE YOU?
AYA, YOU CAN'T TEACH AN OLD DOG NEW TRICKS.
MAMAN, AS LONG AS WOMEN ACCEPT THIS SITUATION, MEN WON'T CHANGE THEIR WAYS, THAT'S FOR SURE.
AYA, YOUR FATHER'S ALWAYS BEEN A SKIRT-CHASER.
THIS ISN'T JUST CHASING SKIRTS, IT'S...
IT'S MY FAULT, I'VE LET MYSELF GO THESE PAST YEARS...
-...HE WENT LOOKING FOR A COMPACT MODEL.
-MAMAN, THAT JEANNE DOESN'T HOLD A CANDLE TO YOU! WHY NOT SHOW HIM THAT YOU CAN TURN SOME HEADS AS WELL?
AYA! ALL THE SAME, HE'S STILL YOUR FATHER!
RIGHT, SO I OUGHT TO KNOW WHAT I'M TALKING ABOUT.

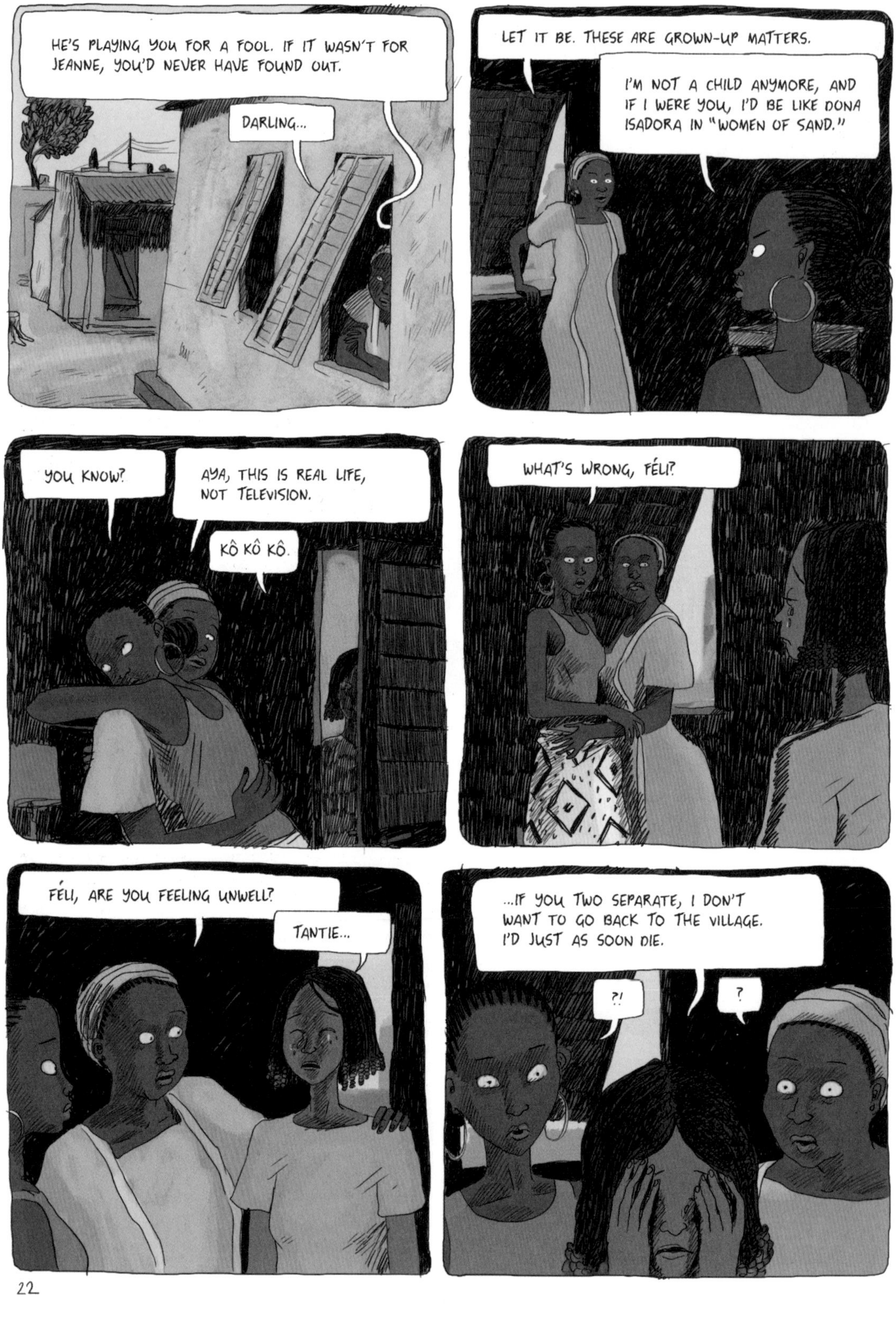
HE'S PLAYING YOU FOR A FOOL. IF IT WASN'T FOR JEANNE, YOU'D NEVER HAVE FOUND OUT.
DARLING...
LET IT BE. THESE ARE GROWN-UP MATTERS.
I'M NOT A CHILD ANYMORE, AND IF I WERE YOU, I'D BE LIKE DONA ISADORA IN "WOMEN OF SAND."
YOU KNOW?
AYA, THIS IS REAL LIFE, NOT TELEVISION.
KÔ KÔ KÔ.
WHAT'S WRONG, FÉLI?
FÉLI, ARE YOU FEELING UNWELL?
TANTIE...
...IF YOU TWO SEPARATE, I DON'T WANT TO GO BACK TO THE VILLAGE. I'D JUST AS SOON DIE.
?!
?

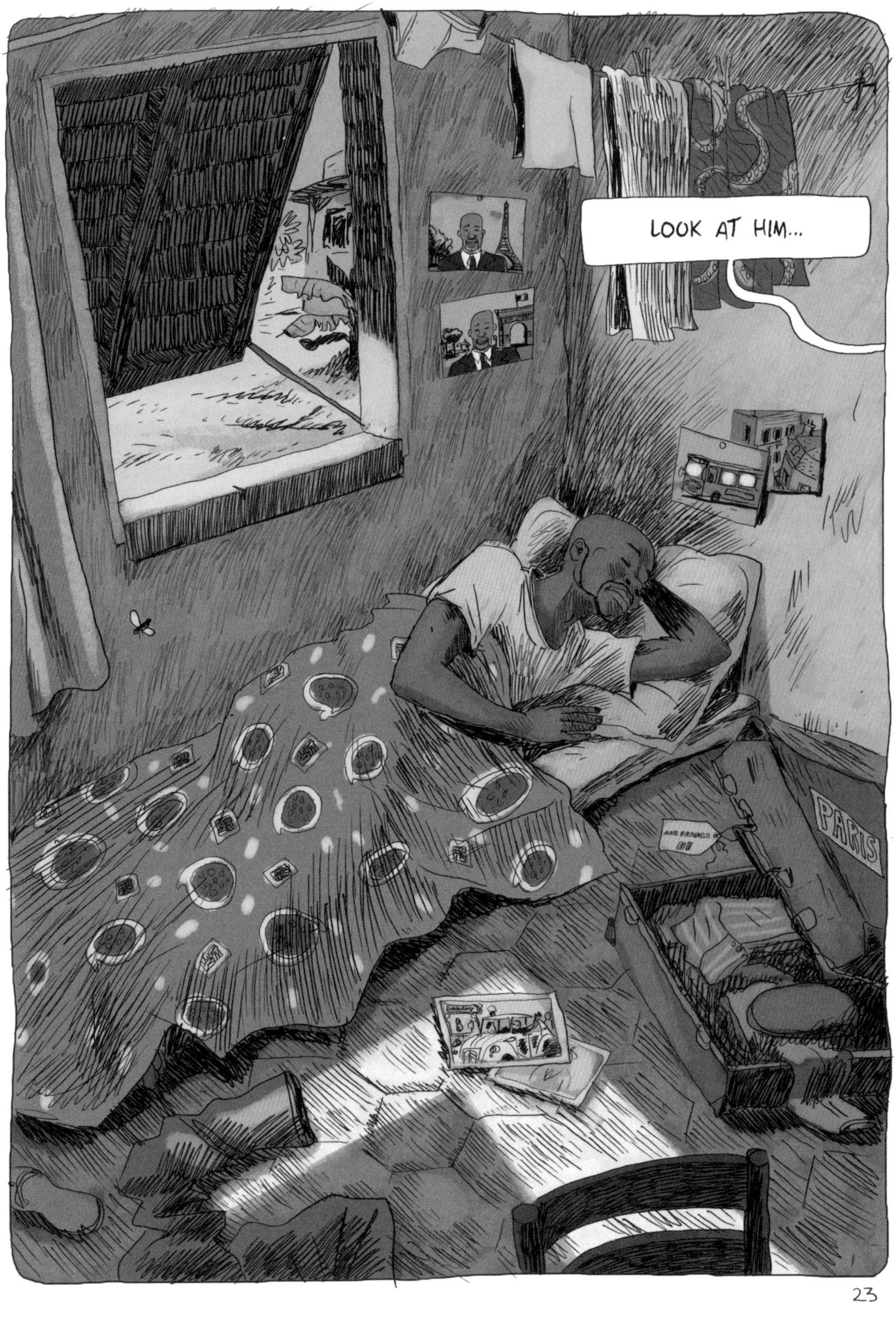
LOOK AT HIM...
PARIS

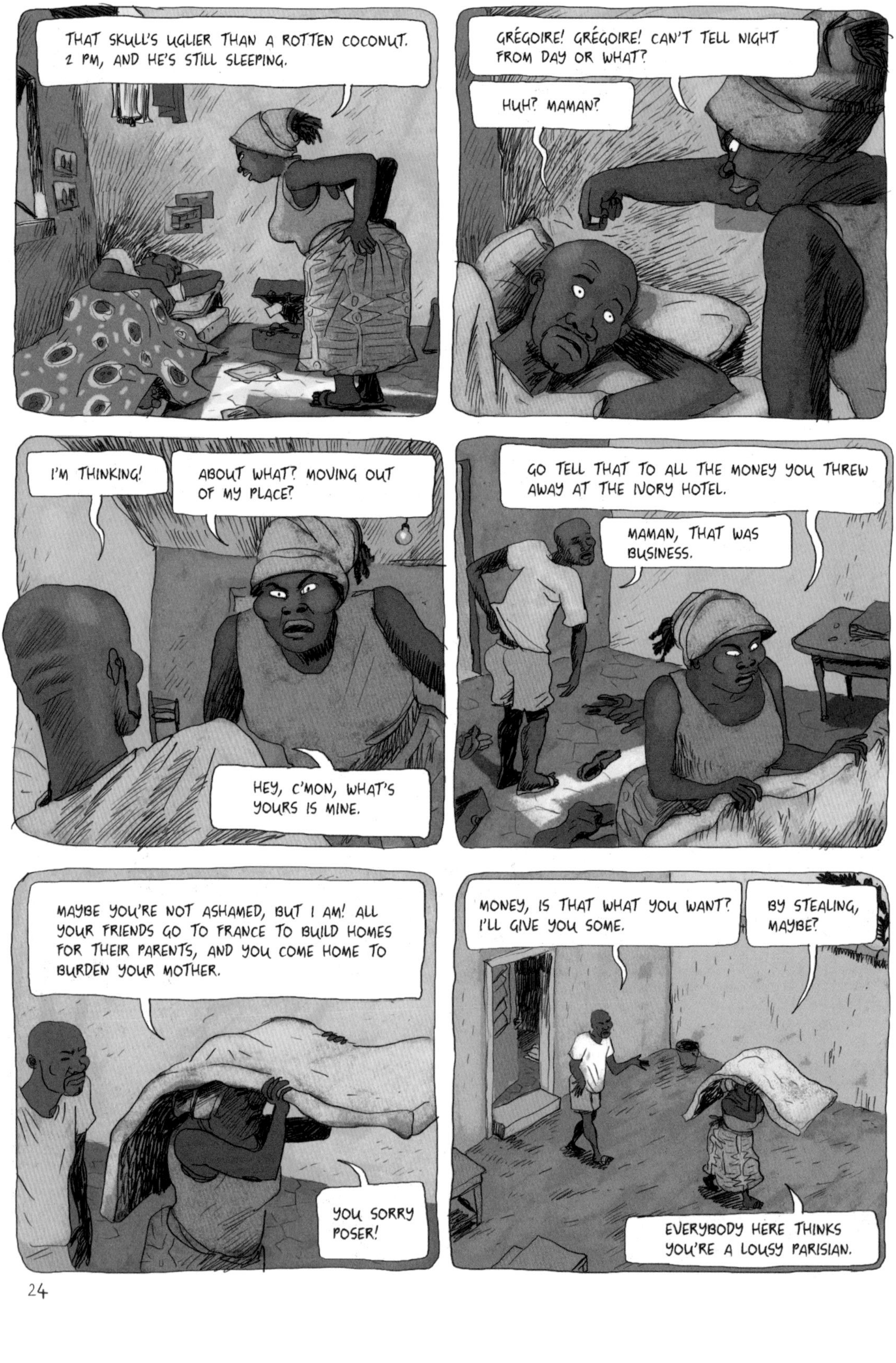
THAT SKULL'S UGLIER THAN A ROTTEN COCONUT. 2 PM, AND HE'S STILL SLEEPING.
GRÉGOIRE! GRÉGOIRE! CAN'T TELL NIGHT FROM DAY OR WHAT?
HUH? MAMAN?
I'M THINKING!
ABOUT WHAT? MOVING OUT OF MY PLACE?
HEY, C'MON, WHAT'S YOURS IS MINE.
GO TELL THAT TO ALL THE MONEY YOU THREW AWAY AT THE IVORY HOTEL.
MAMAN, THAT WAS BUSINESS.
MAYBE YOU'RE NOT ASHAMED, BUT I AM! ALL YOUR FRIENDS GO TO FRANCE TO BUILD HOMES FOR THEIR PARENTS, AND YOU COME HOME TO BURDEN YOUR MOTHER.
YOU SORRY POSER!
MONEY, IS THAT WHAT YOU WANT? I'LL GIVE YOU SOME.
BY STEALING, MAYBE?
EVERYBODY HERE THINKS YOU'RE A LOUSY PARISIAN.

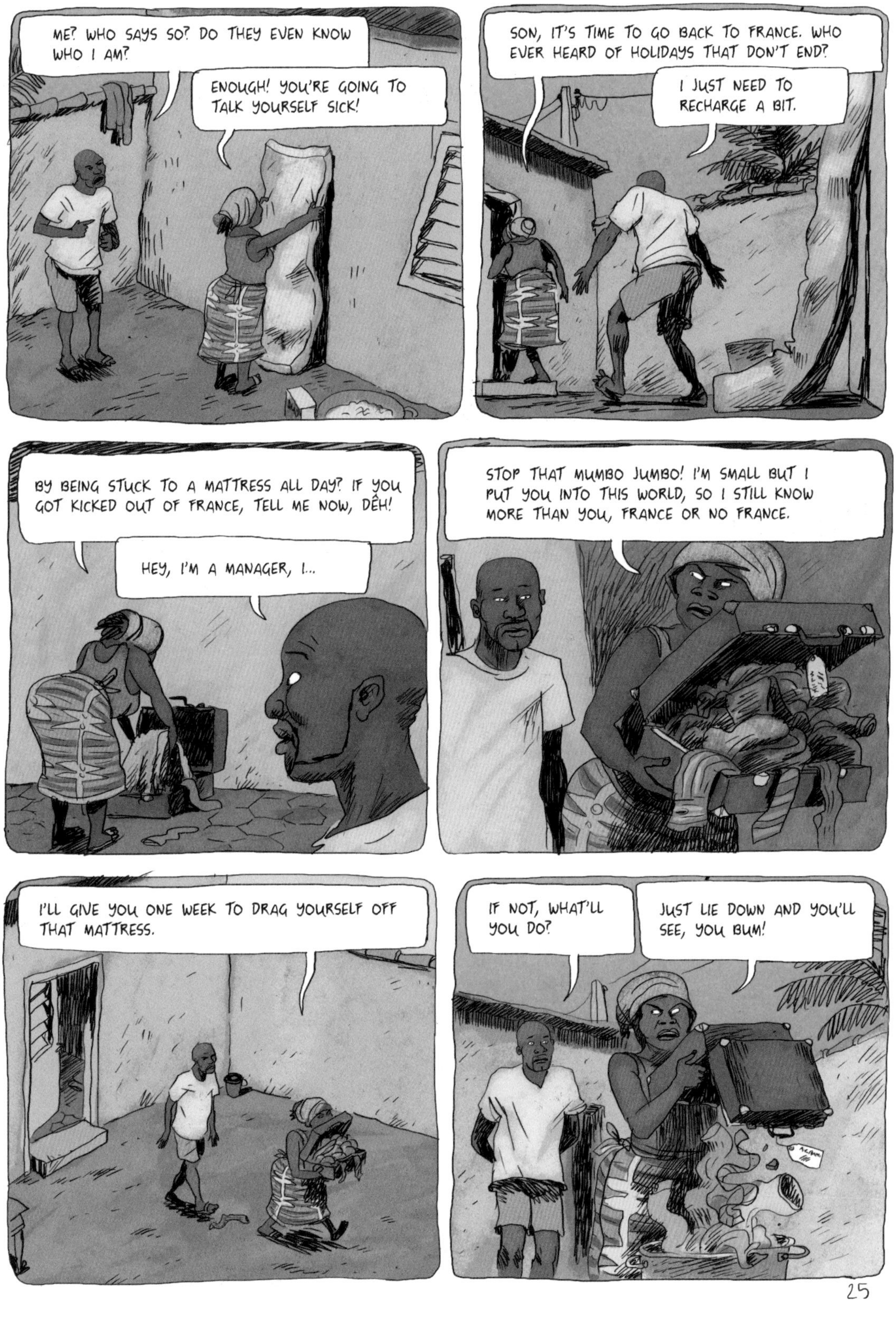
ME? WHO SAYS SO? DO THEY EVEN KNOW WHO I AM?
ENOUGH! YOU'RE GOING TO TALK YOURSELF SICK!
SON, IT'S TIME TO GO BACK TO FRANCE. WHO EVER HEARD OF HOLIDAYS THAT DON'T END?
I JUST NEED TO RECHARGE A BIT.
BY BEING STUCK TO A MATTRESS ALL DAY? IF YOU GOT KICKED OUT OF FRANCE, TELL ME NOW, DÊH!
HEY, I'M A MANAGER, I...
STOP THAT MUMBO JUMBO! I'M SMALL BUT I PUT YOU INTO THIS WORLD, SO I STILL KNOW MORE THAN YOU, FRANCE OR NO FRANCE.
I'LL GIVE YOU ONE WEEK TO DRAG YOURSELF OFF THAT MATTRESS.
IF NOT, WHAT'LL YOU DO?
JUST LIE DOWN AND YOU'LL SEE, YOU BUM!

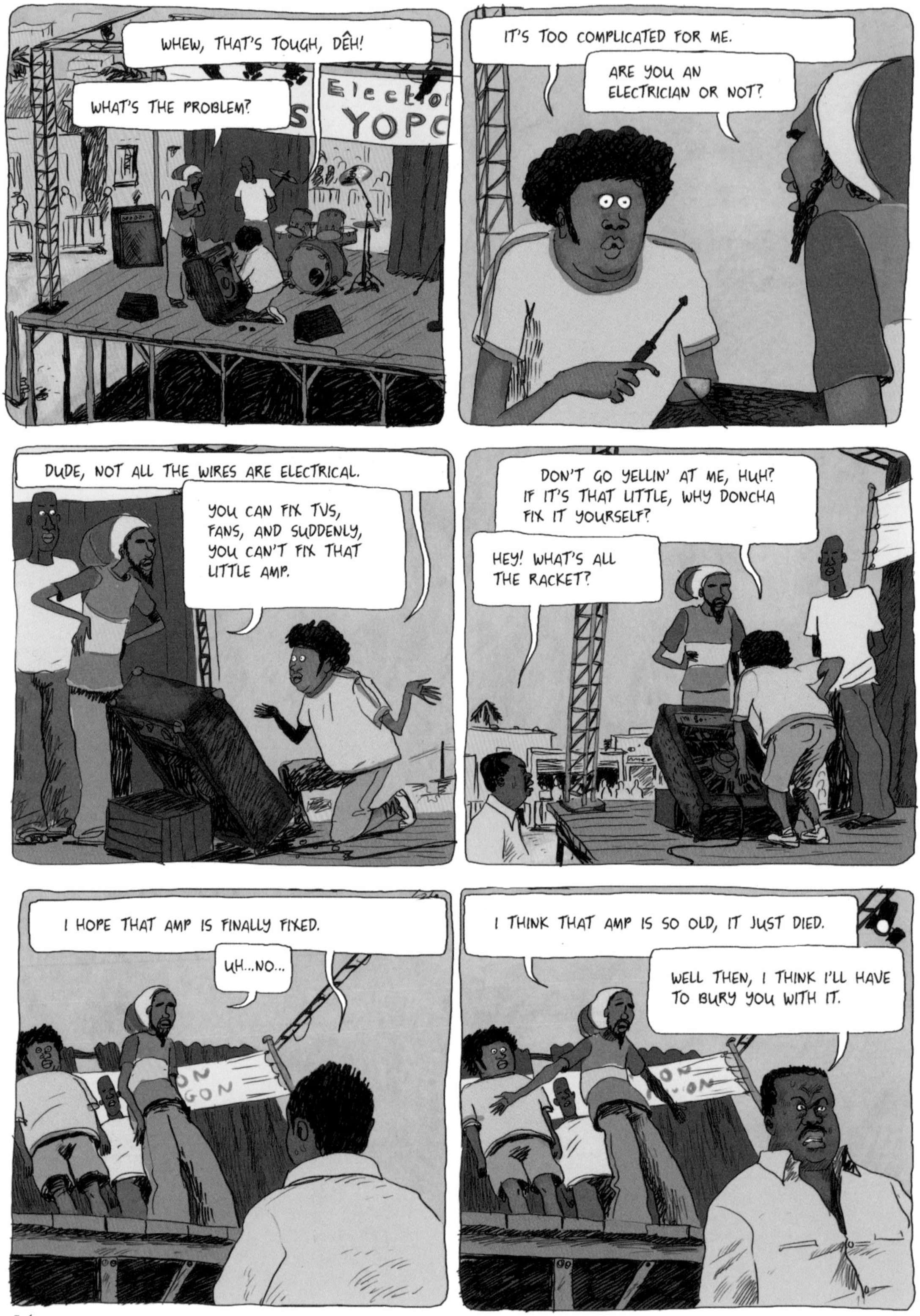
WHEW, THAT'S TOUGH, DÊH!
WHAT'S THE PROBLEM?
IT'S TOO COMPLICATED FOR ME.
ARE YOU AN ELECTRICIAN OR NOT?
DUDE, NOT ALL THE WIRES ARE ELECTRICAL.
YOU CAN FIX TVS, FANS, AND SUDDENLY, YOU CAN'T FIX THAT LITTLE AMP.
DON'T GO YELLIN' AT ME, HUH? IF IT'S THAT LITTLE, WHY DONCHA FIX IT YOURSELF?
HEY! WHAT'S ALL THE RACKET?
I HOPE THAT AMP IS FINALLY FIXED.
UH...NO...
I THINK THAT AMP IS SO OLD, IT JUST DIED.
WELL THEN, I THINK I'LL HAVE TO BURY YOU WITH IT.

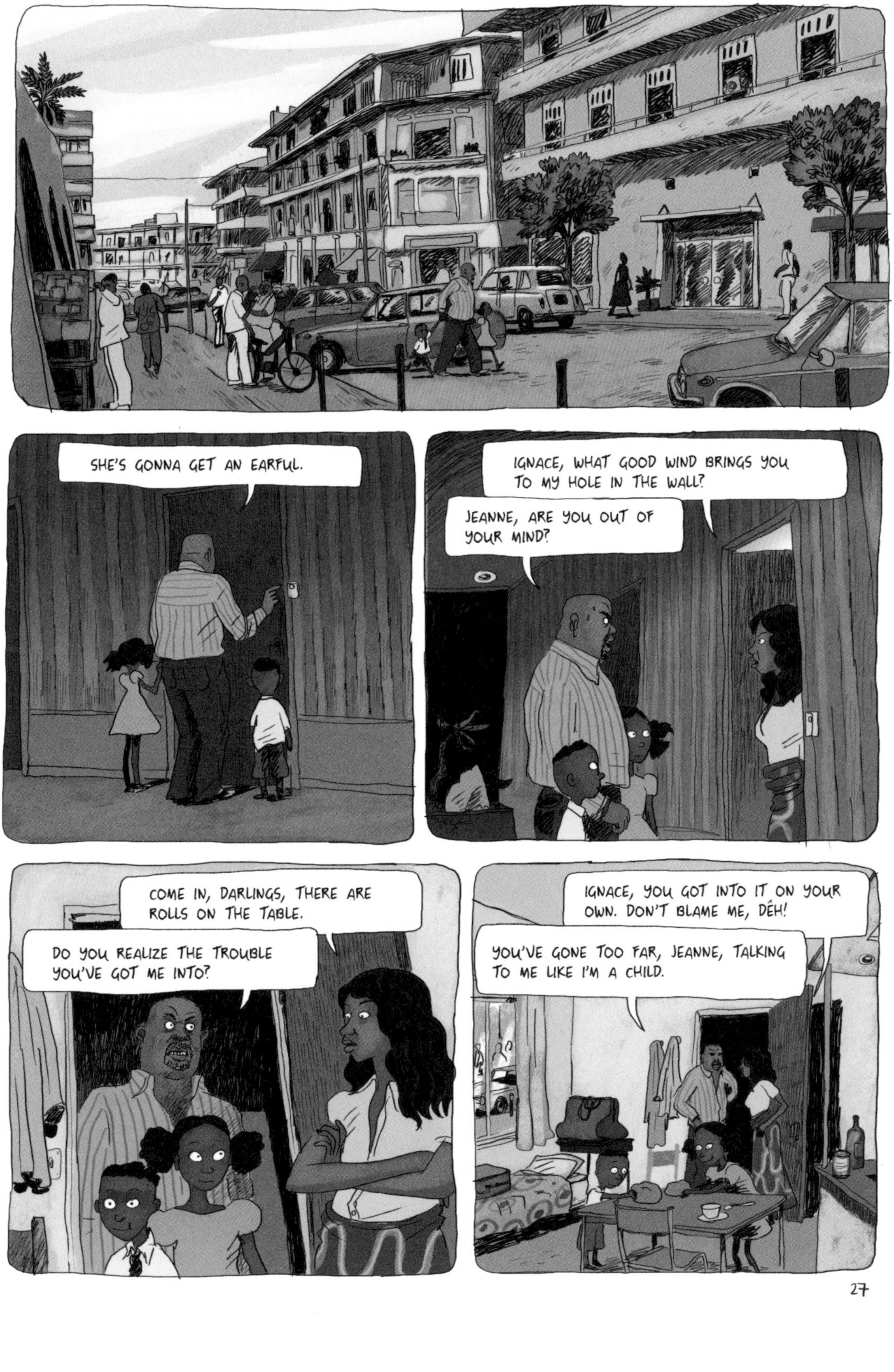
SHE'S GONNA GET AN EARFUL.
IGNACE, WHAT GOOD WIND BRINGS YOU TO MY HOLE IN THE WALL?
JEANNE, ARE YOU OUT OF YOUR MIND?
COME IN, DARLINGS, THERE ARE ROLLS ON THE TABLE.
DO YOU REALIZE THE TROUBLE YOU'VE GOT ME INTO?
IGNACE, YOU GOT INTO IT ON YOUR OWN. DON'T BLAME ME, DÊH!
YOU'VE GONE TOO FAR, JEANNE, TALKING TO ME LIKE I'M A CHILD.

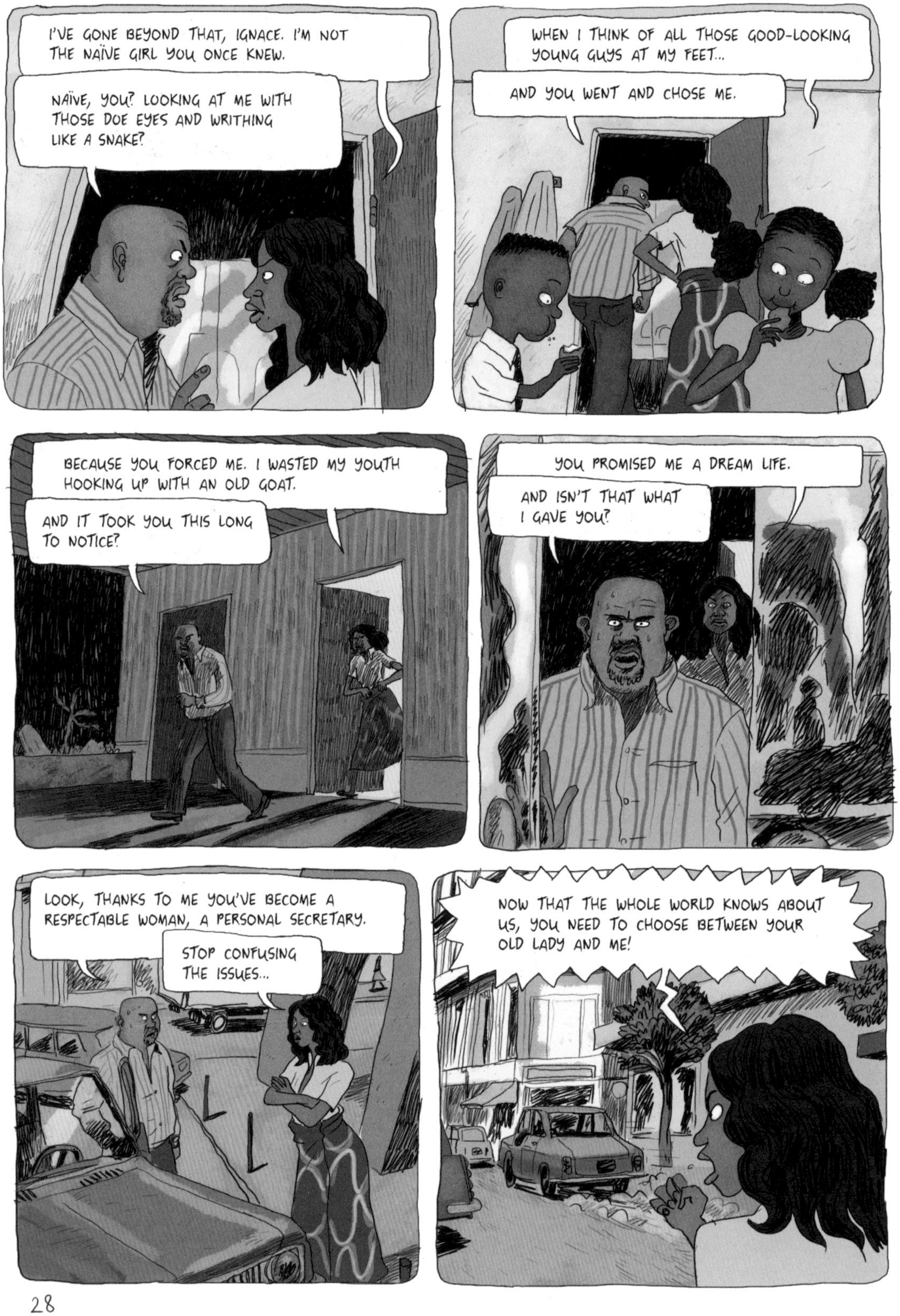
I'VE GONE BEYOND THAT, IGNACE. I'M NOT THE NAÏVE GIRL YOU ONCE KNEW.
NAÏVE, YOU? LOOKING AT ME WITH THOSE DOE EYES AND WRITHING LIKE A SNAKE?
WHEN I THINK OF ALL THOSE GOOD-LOOKING YOUNG GUYS AT MY FEET...
AND YOU WENT AND CHOSE ME.
BECAUSE YOU FORCED ME. I WASTED MY YOUTH HOOKING UP WITH AN OLD GOAT.
AND IT TOOK YOU THIS LONG TO NOTICE?
YOU PROMISED ME A DREAM LIFE.
AND ISN'T THAT WHAT I GAVE YOU?
LOOK, THANKS TO ME YOU'VE BECOME A RESPECTABLE WOMAN, A PERSONAL SECRETARY.
STOP CONFUSING THE ISSUES...
NOW THAT THE WHOLE WORLD KNOWS ABOUT US, YOU NEED TO CHOOSE BETWEEN YOUR OLD LADY AND ME!

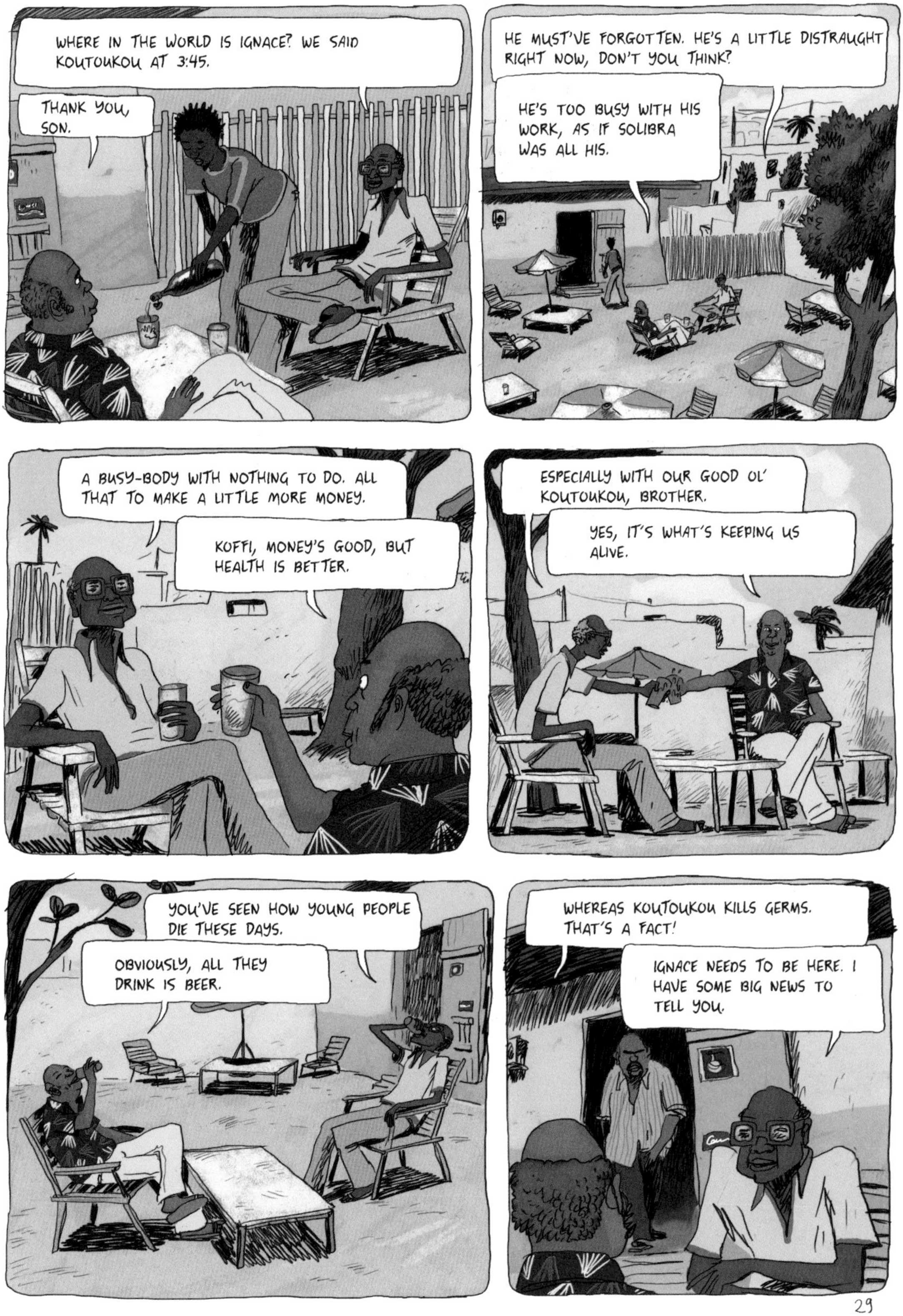
WHERE IN THE WORLD IS IGNACE? WE SAID KOUTOUKOU AT 3:45.
THANK YOU, SON.
HE MUST'VE FORGOTTEN. HE'S A LITTLE DISTRAUGHT RIGHT NOW, DON'T YOU THINK?
HE'S TOO BUSY WITH HIS WORK, AS IF SOLIBRA WAS ALL HIS.
A BUSY-BODY WITH NOTHING TO DO. ALL THAT TO MAKE A LITTLE MORE MONEY.
KOFFI, MONEY'S GOOD, BUT HEALTH IS BETTER.
ESPECIALLY WITH OUR GOOD OL' KOUTOUKOU, BROTHER.
YES, IT'S WHAT'S KEEPING US ALIVE.
YOU'VE SEEN HOW YOUNG PEOPLE DIE THESE DAYS.
OBVIOUSLY, ALL THEY DRINK IS BEER.
WHEREAS KOUTOUKOU KILLS GERMS. THAT'S A FACT!
IGNACE NEEDS TO BE HERE. I HAVE SOME BIG NEWS TO TELL YOU.

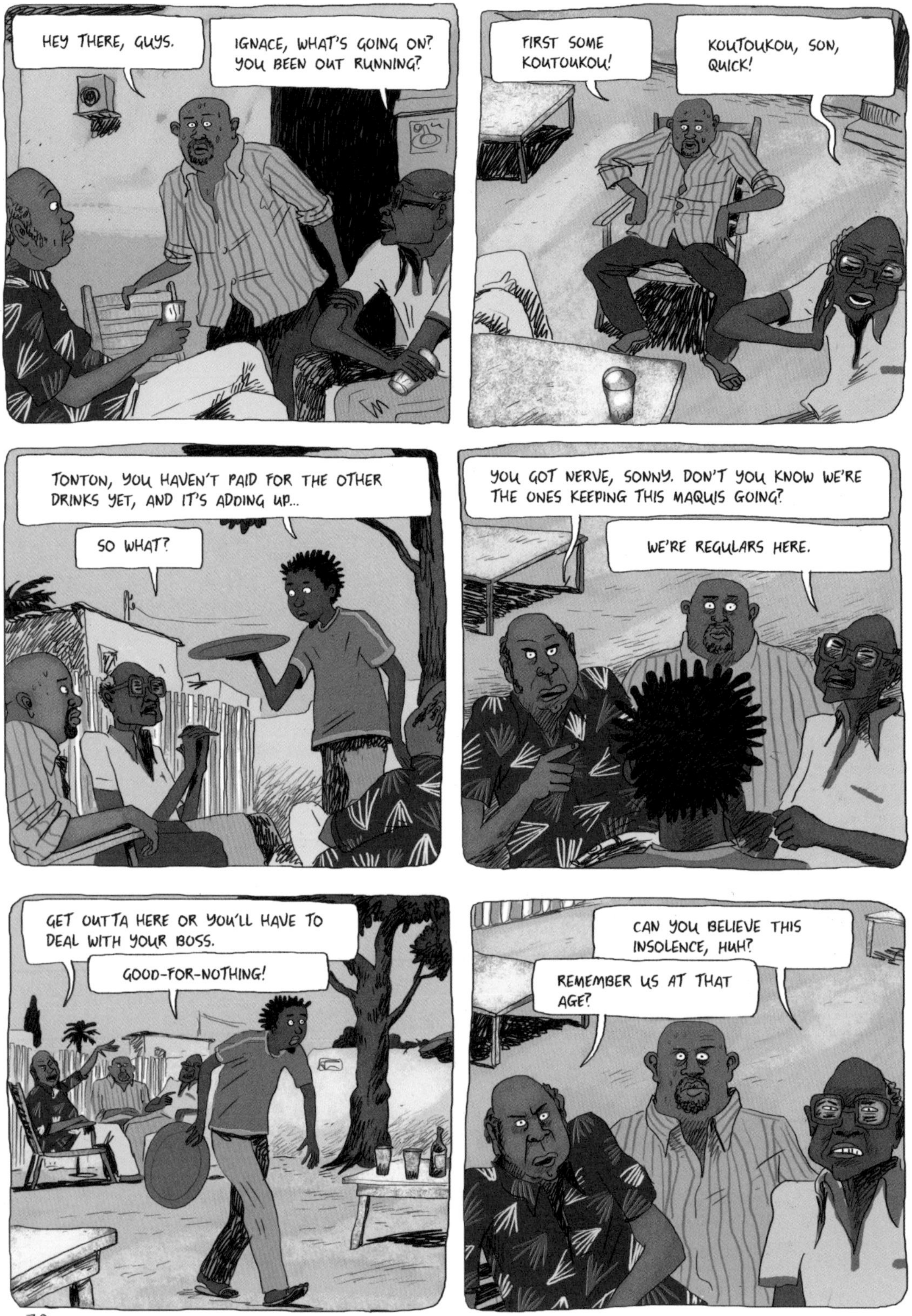
HEY THERE, GUYS.
IGNACE, WHAT'S GOING ON? YOU BEEN OUT RUNNING?
FIRST SOME KOUTOUKOU!
KOUTOUKOU, SON, QUICK!
TONTON, YOU HAVEN'T PAID FOR THE OTHER DRINKS YET, AND IT'S ADDING UP...
SO WHAT?
YOU GOT NERVE, SONNY. DON'T YOU KNOW WE'RE THE ONES KEEPING THIS MAQUIS GOING?
WE'RE REGULARS HERE.
GET OUTTA HERE OR YOU'LL HAVE TO DEAL WITH YOUR BOSS.
GOOD-FOR-NOTHING!
CAN YOU BELIEVE THIS INSOLENCE, HUH?
REMEMBER US AT THAT AGE?

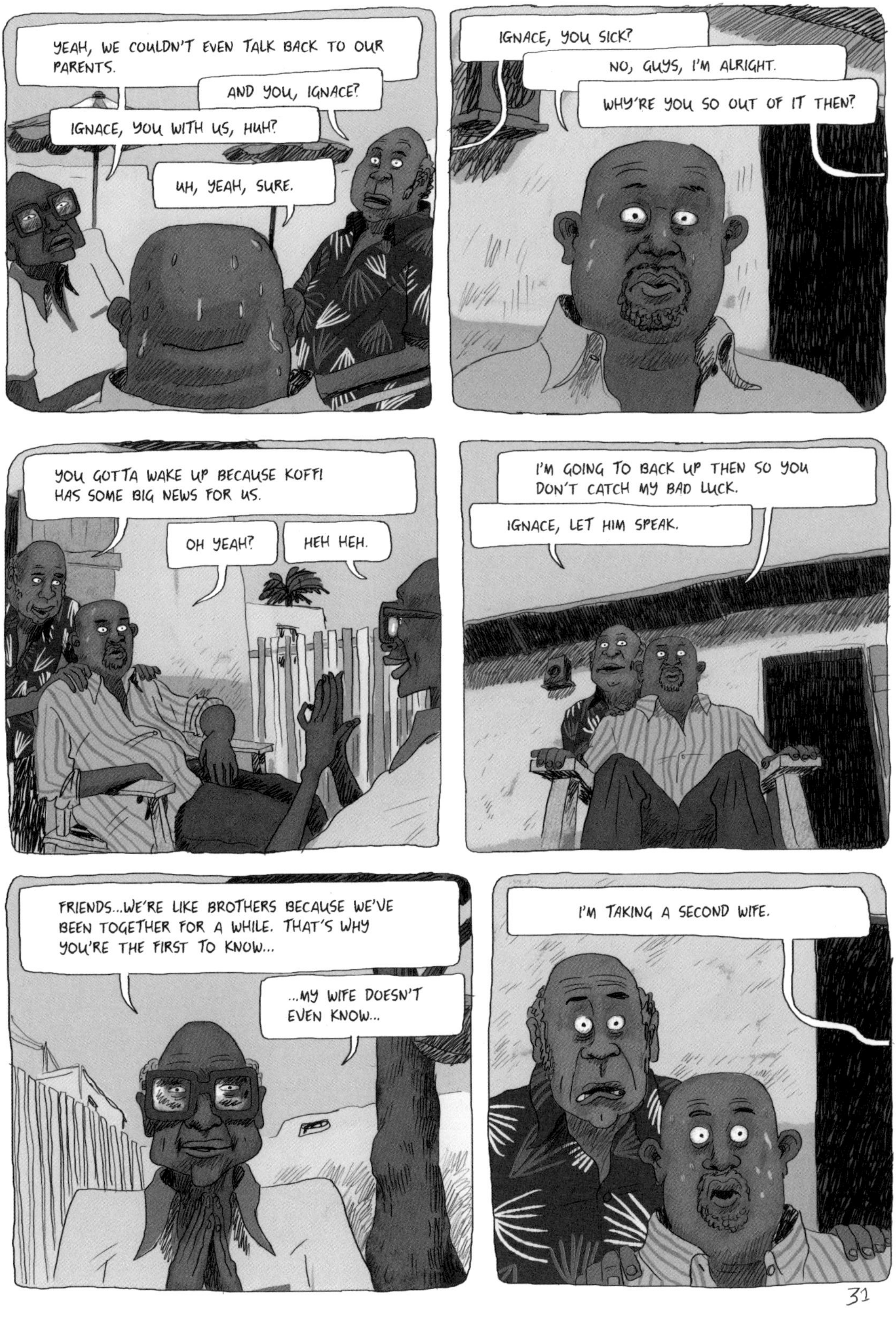

YEAH, WE COULDN'T EVEN TALK BACK TO OUR PARENTS.
AND YOU, IGNACE?
IGNACE, YOU WITH US, HUH?
UH, YEAH, SURE.
IGNACE, YOU SICK?
NO, GUYS, I'M ALRIGHT.
WHY'RE YOU SO OUT OF IT THEN?
YOU GOTTA WAKE UP BECAUSE KOFFI HAS SOME BIG NEWS FOR US.
OH YEAH?
HEH HEH.
I'M GOING TO BACK UP THEN SO YOU DON'T CATCH MY BAD LUCK.
IGNACE, LET HIM SPEAK.
FRIENDS...WE'RE LIKE BROTHERS BECAUSE WE'VE BEEN TOGETHER FOR A WHILE. THAT'S WHY YOU'RE THE FIRST TO KNOW...
...MY WIFE DOESN'T EVEN KNOW...
I'M TAKING A SECOND WIFE.

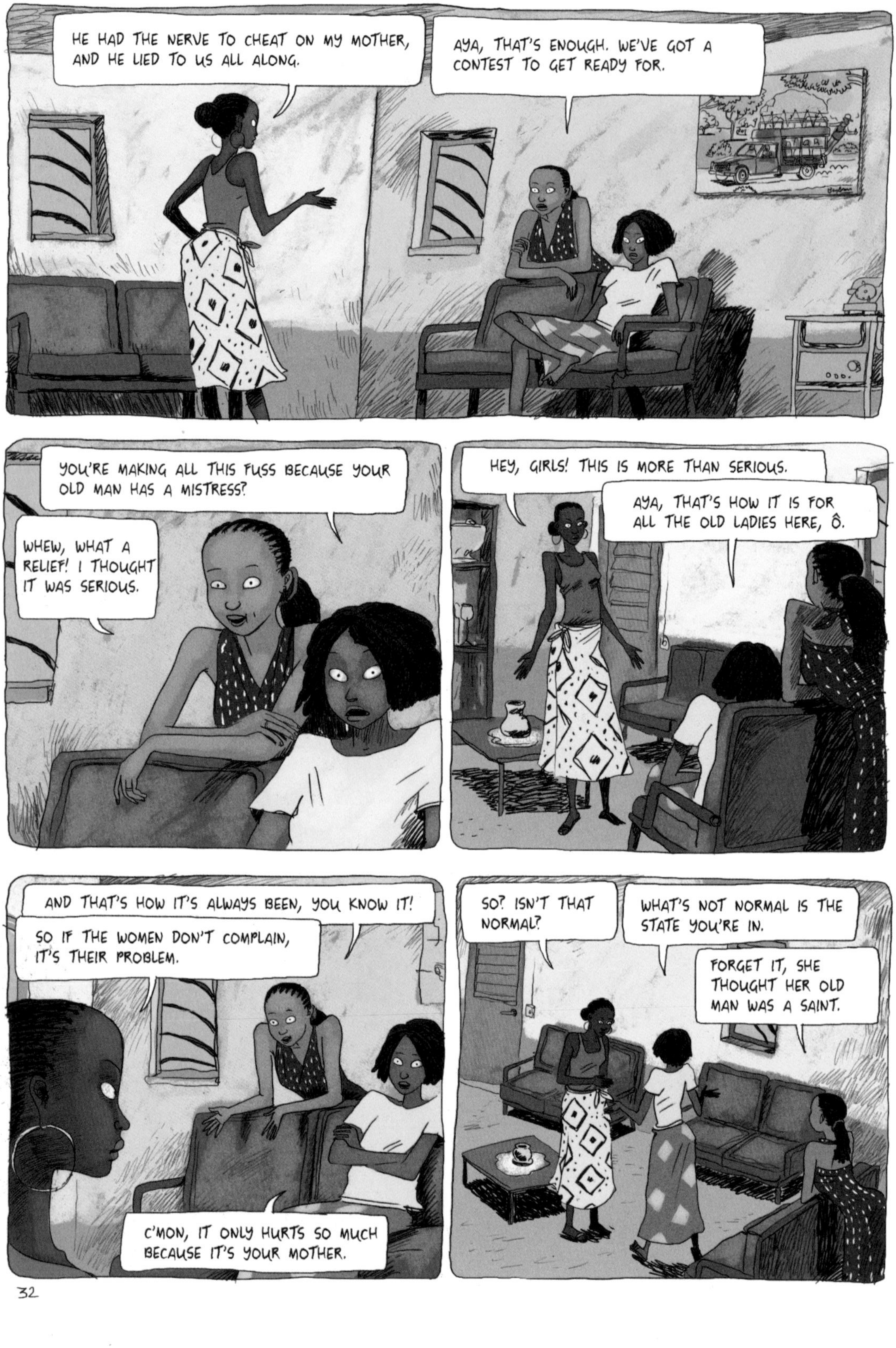

HE HAD THE NERVE TO CHEAT ON MY MOTHER, AND HE LIED TO US ALL ALONG.
AYA, THAT'S ENOUGH. WE'VE GOT A CONTEST TO GET READY FOR.
YOU'RE MAKING ALL THIS FUSS BECAUSE YOUR OLD MAN HAS A MISTRESS?
WHEW, WHAT A RELIEF! I THOUGHT IT WAS SERIOUS.
HEY, GIRLS! THIS IS MORE THAN SERIOUS.
AYA, THAT'S HOW IT IS FOR ALL THE OLD LADIES HERE, Ô.
AND THAT'S HOW IT'S ALWAYS BEEN, YOU KNOW IT!
SO IF THE WOMEN DON'T COMPLAIN, IT'S THEIR PROBLEM.
C'MON, IT ONLY HURTS SO MUCH BECAUSE IT'S YOUR MOTHER.
SO? ISN'T THAT NORMAL?
WHAT'S NOT NORMAL IS THE STATE YOU'RE IN.
FORGET IT, SHE THOUGHT HER OLD MAN WAS A SAINT.

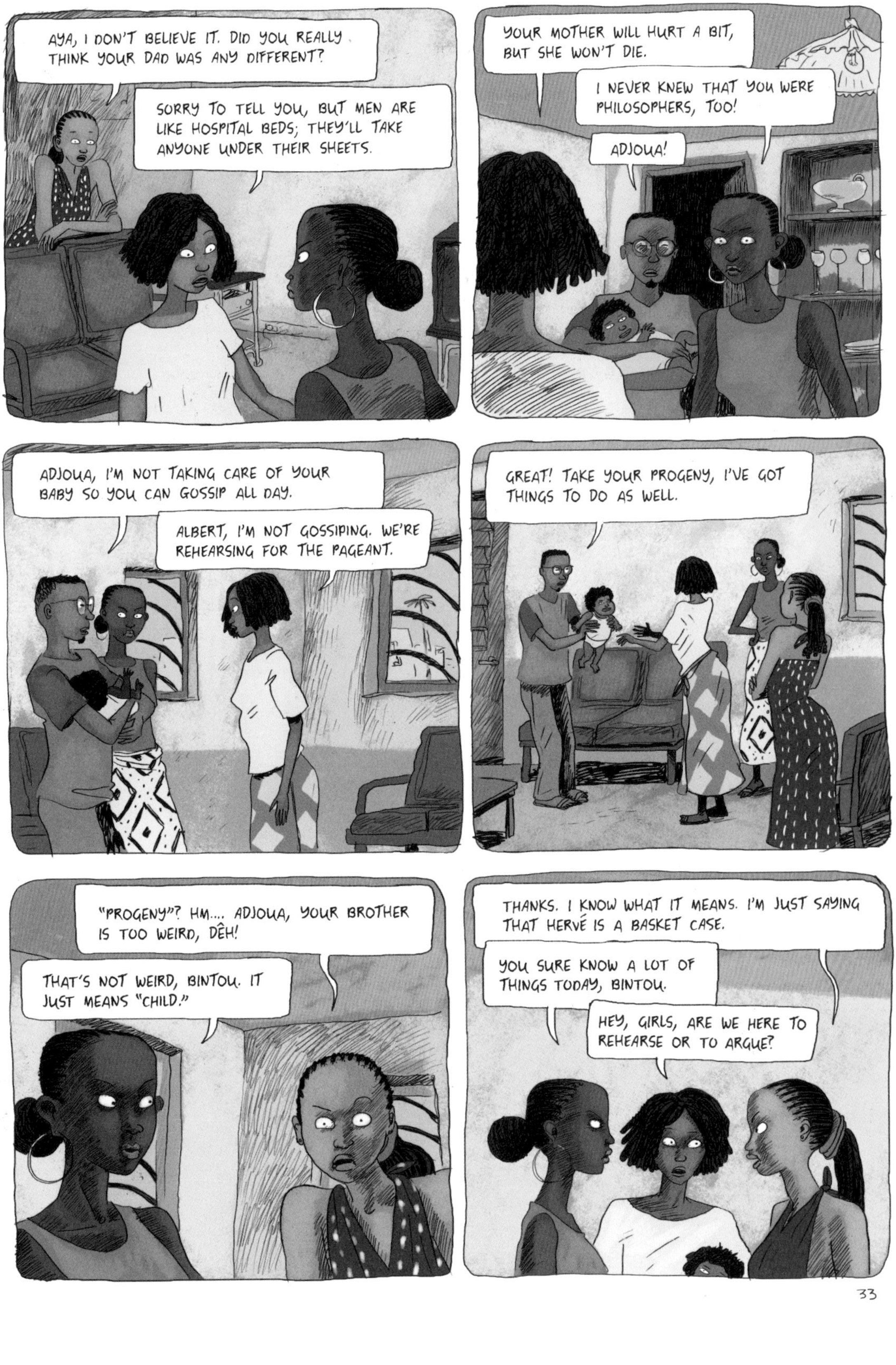
AYA, I DON'T BELIEVE IT. DID YOU REALLY THINK YOUR DAD WAS ANY DIFFERENT?
SORRY TO TELL YOU, BUT MEN ARE LIKE HOSPITAL BEDS; THEY'LL TAKE ANYONE UNDER THEIR SHEETS.
YOUR MOTHER WILL HURT A BIT, BUT SHE WON'T DIE.
I NEVER KNEW THAT YOU WERE PHILOSOPHERS, TOO!
ADJOUA!
ADJOUA, I'M NOT TAKING CARE OF YOUR BABY SO YOU CAN GOSSIP ALL DAY.
ALBERT, I'M NOT GOSSIPING. WE'RE REHEARSING FOR THE PAGEANT.
GREAT! TAKE YOUR PROGENY, I'VE GOT THINGS TO DO AS WELL.
"PROGENY"? HM.... ADJOUA, YOUR BROTHER IS TOO WEIRD, DÊH!
THAT'S NOT WEIRD, BINTOU. IT JUST MEANS "CHILD."
THANKS. I KNOW WHAT IT MEANS. I'M JUST SAYING THAT HERVÉ IS A BASKET CASE.
YOU SURE KNOW A LOT OF THINGS TODAY, BINTOU.
HEY, GIRLS, ARE WE HERE TO REHEARSE OR TO ARGUE?

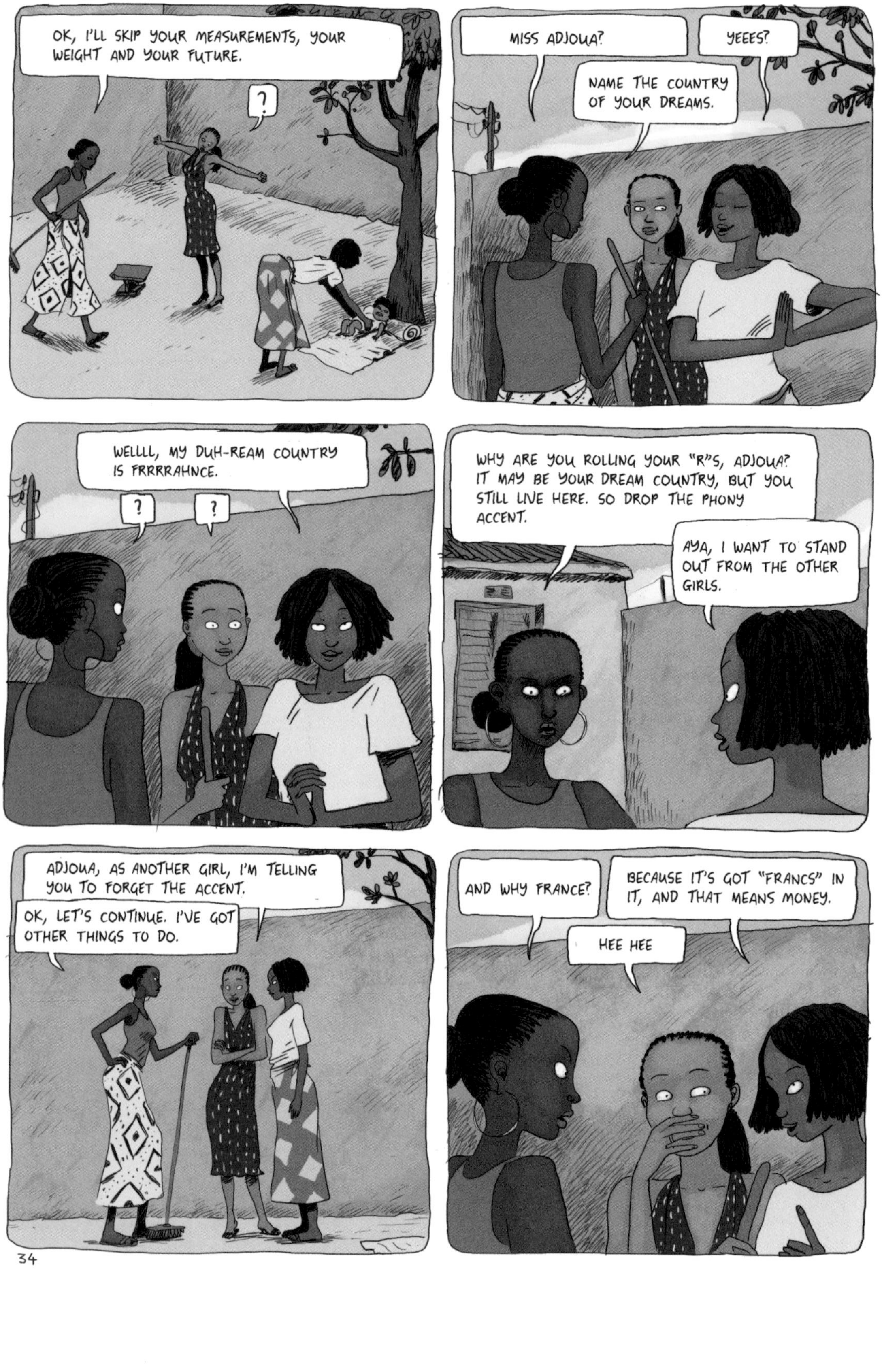
OK, I'LL SKIP YOUR MEASUREMENTS, YOUR WEIGHT AND YOUR FUTURE.
?
MISS ADJOUA?
YEEES?
NAME THE COUNTRY OF YOUR DREAMS.
WELLLL, MY DUH-REAM COUNTRY IS FRRRRAHNCE.
?
?
WHY ARE YOU ROLLING YOUR "R"S, ADJOUA? IT MAY BE YOUR DREAM COUNTRY, BUT YOU STILL LIVE HERE. SO DROP THE PHONY ACCENT.
AYA, I WANT TO STAND OUT FROM THE OTHER GIRLS.
ADJOUA, AS ANOTHER GIRL, I'M TELLING YOU TO FORGET THE ACCENT.
OK, LET'S CONTINUE. I'VE GOT OTHER THINGS TO DO.
AND WHY FRANCE?
BECAUSE IT'S GOT "FRANCS" IN IT, AND THAT MEANS MONEY.
HEE HEE

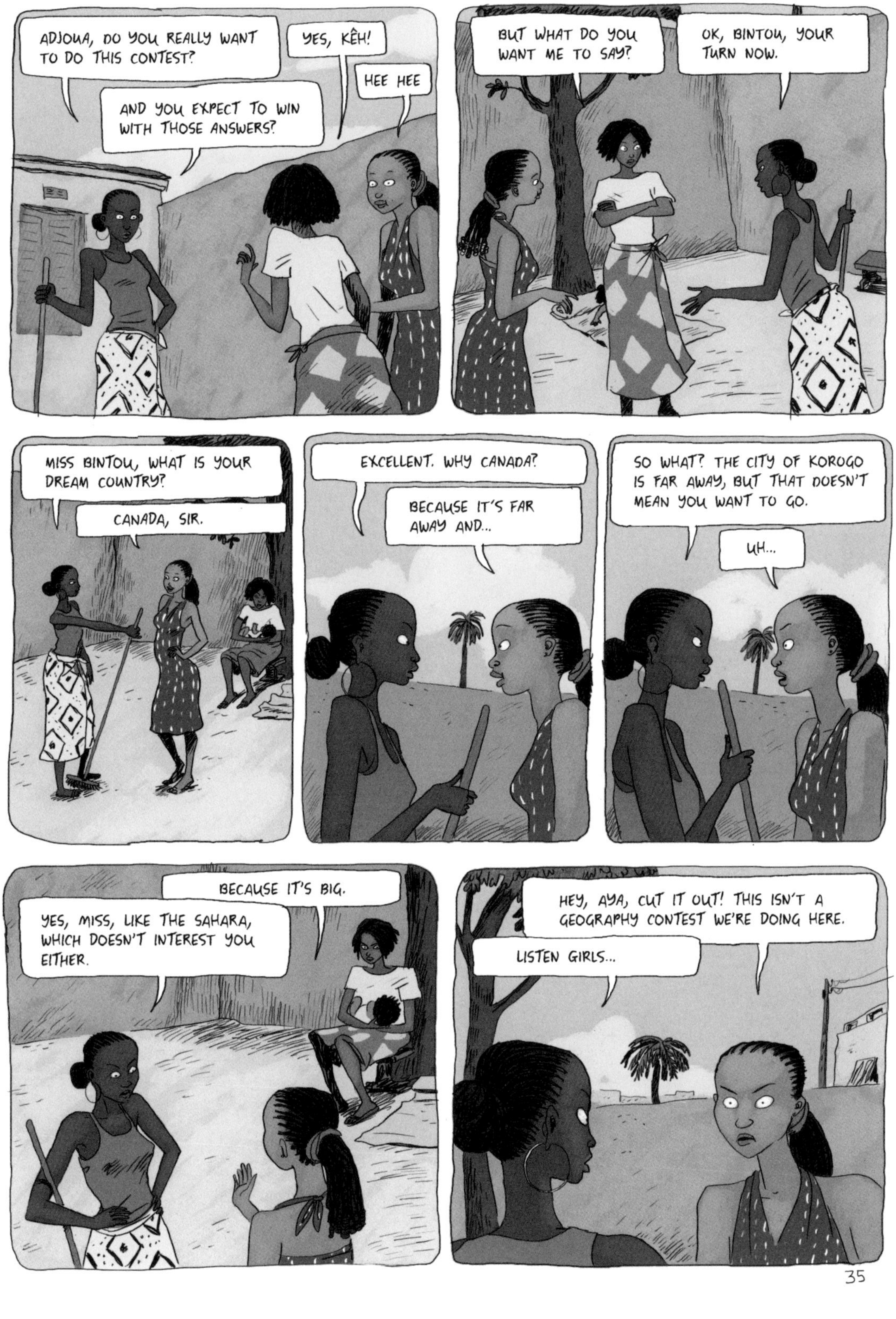
ADJOUA, DO YOU REALLY WANT TO DO THIS CONTEST?
YES, KÊH!
HEE HEE
AND YOU EXPECT TO WIN WITH THOSE ANSWERS?
BUT WHAT DO YOU WANT ME TO SAY?
OK, BINTOU, YOUR TURN NOW.
MISS BINTOU, WHAT IS YOUR DREAM COUNTRY?
CANADA, SIR.
EXCELLENT. WHY CANADA?
BECAUSE IT'S FAR AWAY AND...
SO WHAT? THE CITY OF KOROGO IS FAR AWAY, BUT THAT DOESN'T MEAN YOU WANT TO GO.
UH...
BECAUSE IT'S BIG.
YES, MISS, LIKE THE SAHARA, WHICH DOESN'T INTEREST YOU EITHER.
HEY, AYA, CUT IT OUT! THIS ISN'T A GEOGRAPHY CONTEST WE'RE DOING HERE.
LISTEN GIRLS...

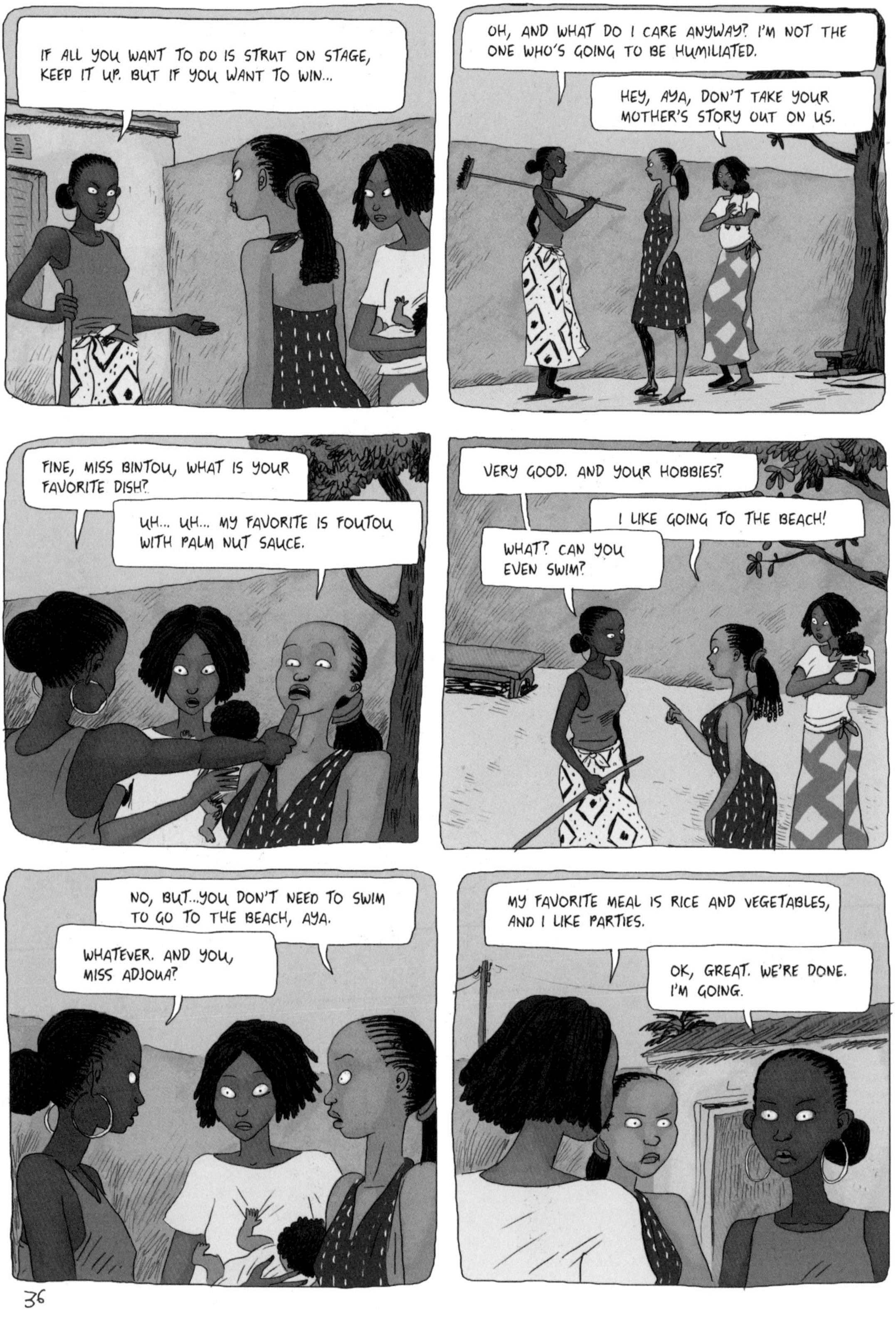
IF ALL YOU WANT TO DO IS STRUT ON STAGE, KEEP IT UP. BUT IF YOU WANT TO WIN...
OH, AND WHAT DO I CARE ANYWAY? I'M NOT THE ONE WHO'S GOING TO BE HUMILIATED.
HEY, AYA, DON'T TAKE YOUR MOTHER'S STORY OUT ON US.
FINE, MISS BINTOU, WHAT IS YOUR FAVORITE DISH?
UH... UH... MY FAVORITE IS FOUTOU WITH PALM NUT SAUCE.
VERY GOOD. AND YOUR HOBBIES?
I LIKE GOING TO THE BEACH!
WHAT? CAN YOU EVEN SWIM?
NO, BUT...YOU DON'T NEED TO SWIM TO GO TO THE BEACH, AYA.
WHATEVER. AND YOU, MISS ADJOUA?
MY FAVORITE MEAL IS RICE AND VEGETABLES, AND I LIKE PARTIES.
OK, GREAT. WE'RE DONE. I'M GOING.

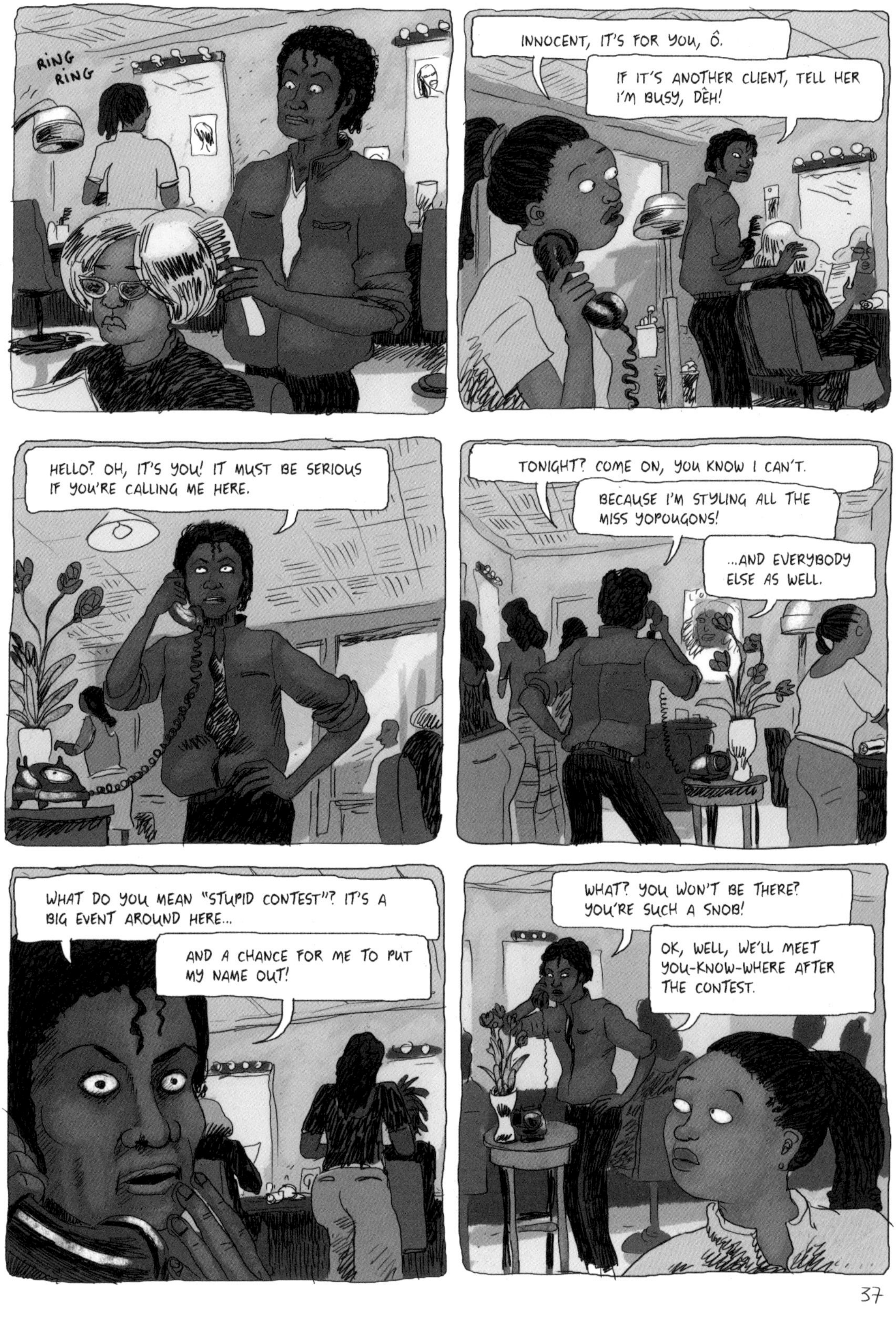
RING RING
INNOCENT, IT'S FOR YOU, Ô.
IF IT'S ANOTHER CLIENT, TELL HER I'M BUSY, DÊH!
HELLO? OH, IT'S YOU! IT MUST BE SERIOUS IF YOU'RE CALLING ME HERE.
TONIGHT? COME ON, YOU KNOW I CAN'T.
BECAUSE I'M STYLING ALL THE MISS YOPOUGONS!
...AND EVERYBODY ELSE AS WELL.
WHAT DO YOU MEAN "STUPID CONTEST"? IT'S A BIG EVENT AROUND HERE...
AND A CHANCE FOR ME TO PUT MY NAME OUT!
WHAT? YOU WON'T BE THERE? YOU'RE SUCH A SNOB!
OK, WELL, WE'LL MEET YOU-KNOW-WHERE AFTER THE CONTEST.

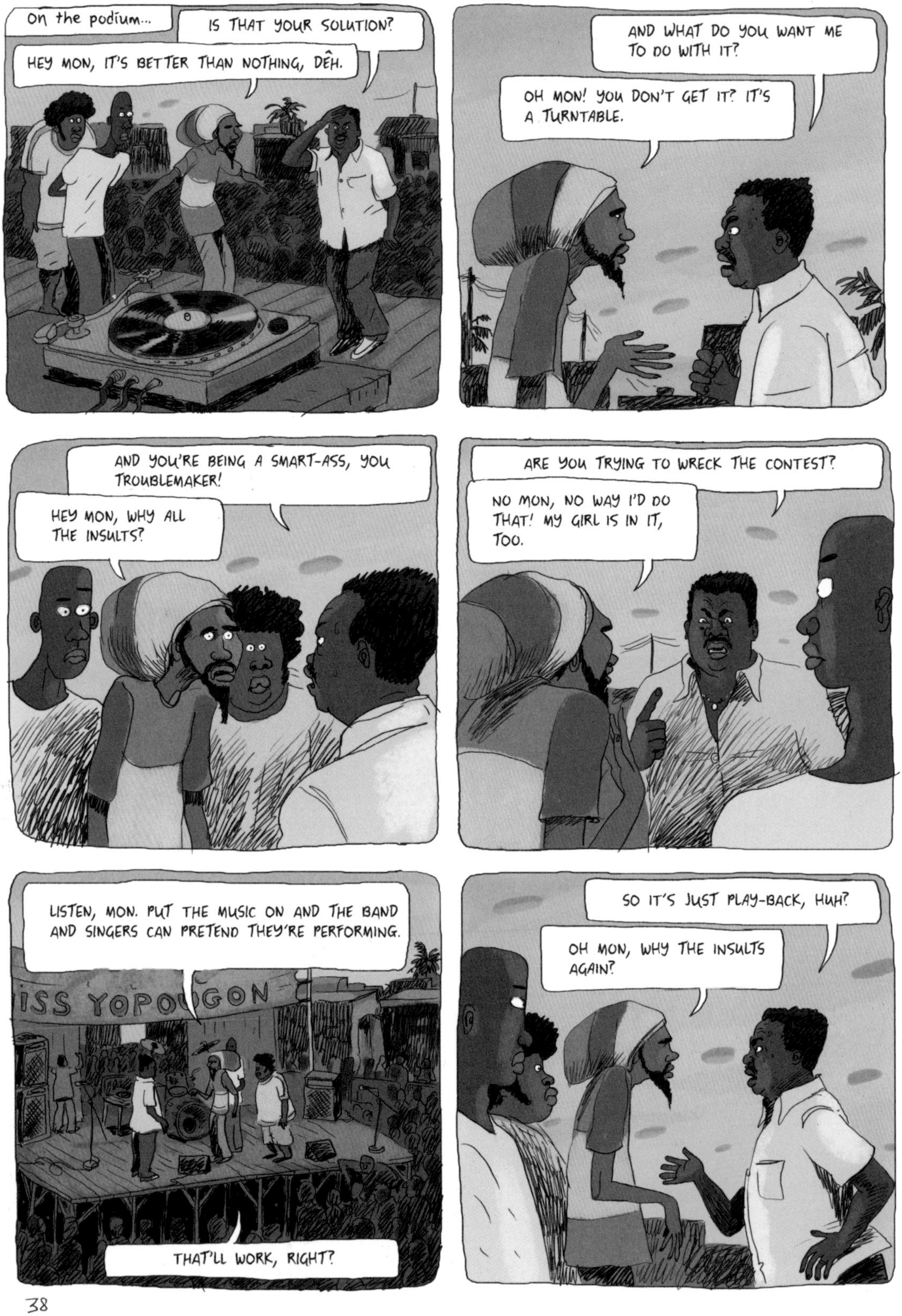
On the podium...
IS THAT YOUR SOLUTION?
HEY MON, IT'S BETTER THAN NOTHING, DÊH.
AND WHAT DO YOU WANT ME TO DO WITH IT?
OH MON! YOU DON'T GET IT? IT'S A TURNTABLE.
AND YOU'RE BEING A SMART-ASS, YOU TROUBLEMAKER!
HEY MON, WHY ALL THE INSULTS?
ARE YOU TRYING TO WRECK THE CONTEST?
NO MON, NO WAY I'D DO THAT! MY GIRL IS IN IT, TOO.
LISTEN, MON. PUT THE MUSIC ON AND THE BAND AND SINGERS CAN PRETEND THEY'RE PERFORMING.
ISS YOPOUGON
THAT'LL WORK, RIGHT?
SO IT'S JUST PLAY-BACK, HUH?
OH MON, WHY THE INSULTS AGAIN?

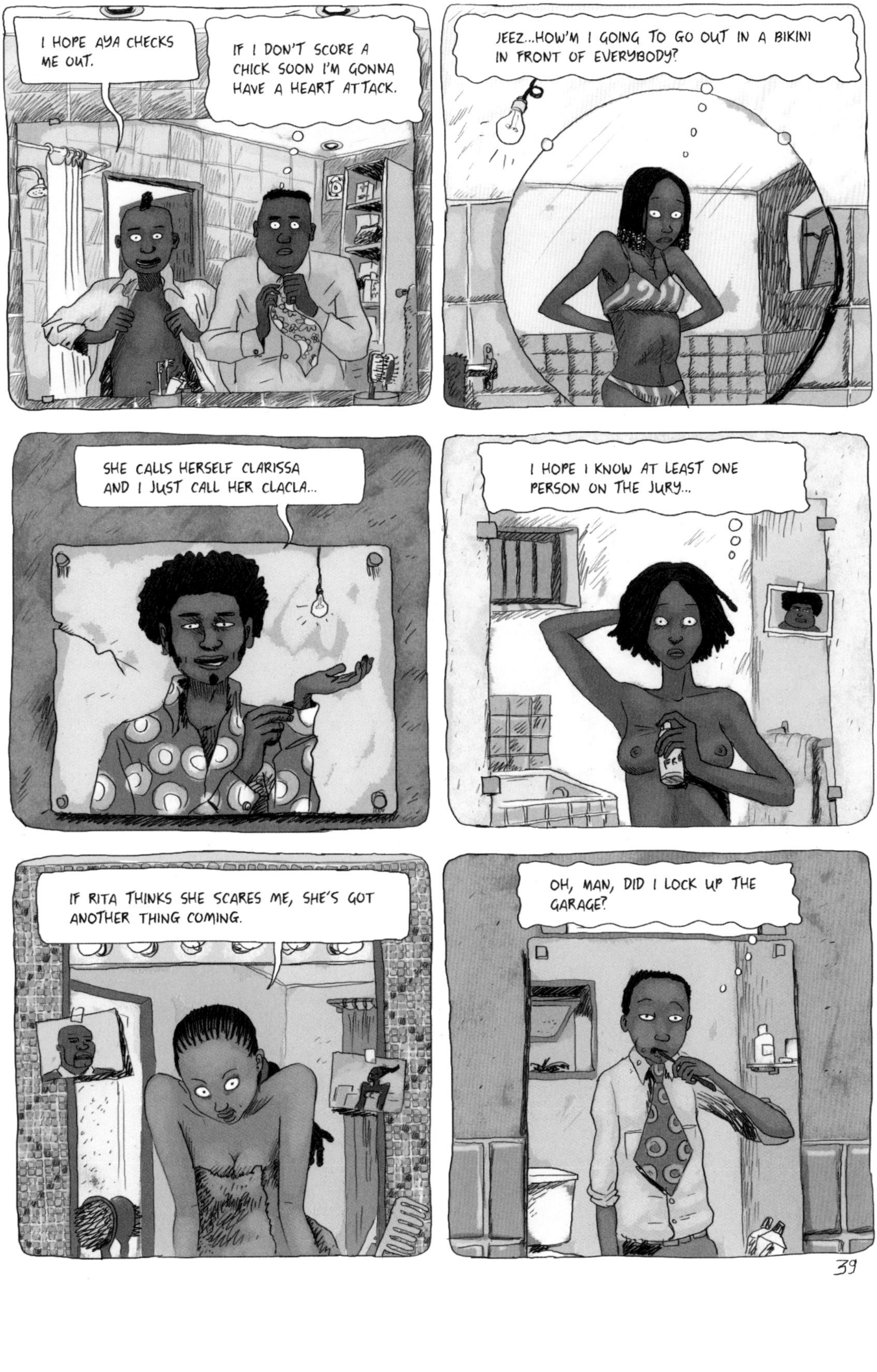
I HOPE AYA CHECKS ME OUT.
IF I DON'T SCORE A CHICK SOON I'M GONNA HAVE A HEART ATTACK.
JEEZ...HOW'M I GOING TO GO OUT IN A BIKINI IN FRONT OF EVERYBODY?
SHE CALLS HERSELF CLARISSA AND I JUST CALL HER CLACLA...
I HOPE I KNOW AT LEAST ONE PERSON ON THE JURY...
IF RITA THINKS SHE SCARES ME, SHE'S GOT ANOTHER THING COMING.
OH, MAN, DID I LOCK UP THE GARAGE?

And the big moment finally arrived....
LADIES AND GENTLEMEN OF YOP CITY
THANK YOU ALL FOR COMING OUT TONIGHT TO CROWN...
MISS YOPOUGON '80!

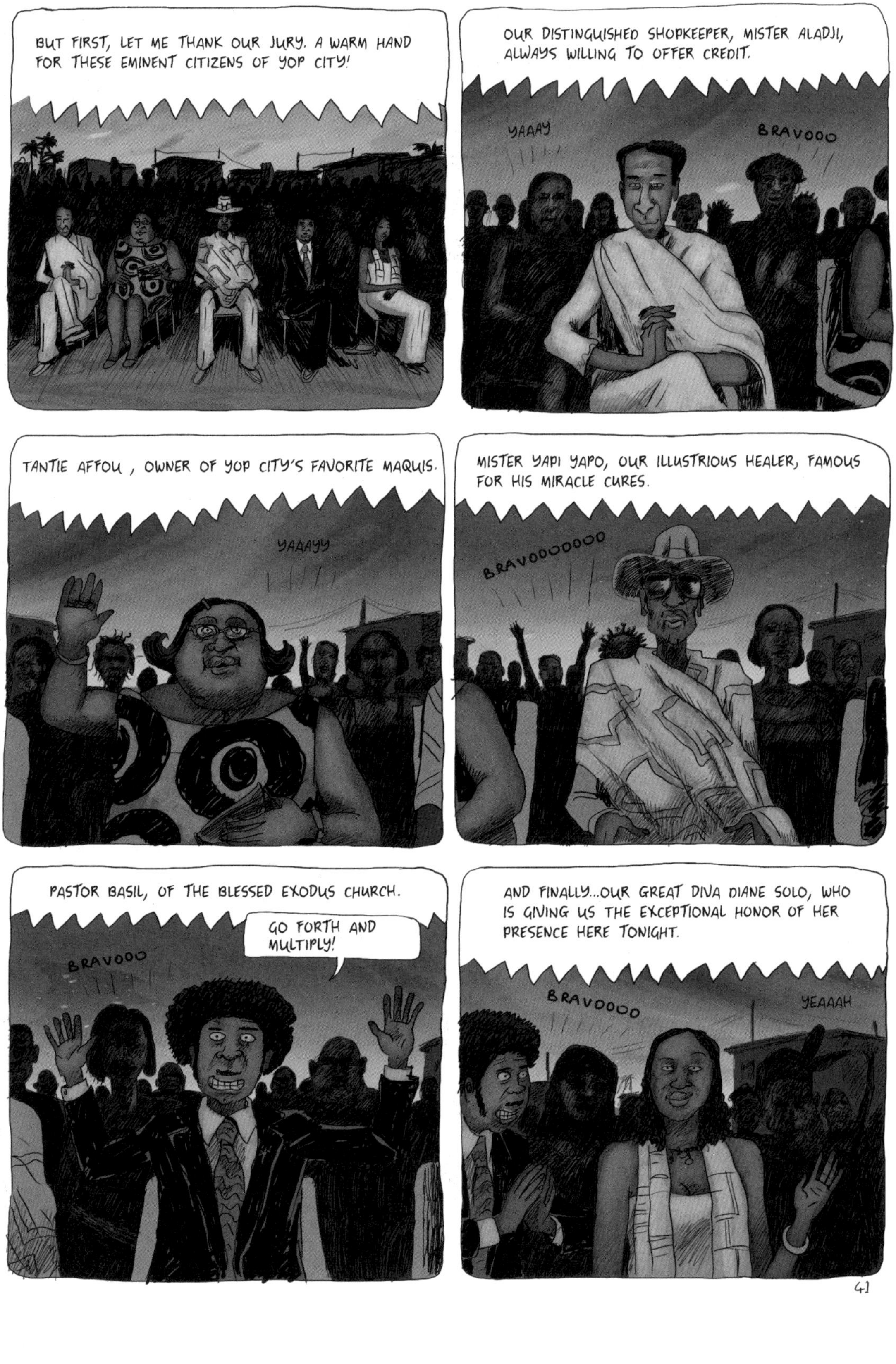
BUT FIRST, LET ME THANK OUR JURY. A WARM HAND FOR THESE EMINENT CITIZENS OF YOP CITY!
OUR DISTINGUISHED SHOPKEEPER, MISTER ALADJI, ALWAYS WILLING TO OFFER CREDIT.
YAAAY
BRAVOOO
TANTIE AFFOU, OWNER OF YOP CITY'S FAVORITE MAQUIS.
YAAAYY
MISTER YAPI YAPO, OUR ILLUSTRIOUS HEALER, FAMOUS FOR HIS MIRACLE CURES.
BRAVOOOOOOOO
PASTOR BASIL, OF THE BLESSED EXODUS CHURCH.
GO FORTH AND MULTIPLY!
BRAVOOO
AND FINALLY...OUR GREAT DIVA DIANE SOLO, WHO IS GIVING US THE EXCEPTIONAL HONOR OF HER PRESENCE HERE TONIGHT.
BRAVOOOO
YEAAAH

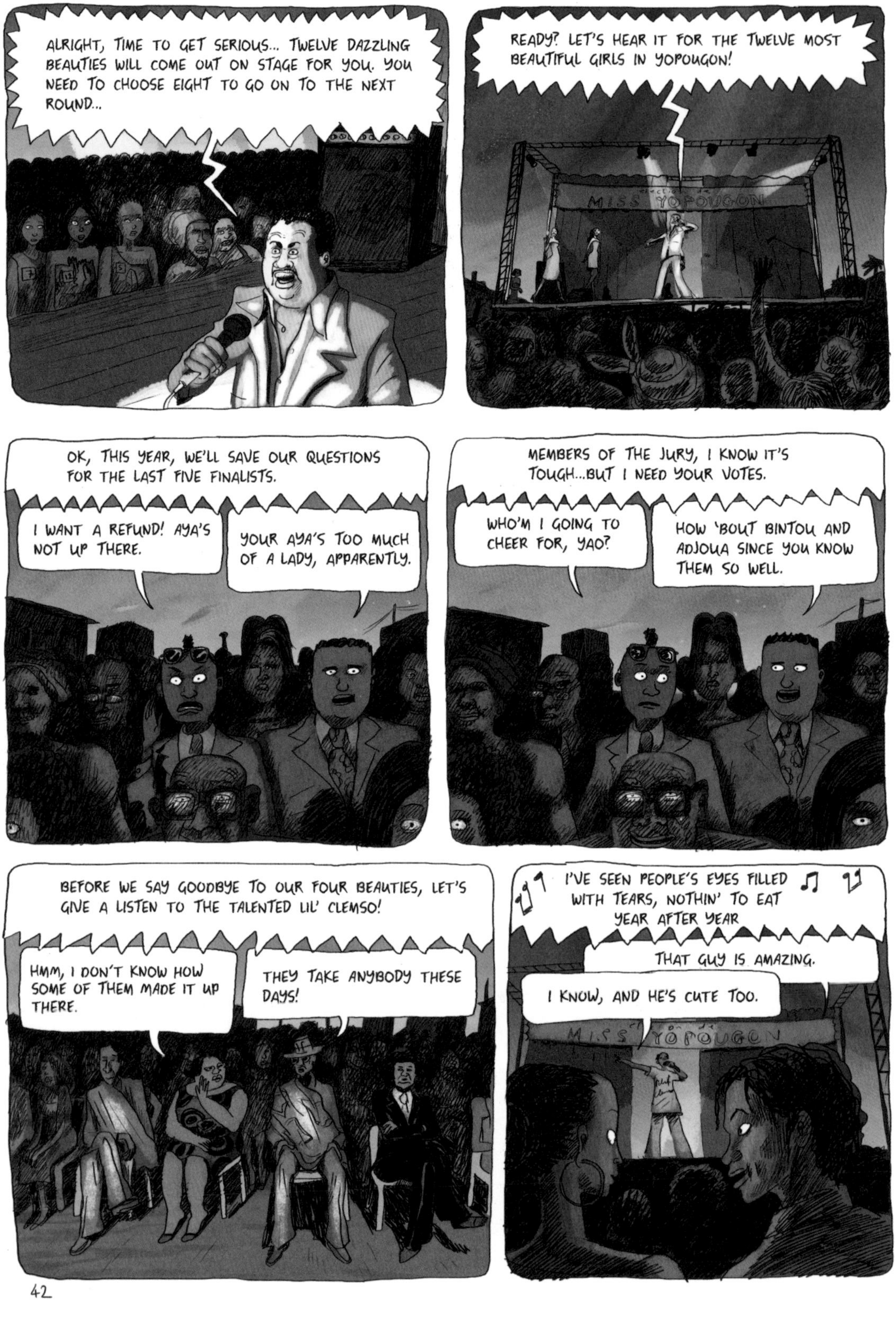
ALRIGHT, TIME TO GET SERIOUS... TWELVE DAZZLING BEAUTIES WILL COME OUT ON STAGE FOR YOU. YOU NEED TO CHOOSE EIGHT TO GO ON TO THE NEXT ROUND...
READY? LET'S HEAR IT FOR THE TWELVE MOST BEAUTIFUL GIRLS IN YOPOUGON!
MISS YOPOUGON
OK, THIS YEAR, WE'LL SAVE OUR QUESTIONS FOR THE LAST FIVE FINALISTS.
I WANT A REFUND! AYA'S NOT UP THERE.
YOUR AYA'S TOO MUCH OF A LADY, APPARENTLY.
MEMBERS OF THE JURY, I KNOW IT'S TOUGH...BUT I NEED YOUR VOTES.
WHO'M I GOING TO CHEER FOR, YAO?
HOW 'BOUT BINTOU AND ADJOUA SINCE YOU KNOW THEM SO WELL.
BEFORE WE SAY GOODBYE TO OUR FOUR BEAUTIES, LET'S GIVE A LISTEN TO THE TALENTED LIL' CLEMSO!
HMM, I DON'T KNOW HOW SOME OF THEM MADE IT UP THERE.
THEY TAKE ANYBODY THESE DAYS!
I'VE SEEN PEOPLE'S EYES FILLED WITH TEARS, NOTHIN' TO EAT YEAR AFTER YEAR
THAT GUY IS AMAZING.
I KNOW, AND HE'S CUTE TOO.
MISS YOPOUGON

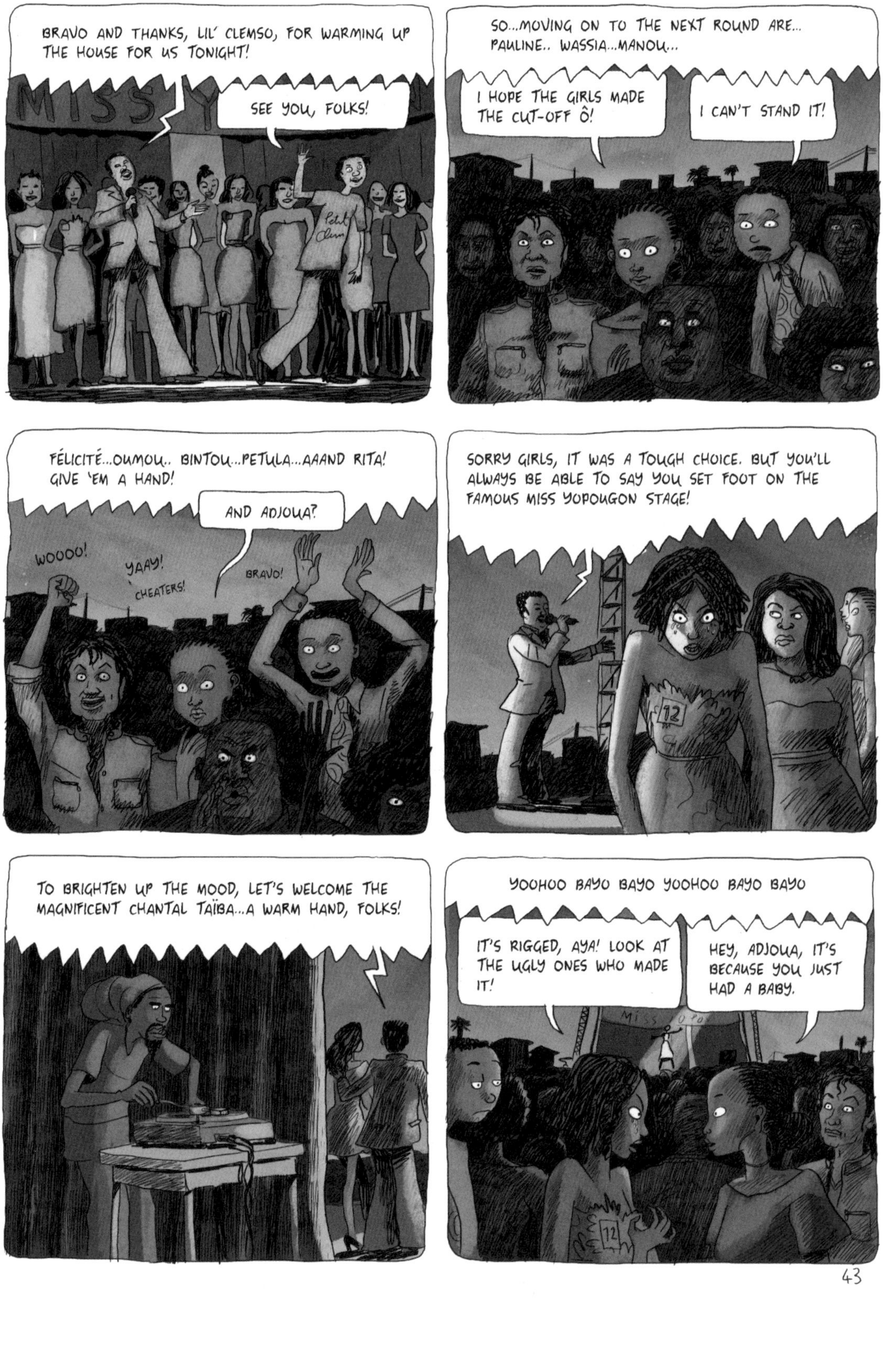
BRAVO AND THANKS, LIL' CLEMSO, FOR WARMING UP THE HOUSE FOR US TONIGHT!
SEE YOU, FOLKS!
SO...MOVING ON TO THE NEXT ROUND ARE... PAULINE.. WASSIA...MANOU...
I HOPE THE GIRLS MADE THE CUT-OFF Ô!
I CAN'T STAND IT!
FÉLICITÉ...OUMOU.. BINTOU...PETULA...AAAND RITA! GIVE 'EM A HAND!
AND ADJOUA?
WOOOO!
YAAY!
CHEATERS!
BRAVO!
SORRY GIRLS, IT WAS A TOUGH CHOICE. BUT YOU'LL ALWAYS BE ABLE TO SAY YOU SET FOOT ON THE FAMOUS MISS YOPOUGON STAGE!
12
TO BRIGHTEN UP THE MOOD, LET'S WELCOME THE MAGNIFICENT CHANTAL TAÏBA...A WARM HAND, FOLKS!
YOOHOO BAYO BAYO YOOHOO BAYO BAYO
IT'S RIGGED, AYA! LOOK AT THE UGLY ONES WHO MADE IT!
HEY, ADJOUA, IT'S BECAUSE YOU JUST HAD A BABY.
12

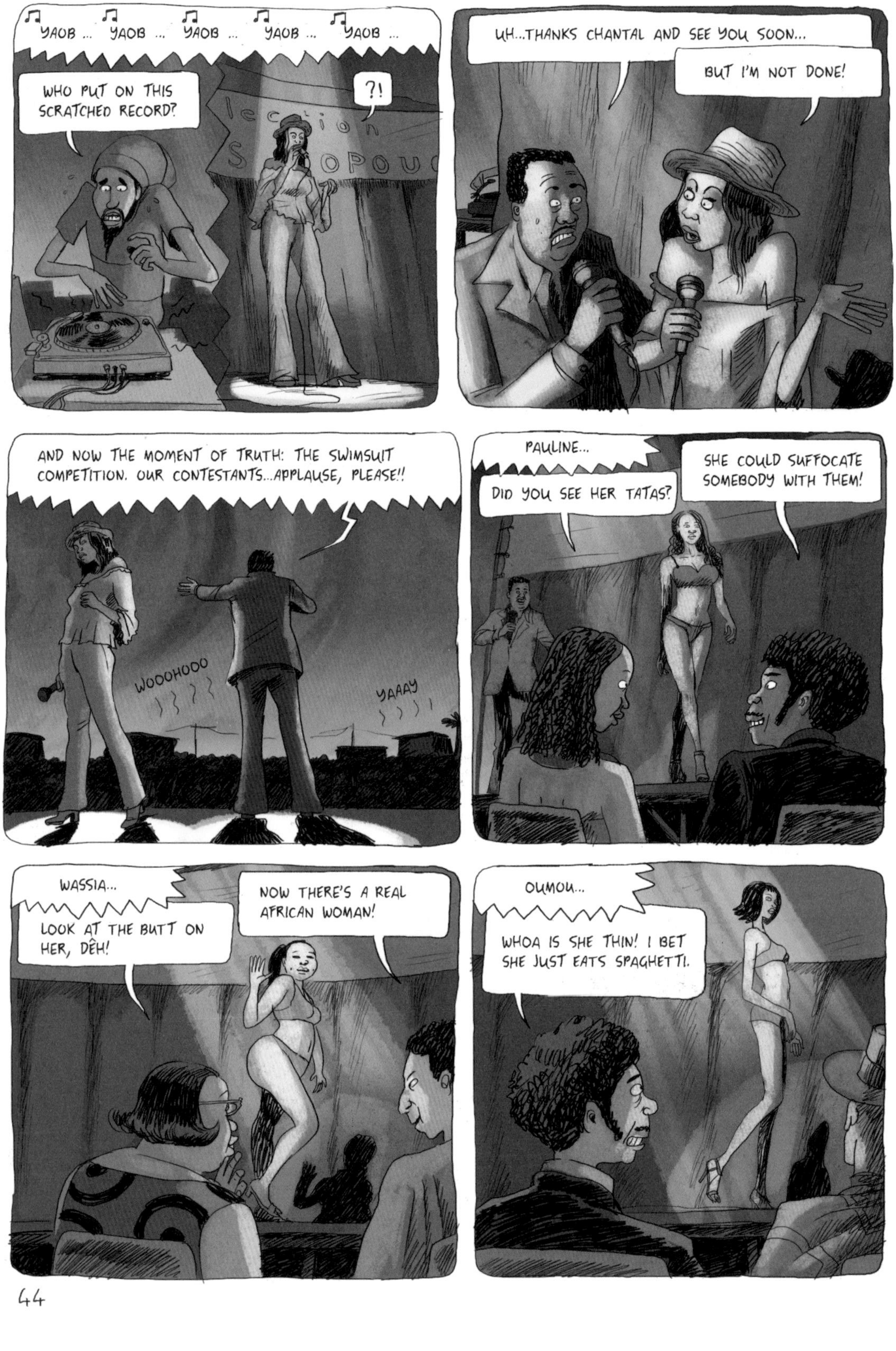

♫ YAOB ... ♫ YAOB ... ♫ YAOB ... ♫ YAOB ... ♫ YAOB ...
WHO PUT ON THIS SCRATCHED RECORD?
?!
UH...THANKS CHANTAL AND SEE YOU SOON...
BUT I'M NOT DONE!
AND NOW THE MOMENT OF TRUTH: THE SWIMSUIT COMPETITION. OUR CONTESTANTS...APPLAUSE, PLEASE!!
WOOOHOOO
YAAAY
PAULINE...
DID YOU SEE HER TATAS?
SHE COULD SUFFOCATE SOMEBODY WITH THEM!
WASSIA...
LOOK AT THE BUTT ON HER, DÊH!
NOW THERE'S A REAL AFRICAN WOMAN!
OUMOU...
WHOA IS SHE THIN! I BET SHE JUST EATS SPAGHETTI.

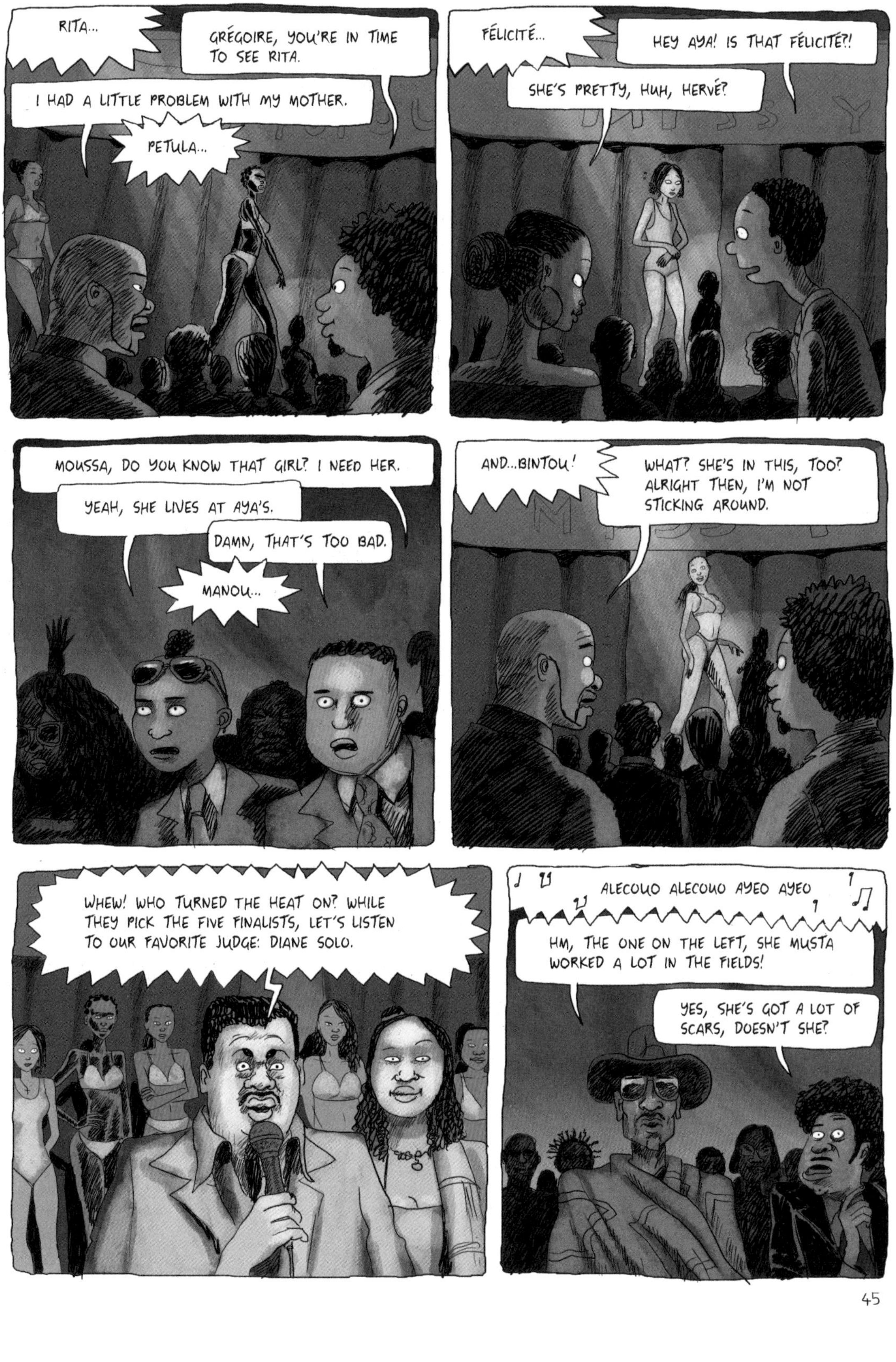
RITA...
GRÉGOIRE, YOU'RE IN TIME TO SEE RITA.
I HAD A LITTLE PROBLEM WITH MY MOTHER.
PETULA...
FÉLICITÉ...
HEY AYA! IS THAT FÉLICITÉ?!
SHE'S PRETTY, HUH, HERVÉ?
MOUSSA, DO YOU KNOW THAT GIRL? I NEED HER.
YEAH, SHE LIVES AT AYA'S.
DAMN, THAT'S TOO BAD.
MANOU...
AND...BINTOU!
WHAT? SHE'S IN THIS, TOO? ALRIGHT THEN, I'M NOT STICKING AROUND.
WHEW! WHO TURNED THE HEAT ON? WHILE THEY PICK THE FIVE FINALISTS, LET'S LISTEN TO OUR FAVORITE JUDGE: DIANE SOLO.
ALECOUO ALECOUO AYEO AYEO
HM, THE ONE ON THE LEFT, SHE MUSTA WORKED A LOT IN THE FIELDS!
YES, SHE'S GOT A LOT OF SCARS, DOESN'T SHE?

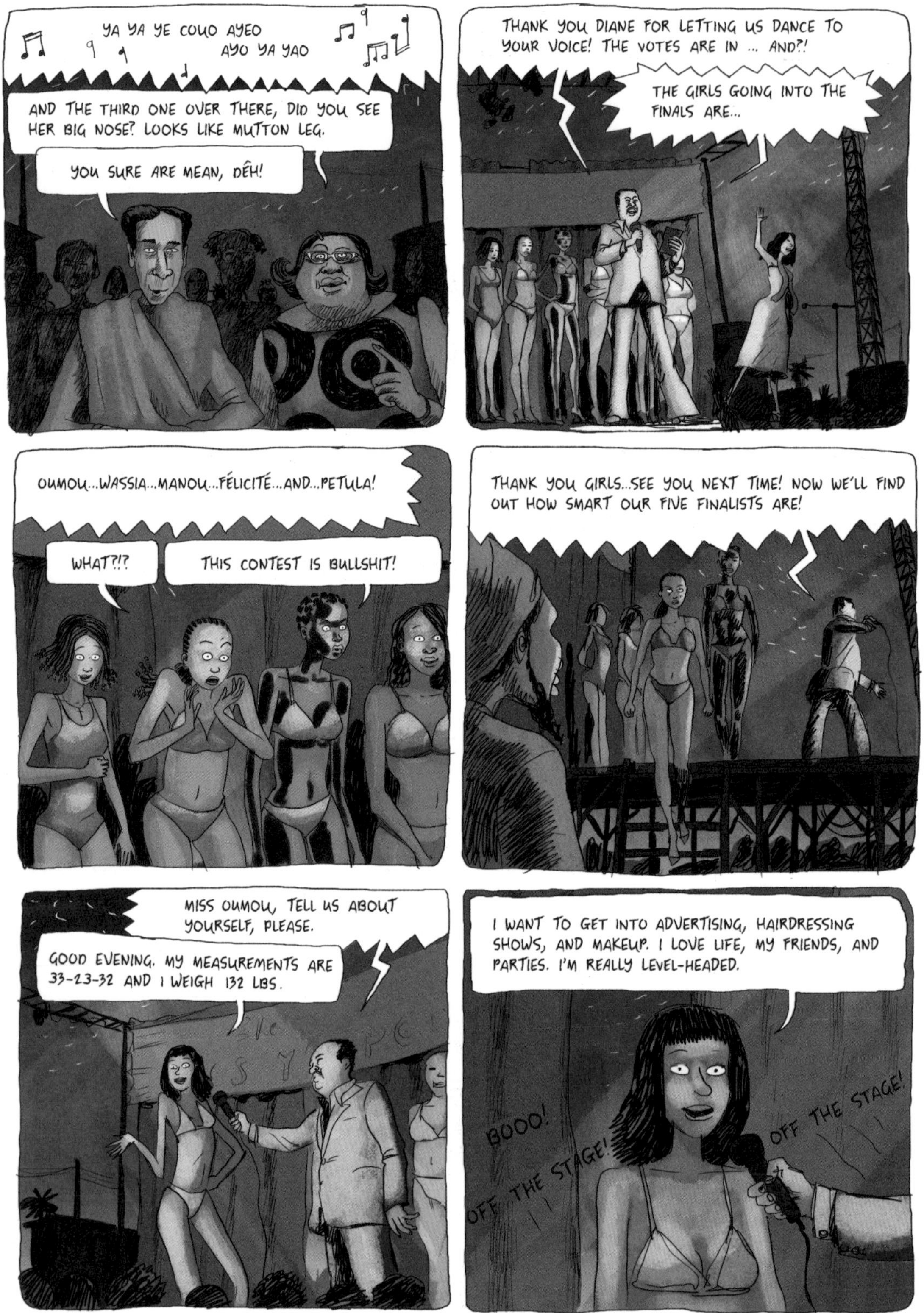
YA YA YE COUO AYEO
AYO YA YAO
AND THE THIRD ONE OVER THERE, DID YOU SEE HER BIG NOSE? LOOKS LIKE MUTTON LEG.
YOU SURE ARE MEAN, DÊH!
THANK YOU DIANE FOR LETTING US DANCE TO YOUR VOICE! THE VOTES ARE IN ... AND?!
THE GIRLS GOING INTO THE FINALS ARE...
OUMOU...WASSIA...MANOU...FÉLICITÉ...AND...PETULA!
WHAT?!?
THIS CONTEST IS BULLSHIT!
THANK YOU GIRLS...SEE YOU NEXT TIME! NOW WE'LL FIND OUT HOW SMART OUR FIVE FINALISTS ARE!
MISS OUMOU, TELL US ABOUT YOURSELF, PLEASE.
GOOD EVENING. MY MEASUREMENTS ARE 33-23-32 AND I WEIGH 132 LBS.
I WANT TO GET INTO ADVERTISING, HAIRDRESSING SHOWS, AND MAKEUP. I LOVE LIFE, MY FRIENDS, AND PARTIES. I'M REALLY LEVEL-HEADED.
BOOO!
OFF THE STAGE!
OFF THE STAGE!

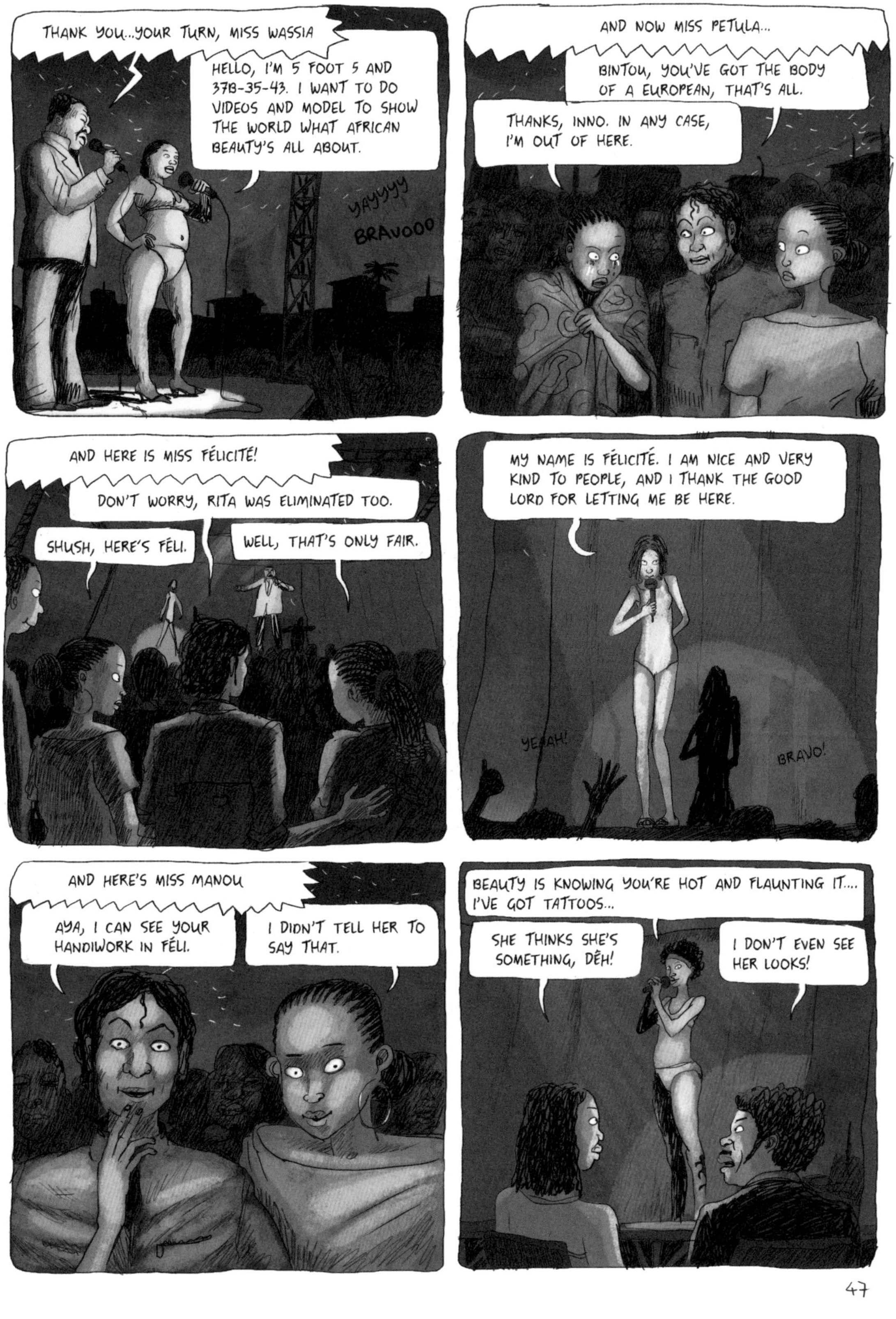
THANK YOU...YOUR TURN, MISS WASSIA
HELLO, I'M 5 FOOT 5 AND 37B-35-43. I WANT TO DO VIDEOS AND MODEL TO SHOW THE WORLD WHAT AFRICAN BEAUTY'S ALL ABOUT.
YAYYYY
BRAVOOO
AND NOW MISS PETULA...
BINTOU, YOU'VE GOT THE BODY OF A EUROPEAN, THAT'S ALL.
THANKS, INNO. IN ANY CASE, I'M OUT OF HERE.
AND HERE IS MISS FÉLICITÉ!
DON'T WORRY, RITA WAS ELIMINATED TOO.
SHUSH, HERE'S FÉLI.
WELL, THAT'S ONLY FAIR.
MY NAME IS FÉLICITÉ. I AM NICE AND VERY KIND TO PEOPLE, AND I THANK THE GOOD LORD FOR LETTING ME BE HERE.
YEAAH!
BRAVO!
AND HERE'S MISS MANOU
AYA, I CAN SEE YOUR HANDIWORK IN FÉLI.
I DIDN'T TELL HER TO SAY THAT.
BEAUTY IS KNOWING YOU'RE HOT AND FLAUNTING IT.... I'VE GOT TATTOOS...
SHE THINKS SHE'S SOMETHING, DÊH!
I DON'T EVEN SEE HER LOOKS!

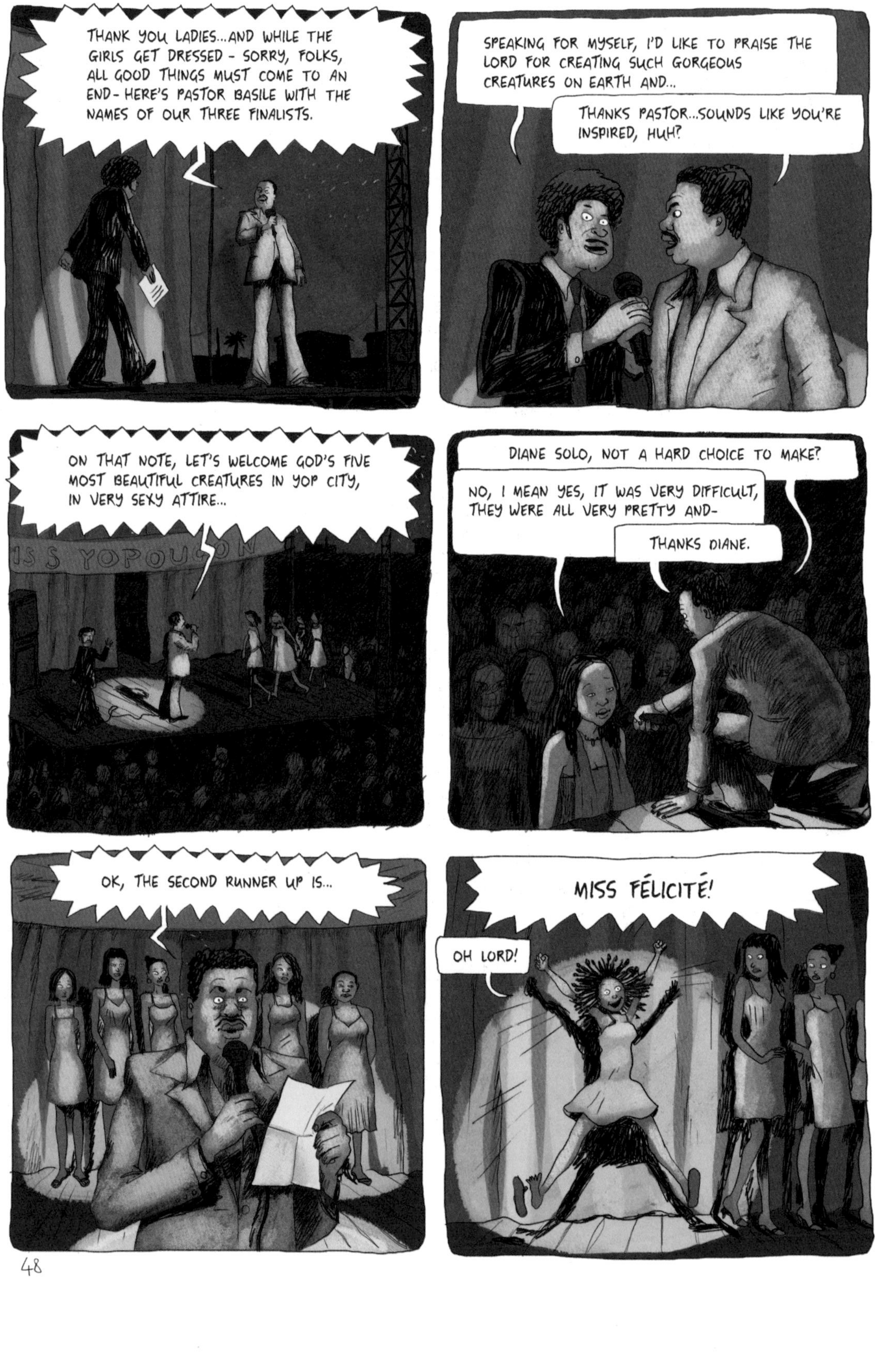
THANK YOU LADIES...AND WHILE THE GIRLS GET DRESSED - SORRY, FOLKS, ALL GOOD THINGS MUST COME TO AN END- HERE'S PASTOR BASILE WITH THE NAMES OF OUR THREE FINALISTS.
SPEAKING FOR MYSELF, I'D LIKE TO PRAISE THE LORD FOR CREATING SUCH GORGEOUS CREATURES ON EARTH AND...
THANKS PASTOR...SOUNDS LIKE YOU'RE INSPIRED, HUH?
ON THAT NOTE, LET'S WELCOME GOD'S FIVE MOST BEAUTIFUL CREATURES IN YOP CITY, IN VERY SEXY ATTIRE...
DIANE SOLO, NOT A HARD CHOICE TO MAKE?
NO, I MEAN YES, IT WAS VERY DIFFICULT, THEY WERE ALL VERY PRETTY AND-
THANKS DIANE.
OK, THE SECOND RUNNER UP IS...
MISS FÉLICITÉ!
OH LORD!

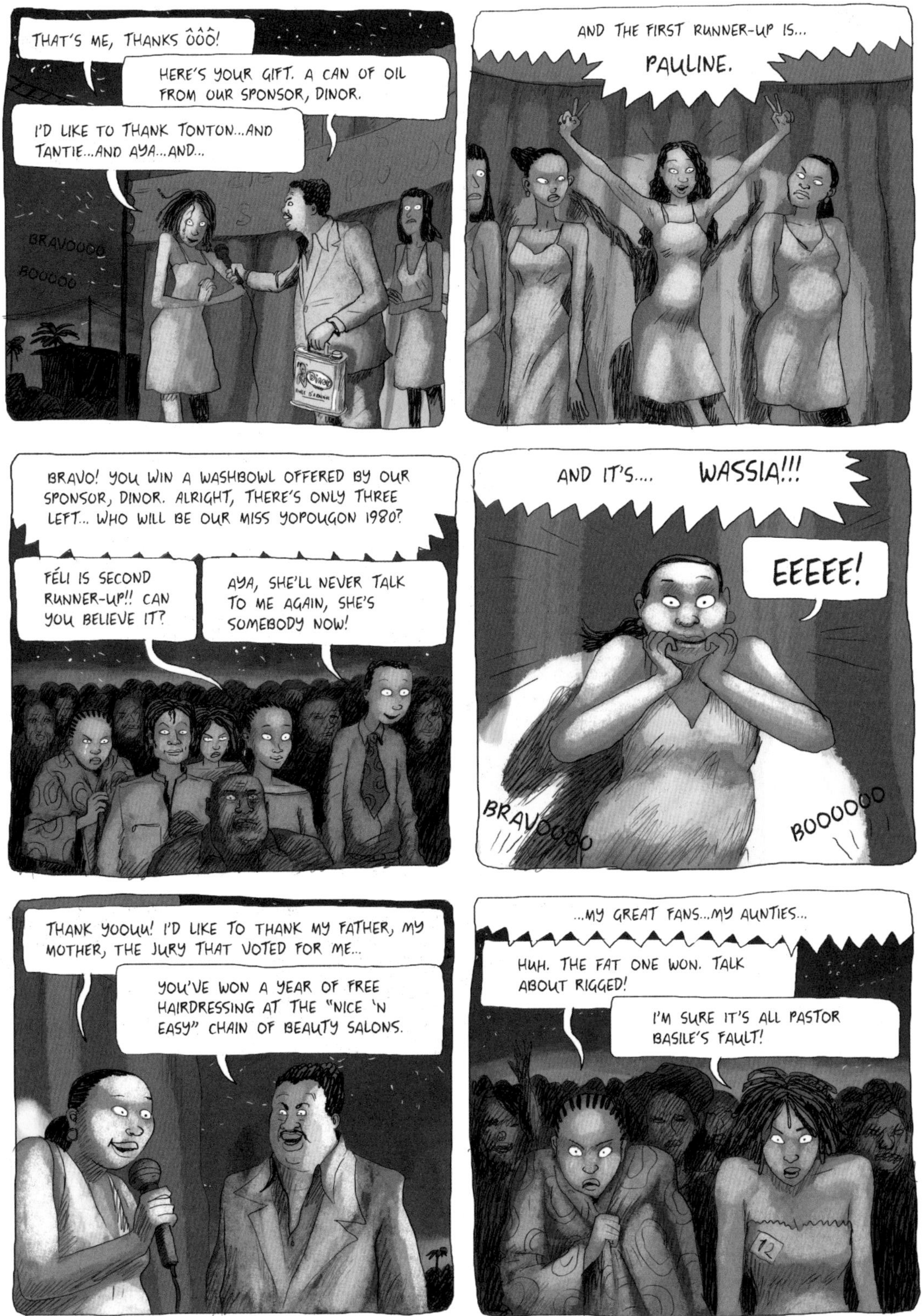
THAT'S ME, THANKS ÔÔÔ!
HERE'S YOUR GIFT. A CAN OF OIL FROM OUR SPONSOR, DINOR.
I'D LIKE TO THANK TONTON...AND TANTIE...AND AYA...AND...
BRAVOOOO
BOOOOO
AND THE FIRST RUNNER-UP IS...
PAULINE.
BRAVO! YOU WIN A WASHBOWL OFFERED BY OUR SPONSOR, DINOR. ALRIGHT, THERE'S ONLY THREE LEFT... WHO WILL BE OUR MISS YOPOUGON 1980?
FÉLI IS SECOND RUNNER-UP!! CAN YOU BELIEVE IT?
AYA, SHE'LL NEVER TALK TO ME AGAIN, SHE'S SOMEBODY NOW!
AND IT'S.... WASSIA!!!
EEEEE!
BRAVOOOO
BOOOOOO
THANK YOOUU! I'D LIKE TO THANK MY FATHER, MY MOTHER, THE JURY THAT VOTED FOR ME...
YOU'VE WON A YEAR OF FREE HAIRDRESSING AT THE "NICE 'N EASY" CHAIN OF BEAUTY SALONS.
...MY GREAT FANS...MY AUNTIES...
HUH. THE FAT ONE WON. TALK ABOUT RIGGED!
I'M SURE IT'S ALL PASTOR BASILE'S FAULT!

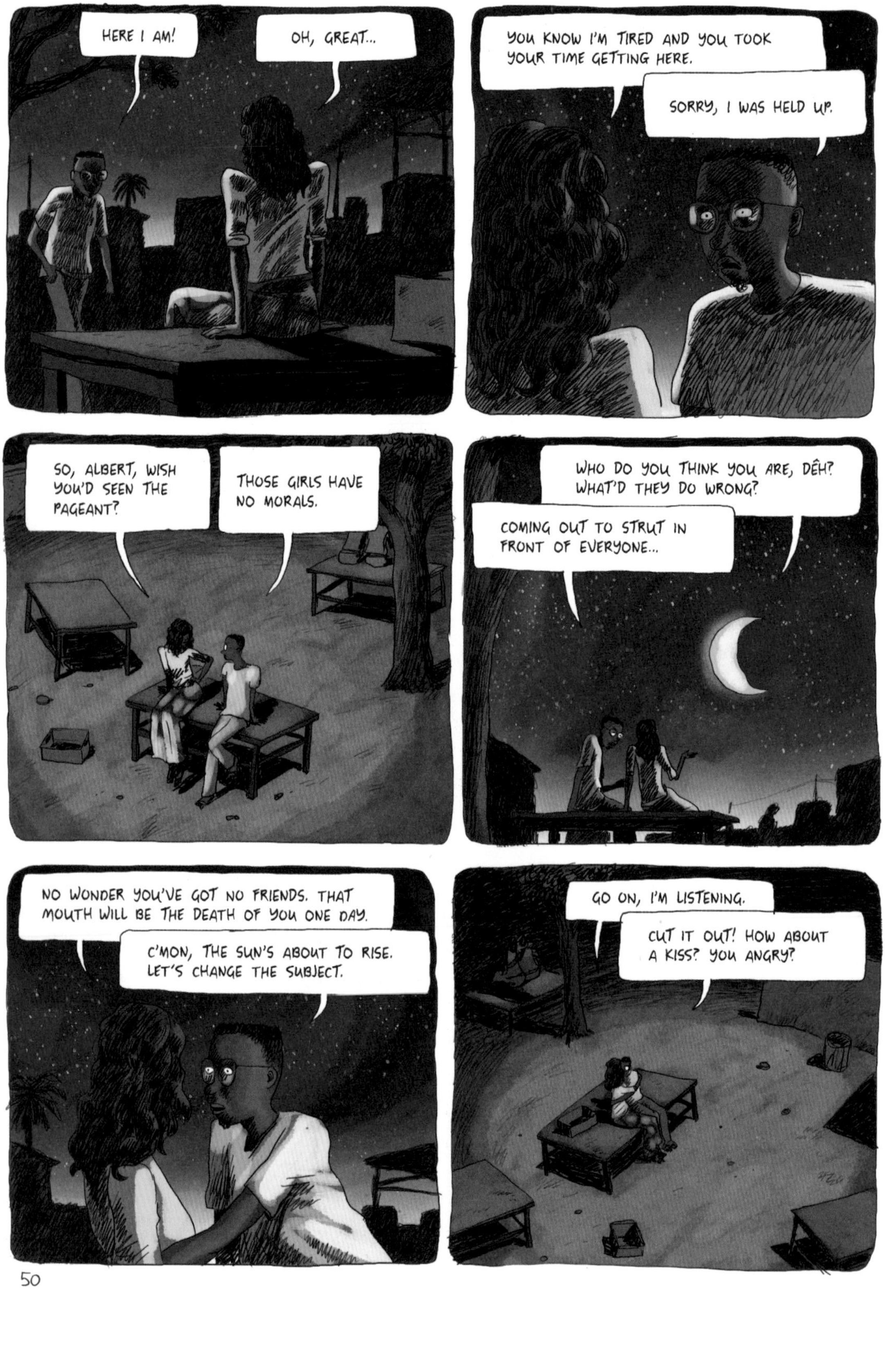
HERE I AM!
OH, GREAT...
YOU KNOW I'M TIRED AND YOU TOOK YOUR TIME GETTING HERE.
SORRY, I WAS HELD UP.
SO, ALBERT, WISH YOU'D SEEN THE PAGEANT?
THOSE GIRLS HAVE NO MORALS.
WHO DO YOU THINK YOU ARE, DÊH? WHAT'D THEY DO WRONG?
COMING OUT TO STRUT IN FRONT OF EVERYONE...
NO WONDER YOU'VE GOT NO FRIENDS. THAT MOUTH WILL BE THE DEATH OF YOU ONE DAY.
C'MON, THE SUN'S ABOUT TO RISE. LET'S CHANGE THE SUBJECT.
GO ON, I'M LISTENING.
CUT IT OUT! HOW ABOUT A KISS? YOU ANGRY?

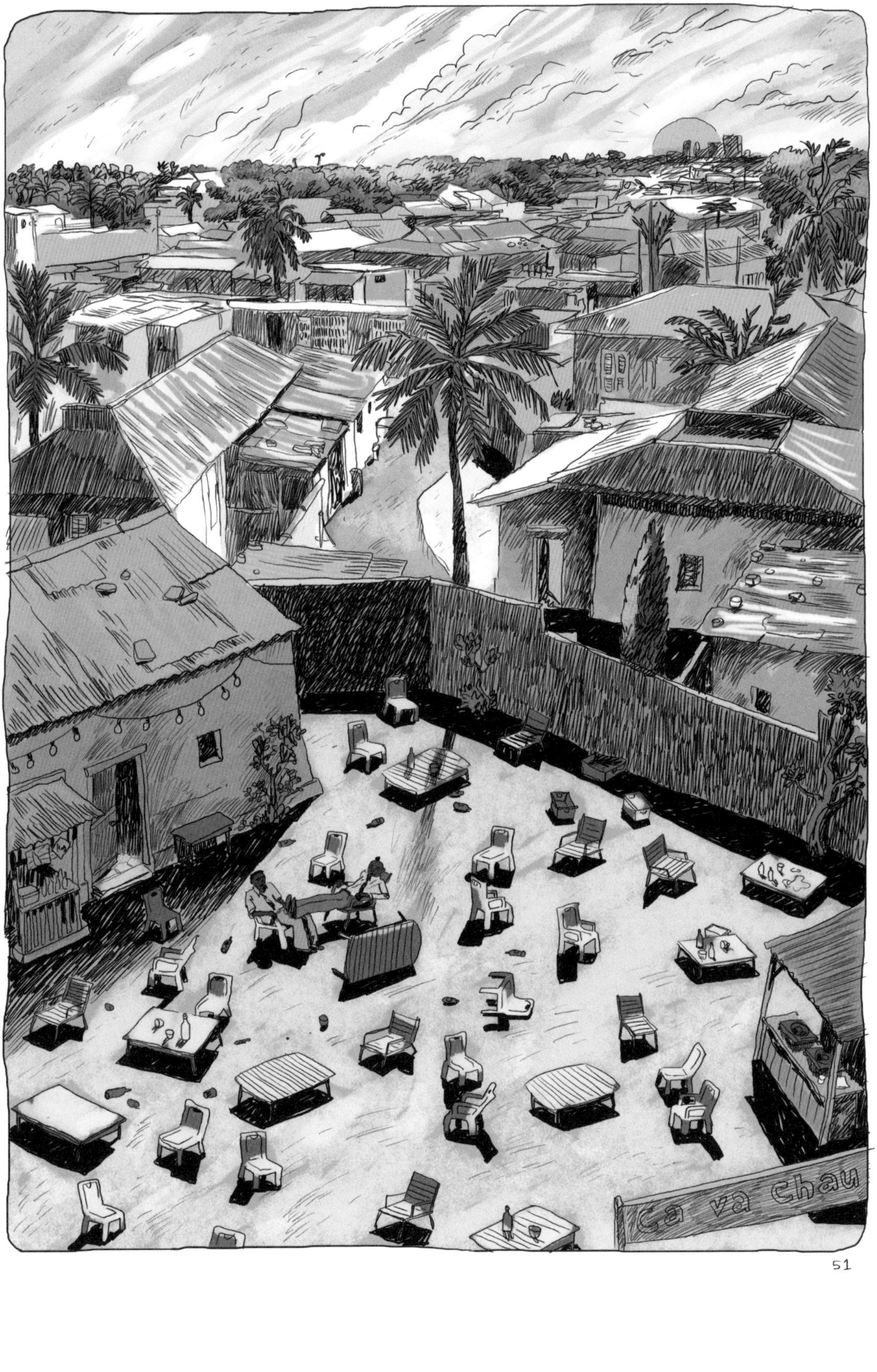
Ça va chau

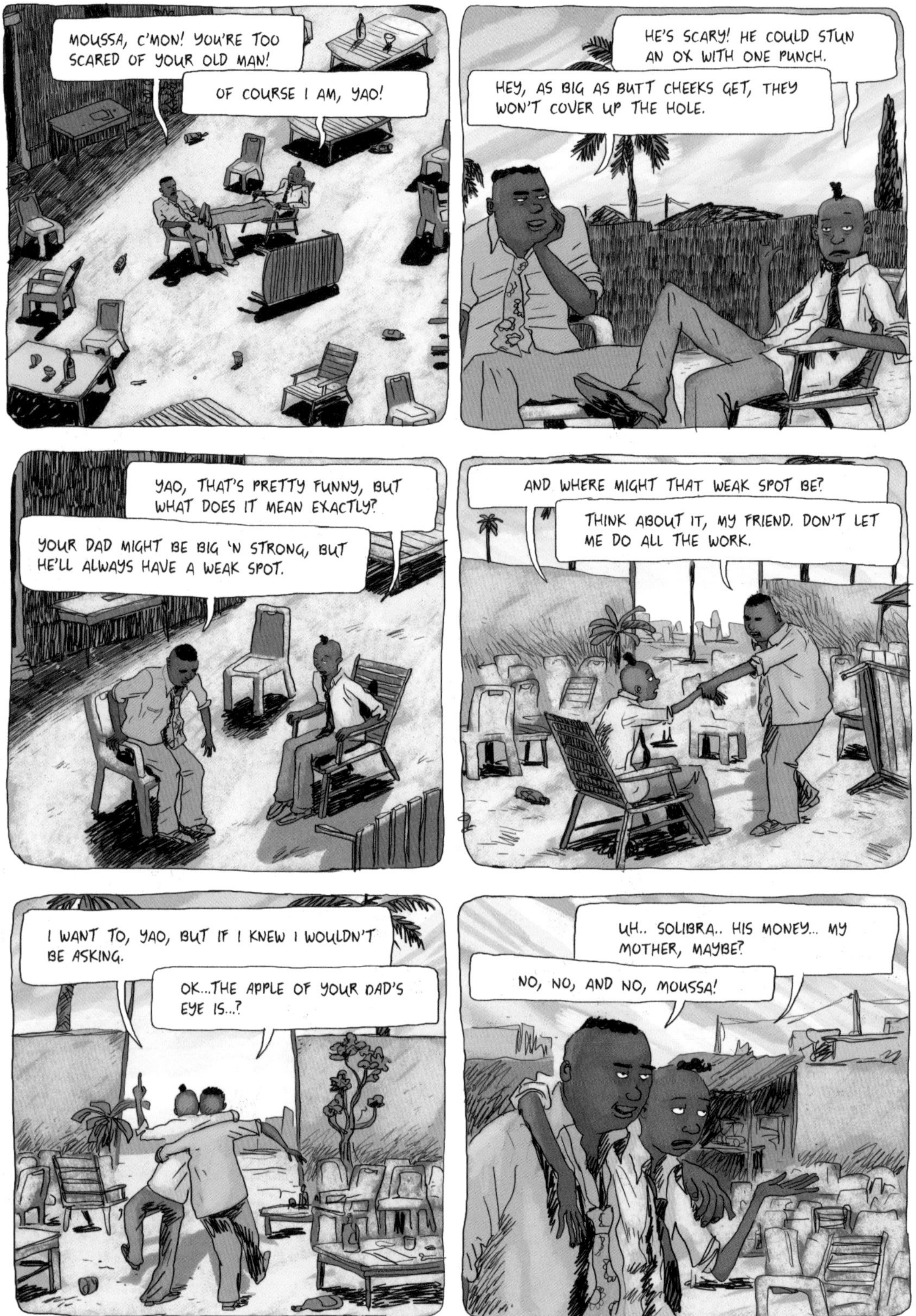
MOUSSA, C'MON! YOU'RE TOO SCARED OF YOUR OLD MAN!
OF COURSE I AM, YAO!
HE'S SCARY! HE COULD STUN AN OX WITH ONE PUNCH.
HEY, AS BIG AS BUTT CHEEKS GET, THEY WON'T COVER UP THE HOLE.
YAO, THAT'S PRETTY FUNNY, BUT WHAT DOES IT MEAN EXACTLY?
YOUR DAD MIGHT BE BIG 'N STRONG, BUT HE'LL ALWAYS HAVE A WEAK SPOT.
AND WHERE MIGHT THAT WEAK SPOT BE?
THINK ABOUT IT, MY FRIEND. DON'T LET ME DO ALL THE WORK.
I WANT TO, YAO, BUT IF I KNEW I WOULDN'T BE ASKING.
OK...THE APPLE OF YOUR DAD'S EYE IS...?
UH.. SOLIBRA.. HIS MONEY... MY MOTHER, MAYBE?
NO, NO, AND NO, MOUSSA!

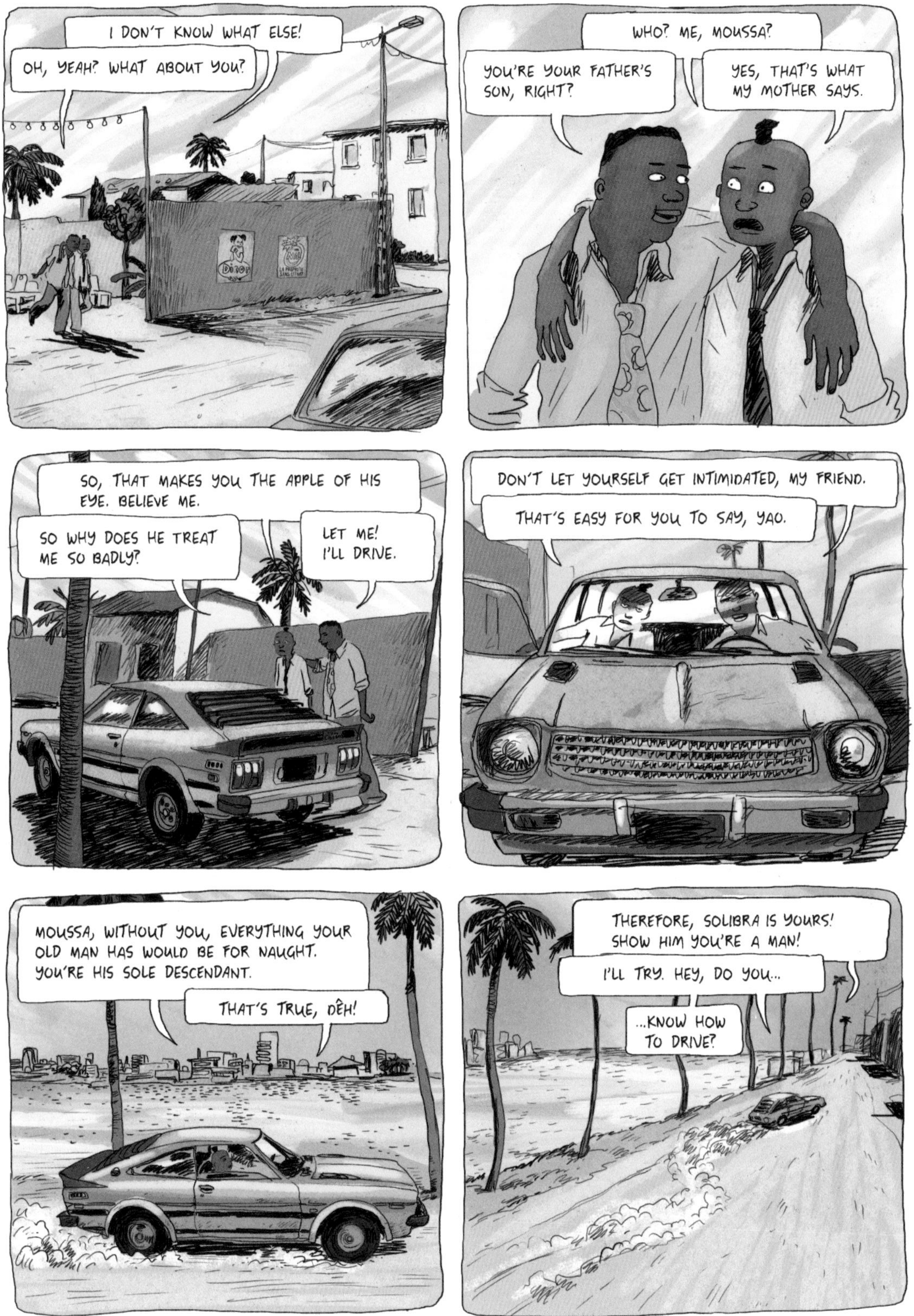

I DON'T KNOW WHAT ELSE!
OH, YEAH? WHAT ABOUT YOU?
WHO? ME, MOUSSA?
YOU'RE YOUR FATHER'S SON, RIGHT?
YES, THAT'S WHAT MY MOTHER SAYS.
SO, THAT MAKES YOU THE APPLE OF HIS EYE. BELIEVE ME.
SO WHY DOES HE TREAT ME SO BADLY?
LET ME! I'LL DRIVE.
DON'T LET YOURSELF GET INTIMIDATED, MY FRIEND.
THAT'S EASY FOR YOU TO SAY, YAO.
MOUSSA, WITHOUT YOU, EVERYTHING YOUR OLD MAN HAS WOULD BE FOR NAUGHT. YOU'RE HIS SOLE DESCENDANT.
THAT'S TRUE, DÊH!
THEREFORE, SOLIBRA IS YOURS! SHOW HIM YOU'RE A MAN!
I'LL TRY. HEY, DO YOU...
...KNOW HOW TO DRIVE?

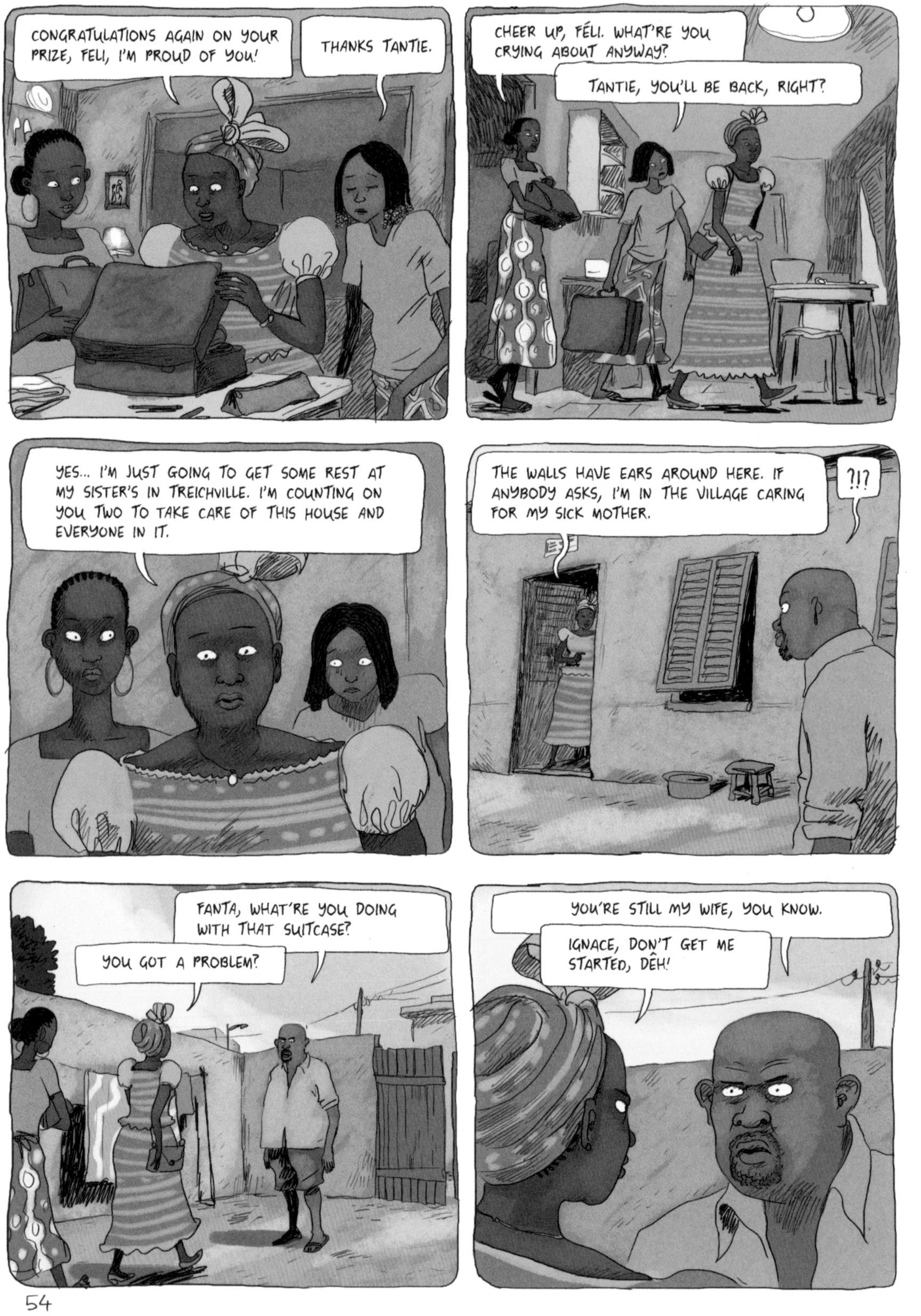
CONGRATULATIONS AGAIN ON YOUR PRIZE, FELI, I'M PROUD OF YOU!
THANKS TANTIE.
CHEER UP, FÉLI. WHAT'RE YOU CRYING ABOUT ANYWAY?
TANTIE, YOU'LL BE BACK, RIGHT?
YES... I'M JUST GOING TO GET SOME REST AT MY SISTER'S IN TREICHVILLE. I'M COUNTING ON YOU TWO TO TAKE CARE OF THIS HOUSE AND EVERYONE IN IT.
THE WALLS HAVE EARS AROUND HERE. IF ANYBODY ASKS, I'M IN THE VILLAGE CARING FOR MY SICK MOTHER.
?!?
FANTA, WHAT'RE YOU DOING WITH THAT SUITCASE?
YOU GOT A PROBLEM?
YOU'RE STILL MY WIFE, YOU KNOW.
IGNACE, DON'T GET ME STARTED, DÊH!

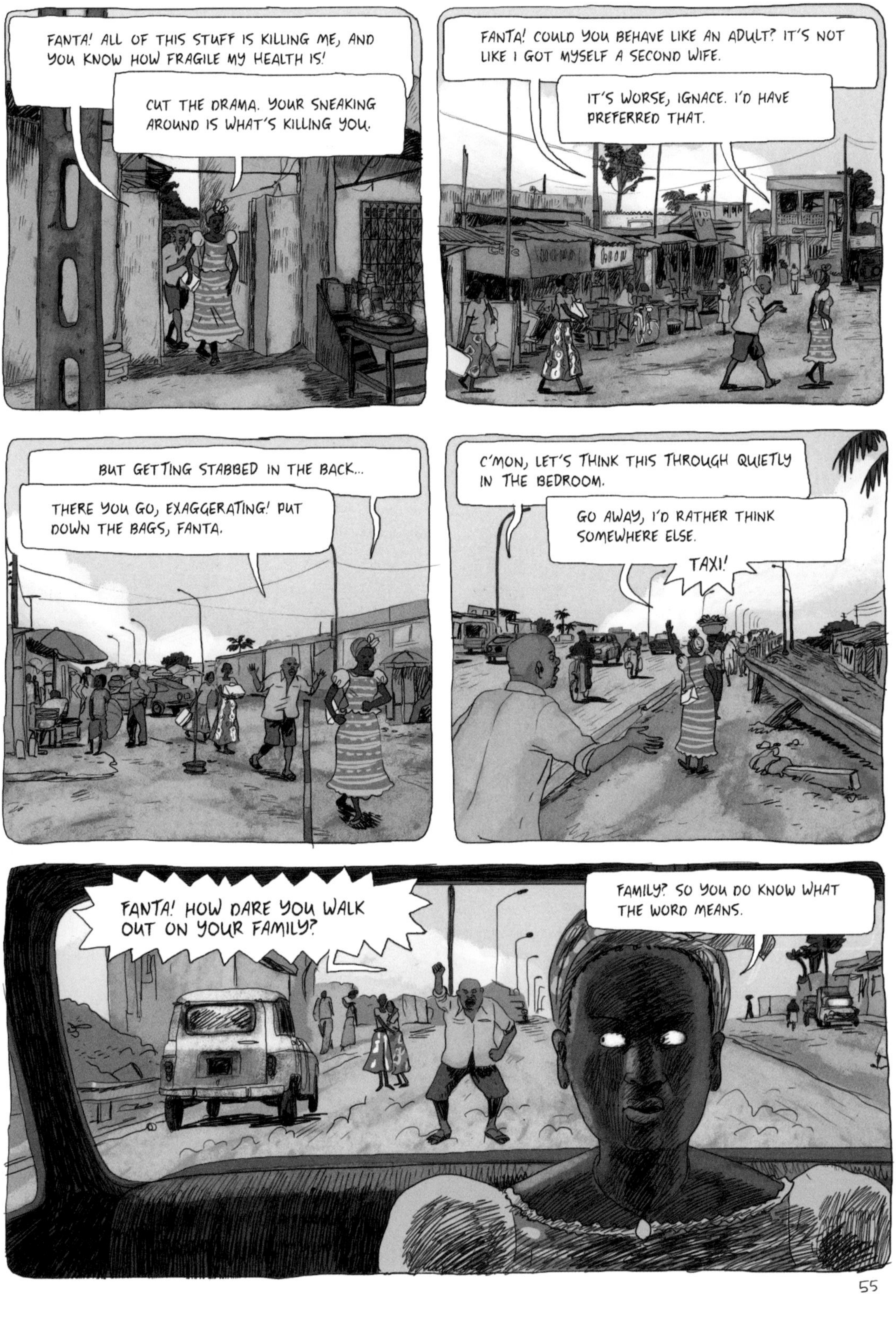
FANTA! ALL OF THIS STUFF IS KILLING ME, AND YOU KNOW HOW FRAGILE MY HEALTH IS!
CUT THE DRAMA. YOUR SNEAKING AROUND IS WHAT'S KILLING YOU.
FANTA! COULD YOU BEHAVE LIKE AN ADULT? IT'S NOT LIKE I GOT MYSELF A SECOND WIFE.
IT'S WORSE, IGNACE. I'D HAVE PREFERRED THAT.
BUT GETTING STABBED IN THE BACK...
THERE YOU GO, EXAGGERATING! PUT DOWN THE BAGS, FANTA.
C'MON, LET'S THINK THIS THROUGH QUIETLY IN THE BEDROOM.
GO AWAY, I'D RATHER THINK SOMEWHERE ELSE.
TAXI!
FANTA! HOW DARE YOU WALK OUT ON YOUR FAMILY?
FAMILY? SO YOU DO KNOW WHAT THE WORD MEANS.

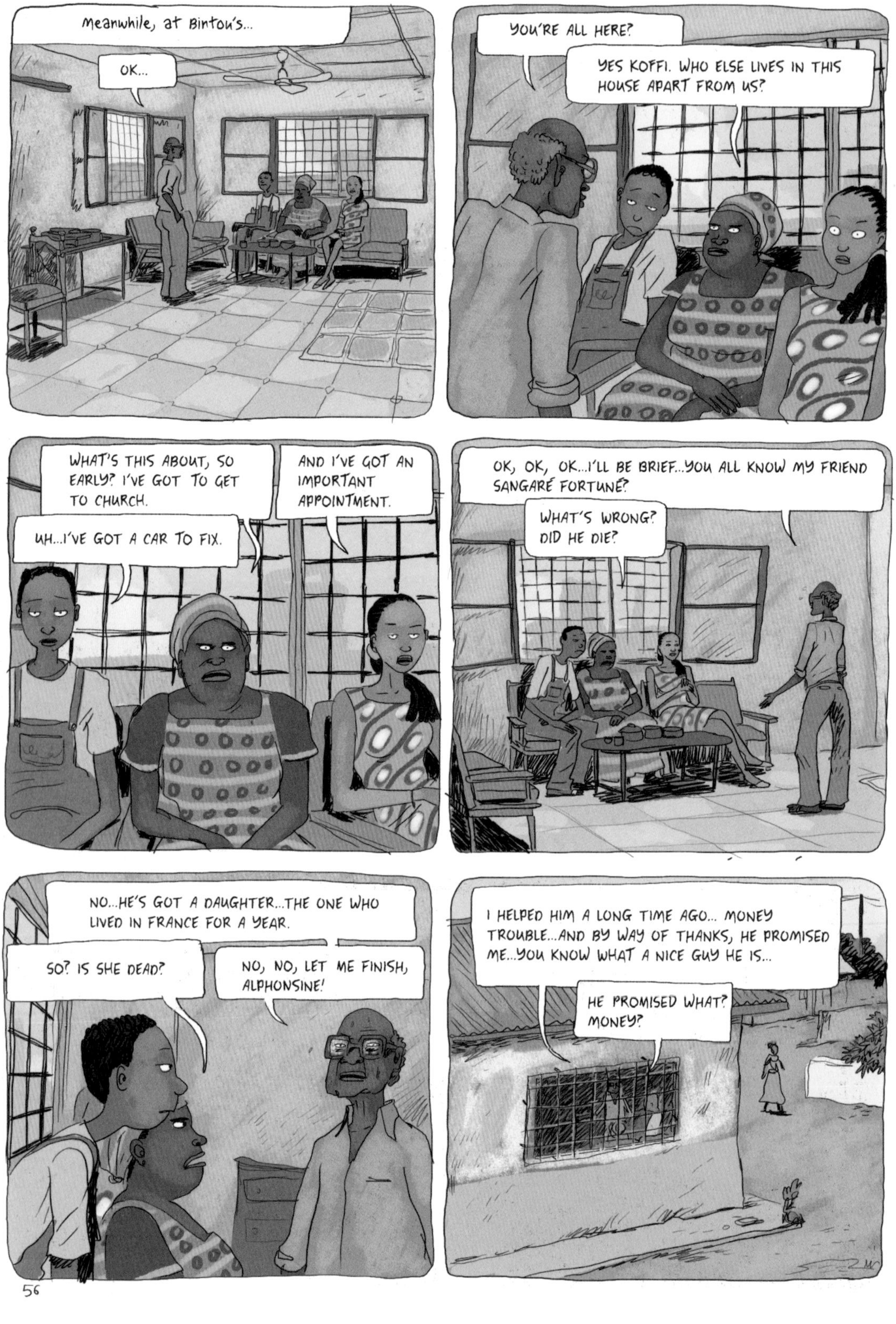
Meanwhile, at Bintou's...
OK...
YOU'RE ALL HERE?
YES KOFFI. WHO ELSE LIVES IN THIS HOUSE APART FROM US?
WHAT'S THIS ABOUT, SO EARLY? I'VE GOT TO GET TO CHURCH.
AND I'VE GOT AN IMPORTANT APPOINTMENT.
UH...I'VE GOT A CAR TO FIX.
OK, OK, OK...I'LL BE BRIEF...YOU ALL KNOW MY FRIEND SANGARÉ FORTUNÉ?
WHAT'S WRONG? DID HE DIE?
NO...HE'S GOT A DAUGHTER...THE ONE WHO LIVED IN FRANCE FOR A YEAR.
SO? IS SHE DEAD?
NO, NO, LET ME FINISH, ALPHONSINE!
I HELPED HIM A LONG TIME AGO... MONEY TROUBLE...AND BY WAY OF THANKS, HE PROMISED ME...YOU KNOW WHAT A NICE GUY HE IS...
HE PROMISED WHAT? MONEY?

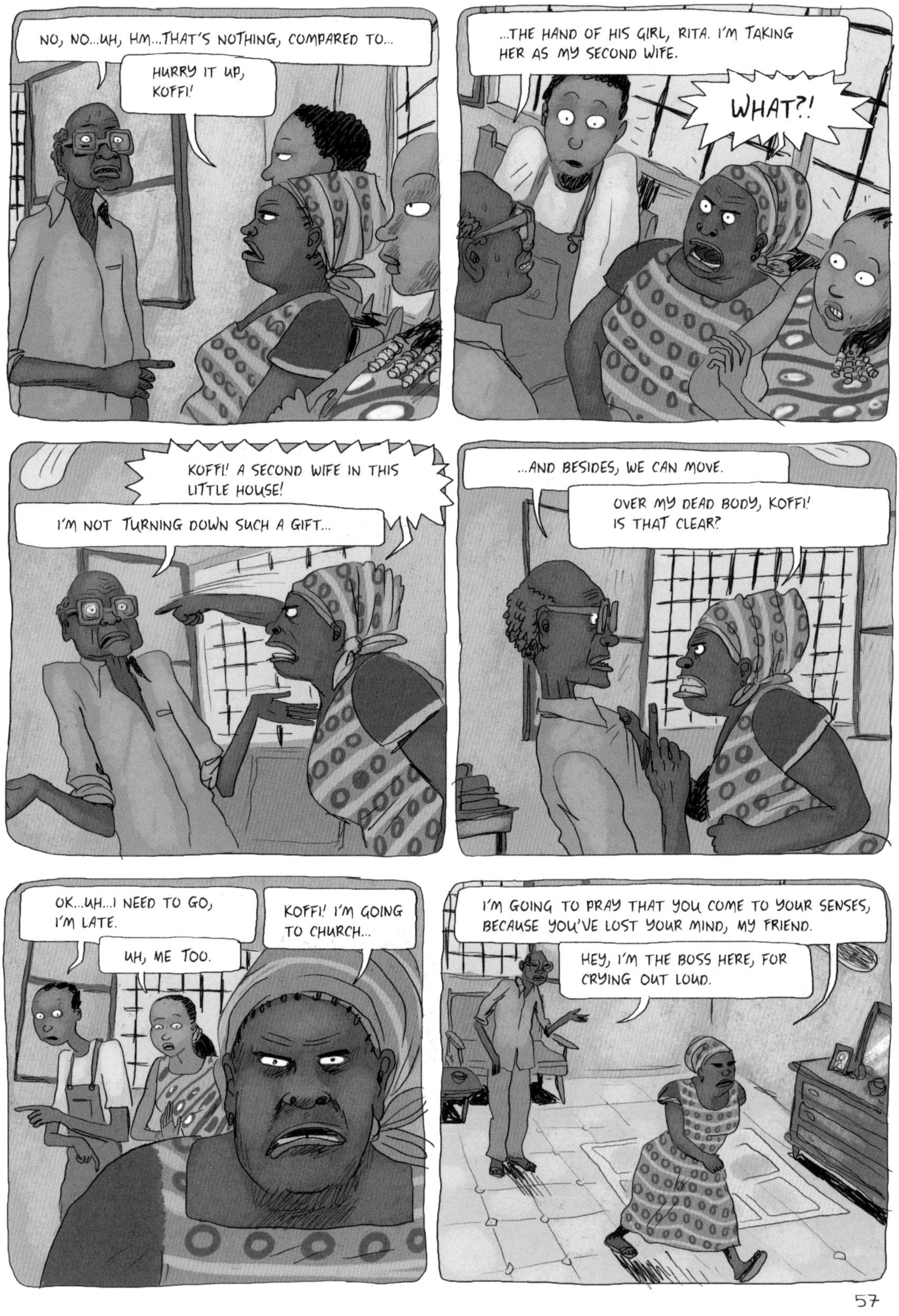
NO, NO...UH, HM...THAT'S NOTHING, COMPARED TO...
HURRY IT UP, KOFFI!
...THE HAND OF HIS GIRL, RITA. I'M TAKING HER AS MY SECOND WIFE.
WHAT?!
KOFFI! A SECOND WIFE IN THIS LITTLE HOUSE!
I'M NOT TURNING DOWN SUCH A GIFT...
...AND BESIDES, WE CAN MOVE.
OVER MY DEAD BODY, KOFFI! IS THAT CLEAR?
OK...UH...I NEED TO GO, I'M LATE.
UH, ME TOO.
KOFFI! I'M GOING TO CHURCH...
I'M GOING TO PRAY THAT YOU COME TO YOUR SENSES, BECAUSE YOU'VE LOST YOUR MIND, MY FRIEND.
HEY, I'M THE BOSS HERE, FOR CRYING OUT LOUD.

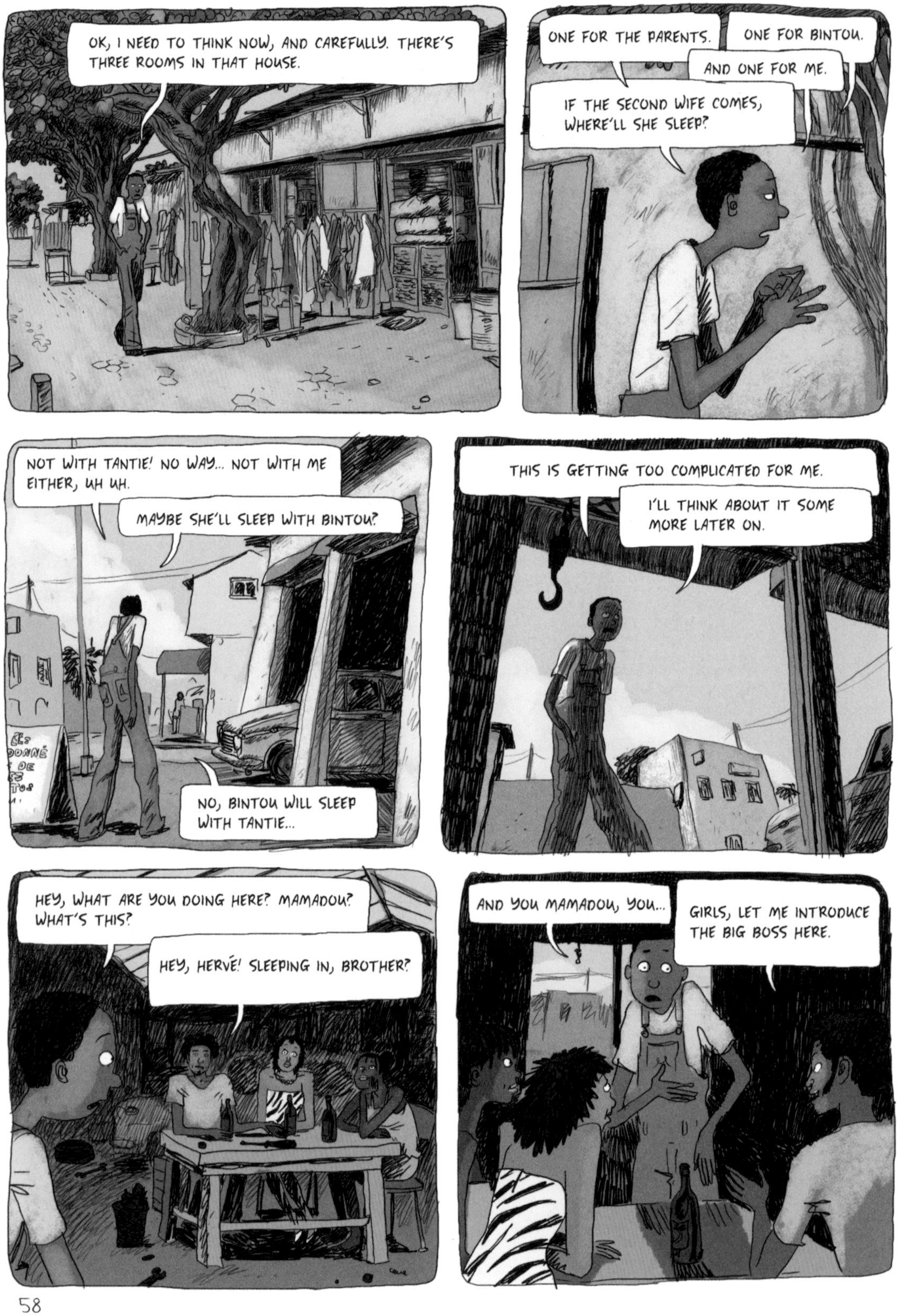
OK, I NEED TO THINK NOW, AND CAREFULLY. THERE'S THREE ROOMS IN THAT HOUSE.
ONE FOR THE PARENTS.
ONE FOR BINTOU.
AND ONE FOR ME.
IF THE SECOND WIFE COMES, WHERE'LL SHE SLEEP?
NOT WITH TANTIE! NO WAY... NOT WITH ME EITHER, UH UH.
MAYBE SHE'LL SLEEP WITH BINTOU?
NO, BINTOU WILL SLEEP WITH TANTIE...
THIS IS GETTING TOO COMPLICATED FOR ME.
I'LL THINK ABOUT IT SOME MORE LATER ON.
HEY, WHAT ARE YOU DOING HERE? MAMADOU? WHAT'S THIS?
HEY, HERVÉ! SLEEPING IN, BROTHER?
AND YOU MAMADOU, YOU...
GIRLS, LET ME INTRODUCE THE BIG BOSS HERE.

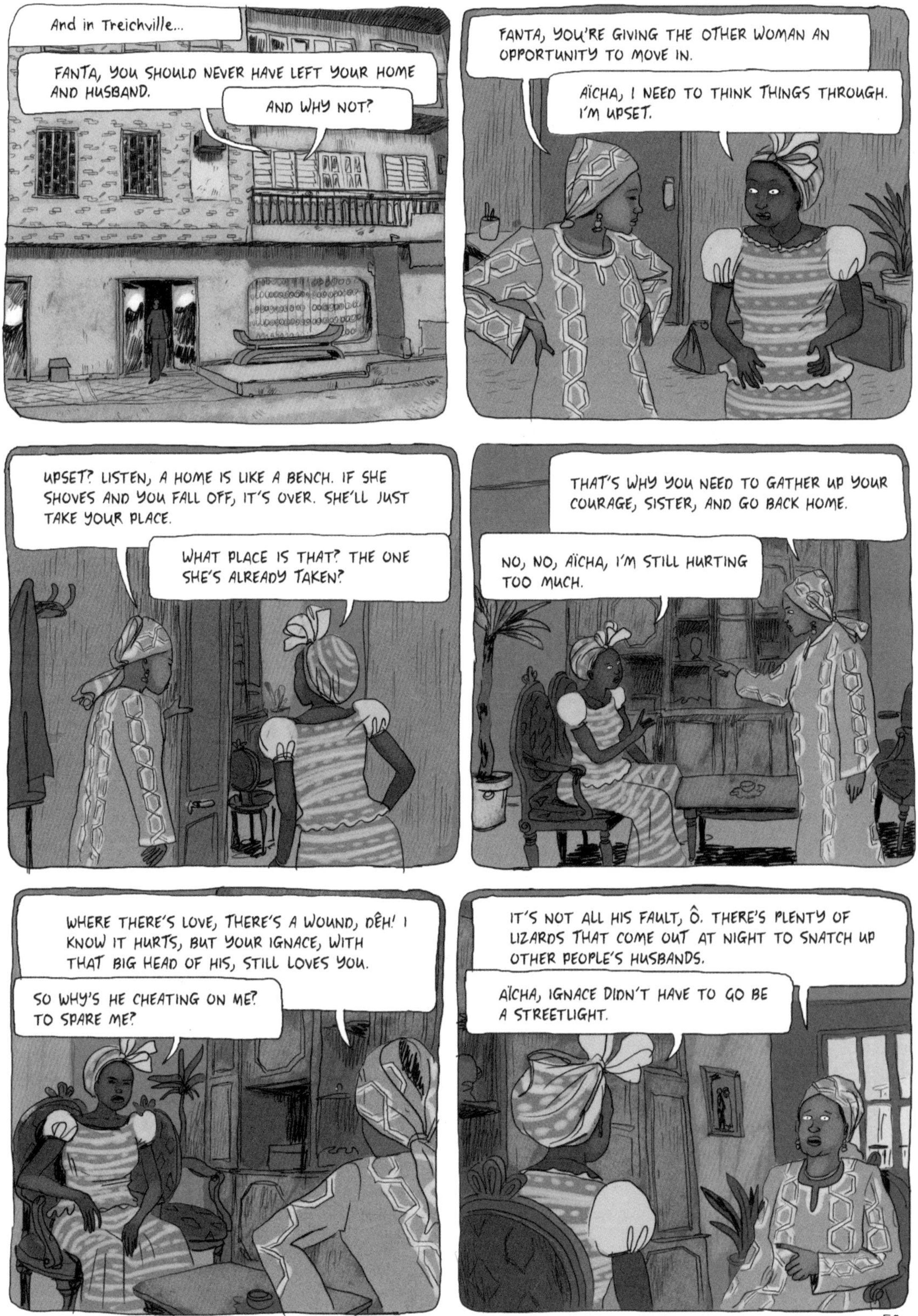
And in Treichville...
FANTA, YOU SHOULD NEVER HAVE LEFT YOUR HOME AND HUSBAND.
AND WHY NOT?
FANTA, YOU'RE GIVING THE OTHER WOMAN AN OPPORTUNITY TO MOVE IN.
AÏCHA, I NEED TO THINK THINGS THROUGH. I'M UPSET.
UPSET? LISTEN, A HOME IS LIKE A BENCH. IF SHE SHOVES AND YOU FALL OFF, IT'S OVER. SHE'LL JUST TAKE YOUR PLACE.
WHAT PLACE IS THAT? THE ONE SHE'S ALREADY TAKEN?
THAT'S WHY YOU NEED TO GATHER UP YOUR COURAGE, SISTER, AND GO BACK HOME.
NO, NO, AÏCHA, I'M STILL HURTING TOO MUCH.
WHERE THERE'S LOVE, THERE'S A WOUND, DÊH! I KNOW IT HURTS, BUT YOUR IGNACE, WITH THAT BIG HEAD OF HIS, STILL LOVES YOU.
SO WHY'S HE CHEATING ON ME? TO SPARE ME?
IT'S NOT ALL HIS FAULT, Ô. THERE'S PLENTY OF LIZARDS THAT COME OUT AT NIGHT TO SNATCH UP OTHER PEOPLE'S HUSBANDS.
AÏCHA, IGNACE DIDN'T HAVE TO GO BE A STREETLIGHT.

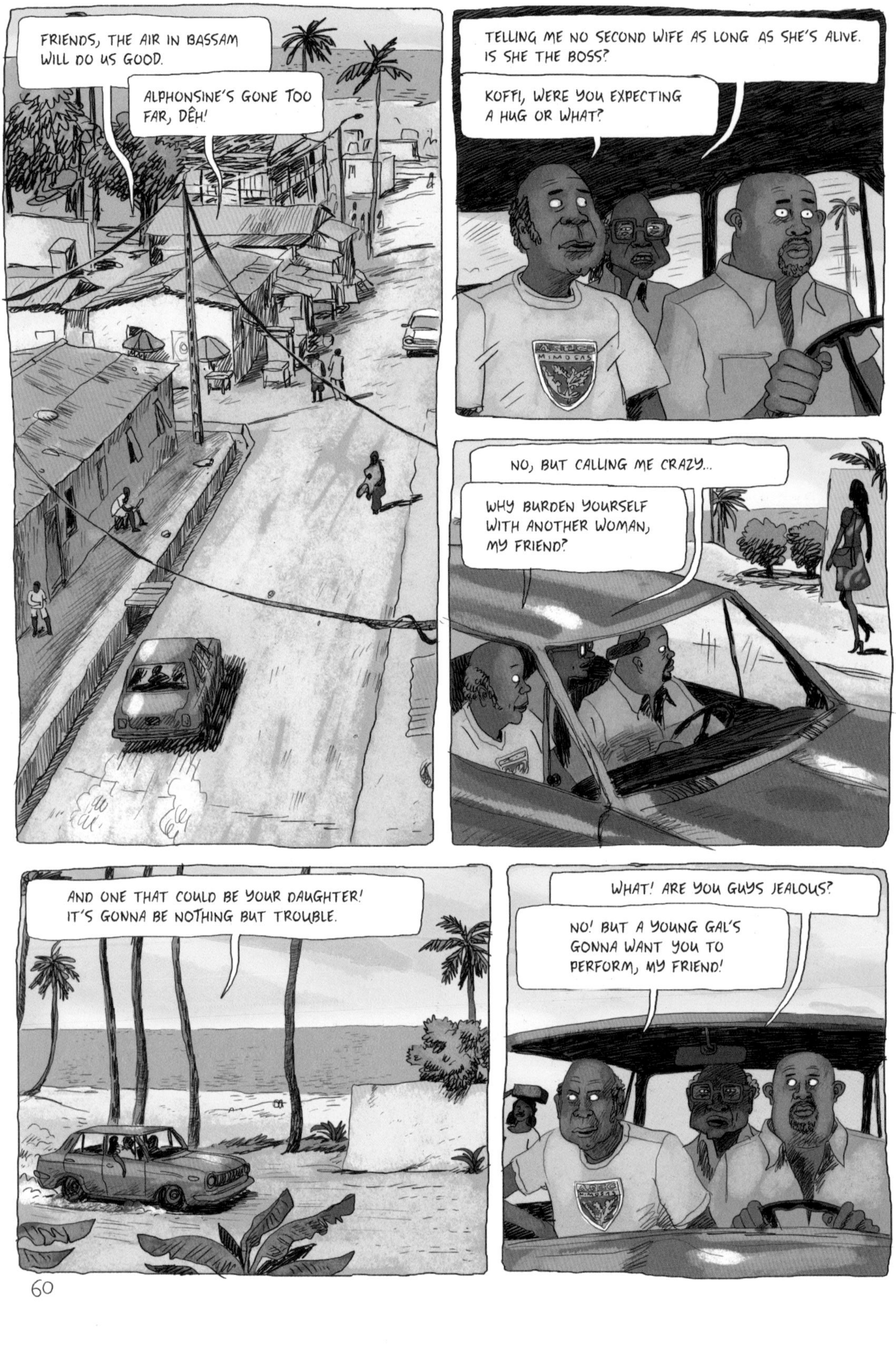

FRIENDS, THE AIR IN BASSAM WILL DO US GOOD.
ALPHONSINE'S GONE TOO FAR, DÊH!
TELLING ME NO SECOND WIFE AS LONG AS SHE'S ALIVE. IS SHE THE BOSS?
KOFFI, WERE YOU EXPECTING A HUG OR WHAT?
NO, BUT CALLING ME CRAZY...
WHY BURDEN YOURSELF WITH ANOTHER WOMAN, MY FRIEND?
AND ONE THAT COULD BE YOUR DAUGHTER! IT'S GONNA BE NOTHING BUT TROUBLE.
WHAT! ARE YOU GUYS JEALOUS?
NO! BUT A YOUNG GAL'S GONNA WANT YOU TO PERFORM, MY FRIEND!

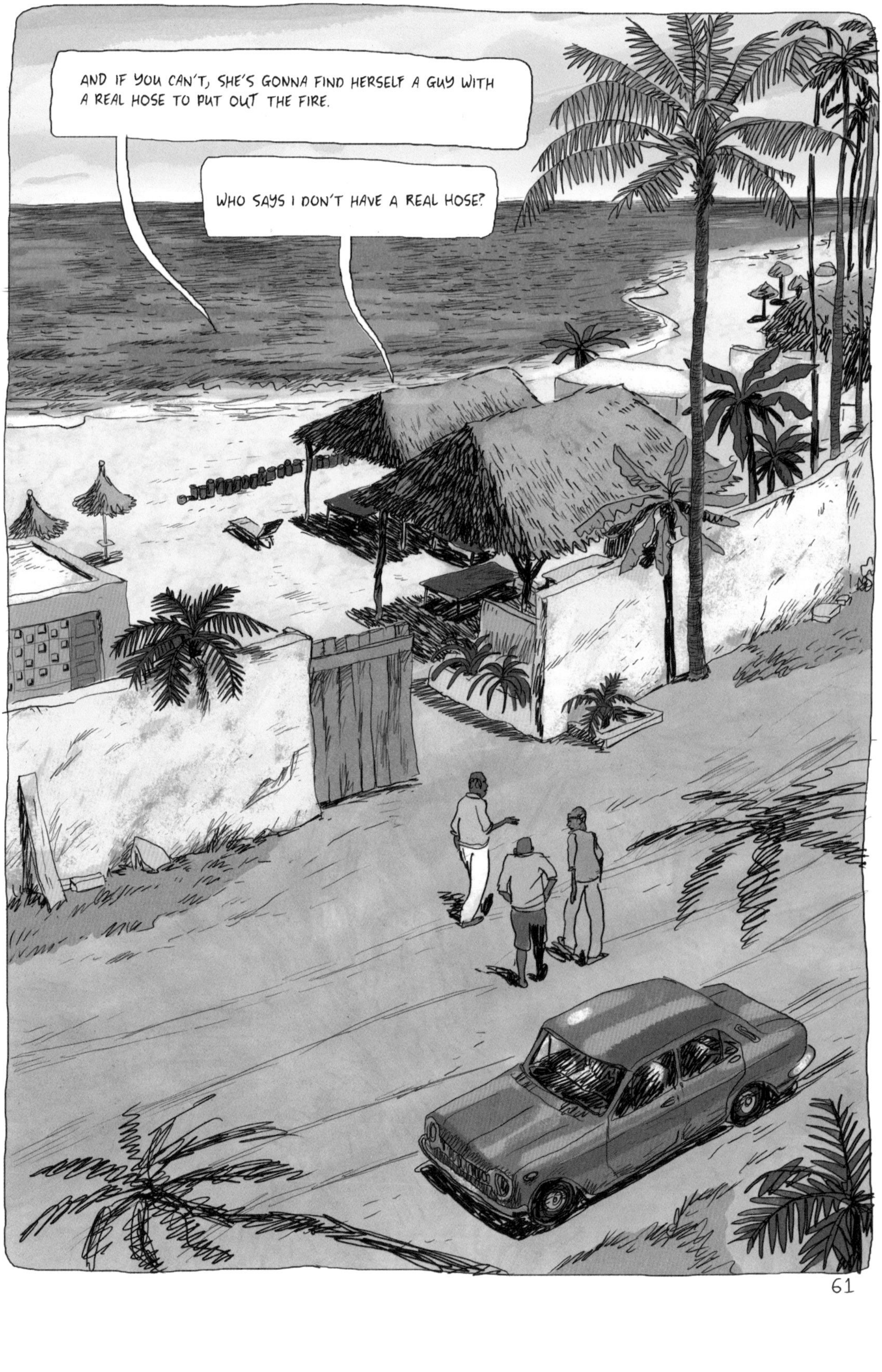
AND IF YOU CAN'T, SHE'S GONNA FIND HERSELF A GUY WITH A REAL HOSE TO PUT OUT THE FIRE.
WHO SAYS I DON'T HAVE A REAL HOSE?

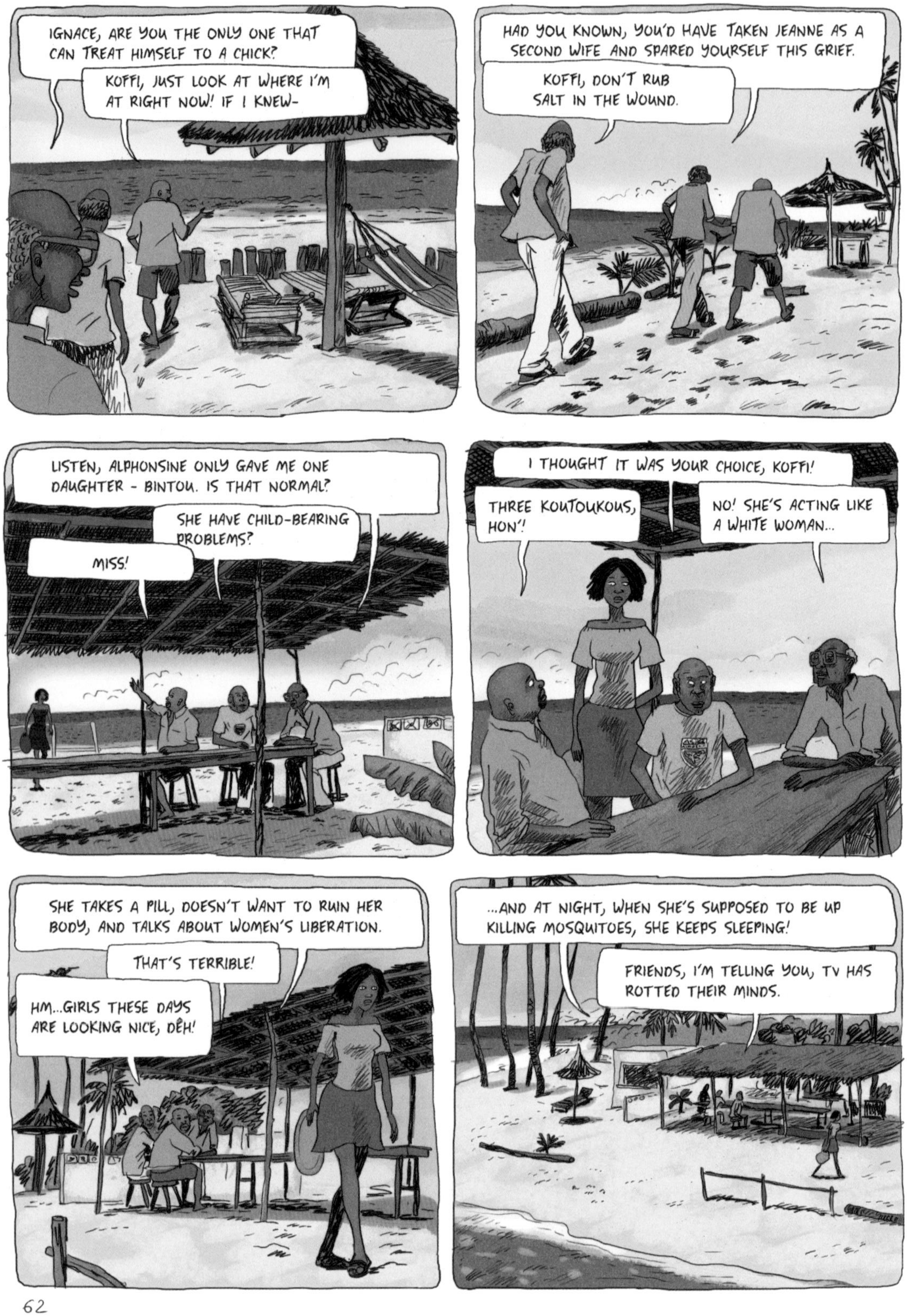
IGNACE, ARE YOU THE ONLY ONE THAT CAN TREAT HIMSELF TO A CHICK?
KOFFI, JUST LOOK AT WHERE I'M AT RIGHT NOW! IF I KNEW-
HAD YOU KNOWN, YOU'D HAVE TAKEN JEANNE AS A SECOND WIFE AND SPARED YOURSELF THIS GRIEF.
KOFFI, DON'T RUB SALT IN THE WOUND.
LISTEN, ALPHONSINE ONLY GAVE ME ONE DAUGHTER - BINTOU. IS THAT NORMAL?
SHE HAVE CHILD-BEARING PROBLEMS?
MISS!
I THOUGHT IT WAS YOUR CHOICE, KOFFI!
THREE KOUTOUKOUS, HON'!
NO! SHE'S ACTING LIKE A WHITE WOMAN...
SHE TAKES A PILL, DOESN'T WANT TO RUIN HER BODY, AND TALKS ABOUT WOMEN'S LIBERATION.
THAT'S TERRIBLE!
HM...GIRLS THESE DAYS ARE LOOKING NICE, DÊH!
...AND AT NIGHT, WHEN SHE'S SUPPOSED TO BE UP KILLING MOSQUITOES, SHE KEEPS SLEEPING!
FRIENDS, I'M TELLING YOU, TV HAS ROTTED THEIR MINDS.

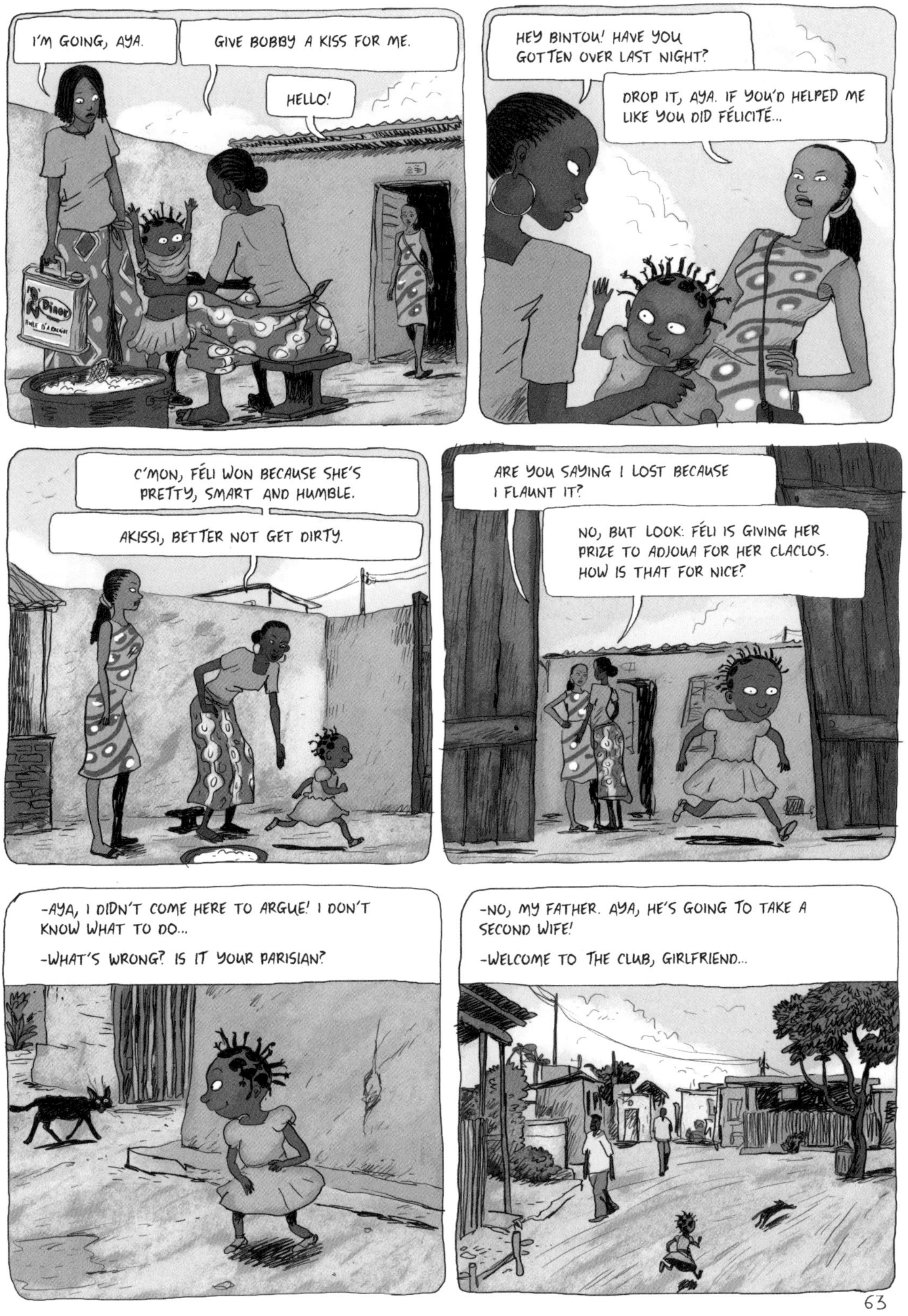
I'M GOING, AYA.
GIVE BOBBY A KISS FOR ME.
HELLO!
HEY BINTOU! HAVE YOU GOTTEN OVER LAST NIGHT?
DROP IT, AYA. IF YOU'D HELPED ME LIKE YOU DID FÉLICITÉ...
C'MON, FÉLI WON BECAUSE SHE'S PRETTY, SMART AND HUMBLE.
AKISSI, BETTER NOT GET DIRTY.
ARE YOU SAYING I LOST BECAUSE I FLAUNT IT?
NO, BUT LOOK: FÉLI IS GIVING HER PRIZE TO ADJOUA FOR HER CLACLOS. HOW IS THAT FOR NICE?
-AYA, I DIDN'T COME HERE TO ARGUE! I DON'T KNOW WHAT TO DO...
-WHAT'S WRONG? IS IT YOUR PARISIAN?
-NO, MY FATHER. AYA, HE'S GOING TO TAKE A SECOND WIFE!
-WELCOME TO THE CLUB, GIRLFRIEND...

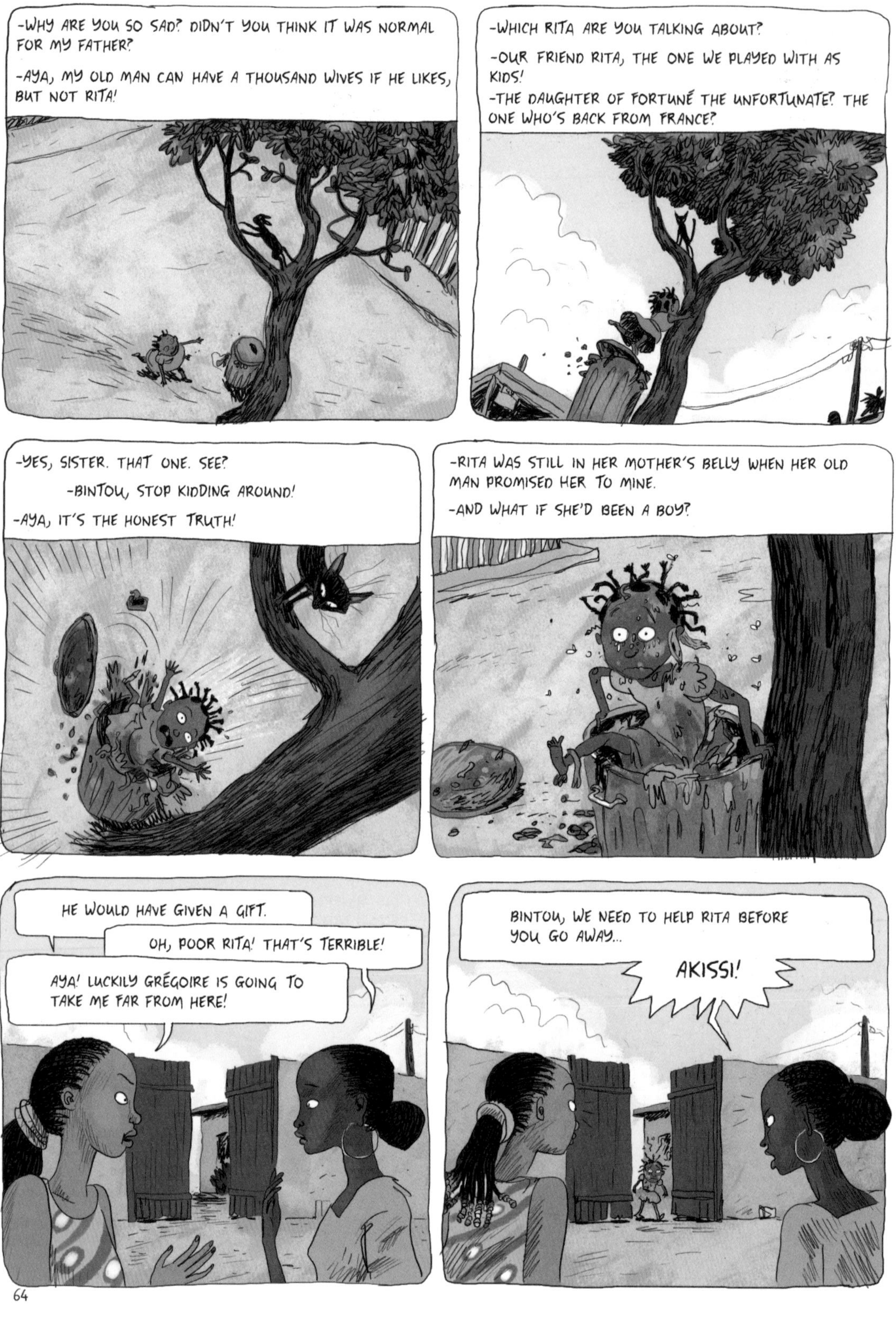
-WHY ARE YOU SO SAD? DIDN'T YOU THINK IT WAS NORMAL FOR MY FATHER?
-AYA, MY OLD MAN CAN HAVE A THOUSAND WIVES IF HE LIKES, BUT NOT RITA!
-WHICH RITA ARE YOU TALKING ABOUT?
-OUR FRIEND RITA, THE ONE WE PLAYED WITH AS KIDS!
-THE DAUGHTER OF FORTUNÉ THE UNFORTUNATE? THE ONE WHO'S BACK FROM FRANCE?
-YES, SISTER. THAT ONE. SEE?
-BINTOU, STOP KIDDING AROUND!
-AYA, IT'S THE HONEST TRUTH!
-RITA WAS STILL IN HER MOTHER'S BELLY WHEN HER OLD MAN PROMISED HER TO MINE.
-AND WHAT IF SHE'D BEEN A BOY?
HE WOULD HAVE GIVEN A GIFT.
OH, POOR RITA! THAT'S TERRIBLE!
AYA! LUCKILY GRÉGOIRE IS GOING TO TAKE ME FAR FROM HERE!
BINTOU, WE NEED TO HELP RITA BEFORE YOU GO AWAY...
AKISSI!

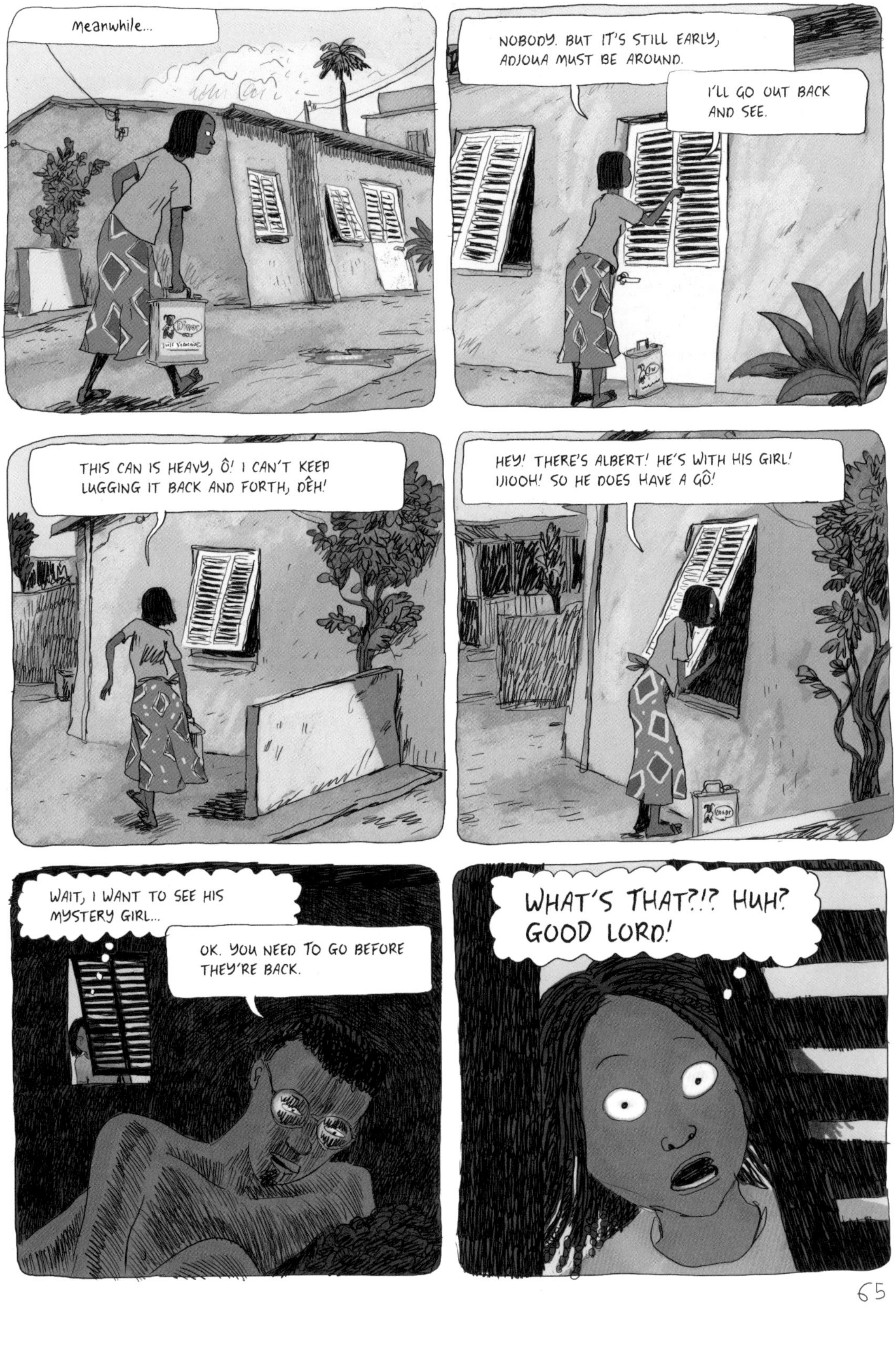
Meanwhile...
NOBODY. BUT IT'S STILL EARLY, ADJOUA MUST BE AROUND.
I'LL GO OUT BACK AND SEE.
THIS CAN IS HEAVY, Ô! I CAN'T KEEP LUGGING IT BACK AND FORTH, DÊH!
HEY! THERE'S ALBERT! HE'S WITH HIS GIRL! UOOH! SO HE DOES HAVE A GÔ!
WAIT, I WANT TO SEE HIS MYSTERY GIRL...
OK. YOU NEED TO GO BEFORE THEY'RE BACK.
WHAT'S THAT?!? HUH? GOOD LORD!

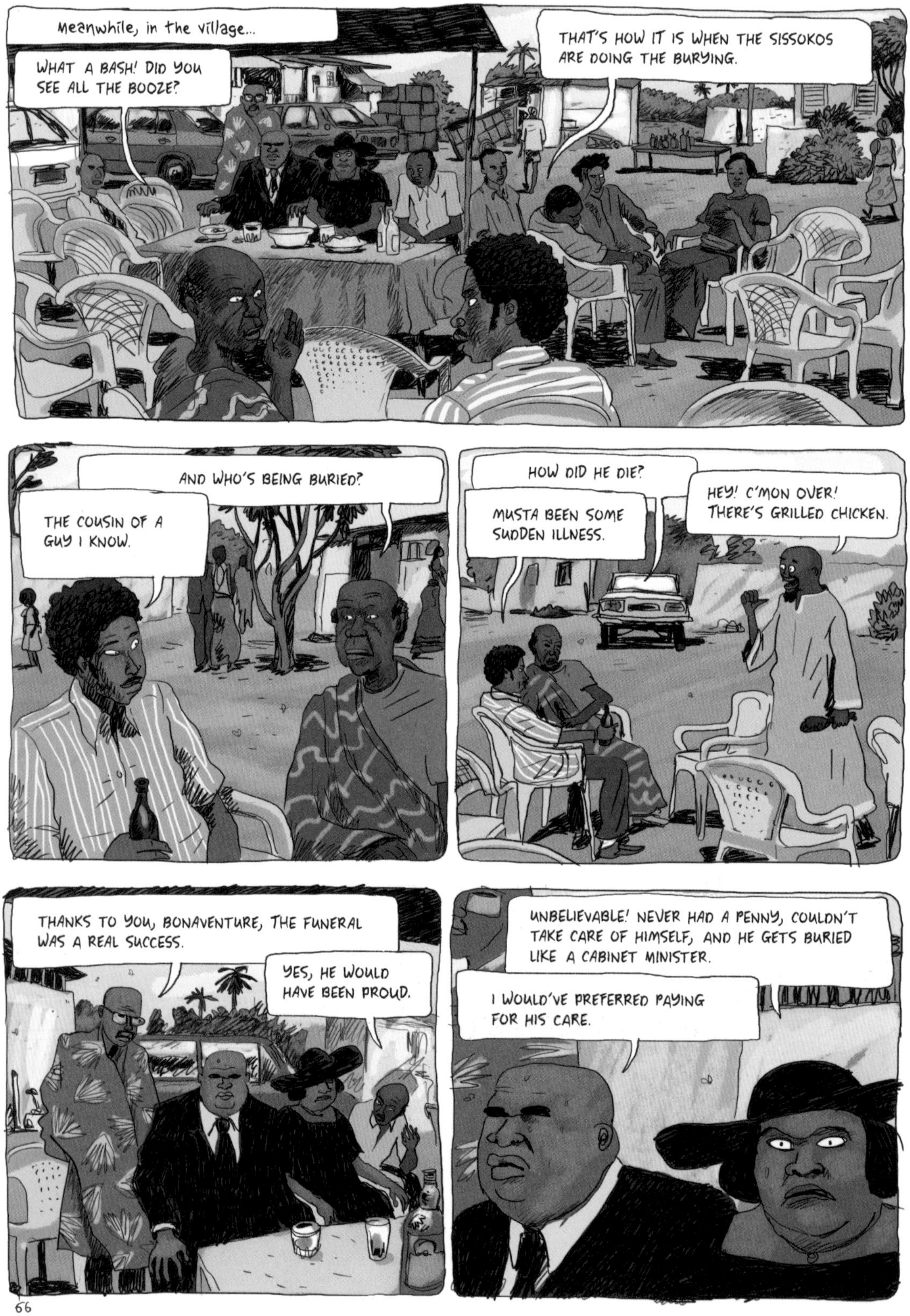
Meanwhile, in the village...
WHAT A BASH! DID YOU SEE ALL THE BOOZE?
THAT'S HOW IT IS WHEN THE SISSOKOS ARE DOING THE BURYING.
AND WHO'S BEING BURIED?
THE COUSIN OF A GUY I KNOW.
HOW DID HE DIE?
MUSTA BEEN SOME SUDDEN ILLNESS.
HEY! C'MON OVER! THERE'S GRILLED CHICKEN.
THANKS TO YOU, BONAVENTURE, THE FUNERAL WAS A REAL SUCCESS.
YES, HE WOULD HAVE BEEN PROUD.
UNBELIEVABLE! NEVER HAD A PENNY, COULDN'T TAKE CARE OF HIMSELF, AND HE GETS BURIED LIKE A CABINET MINISTER.
I WOULD'VE PREFERRED PAYING FOR HIS CARE.

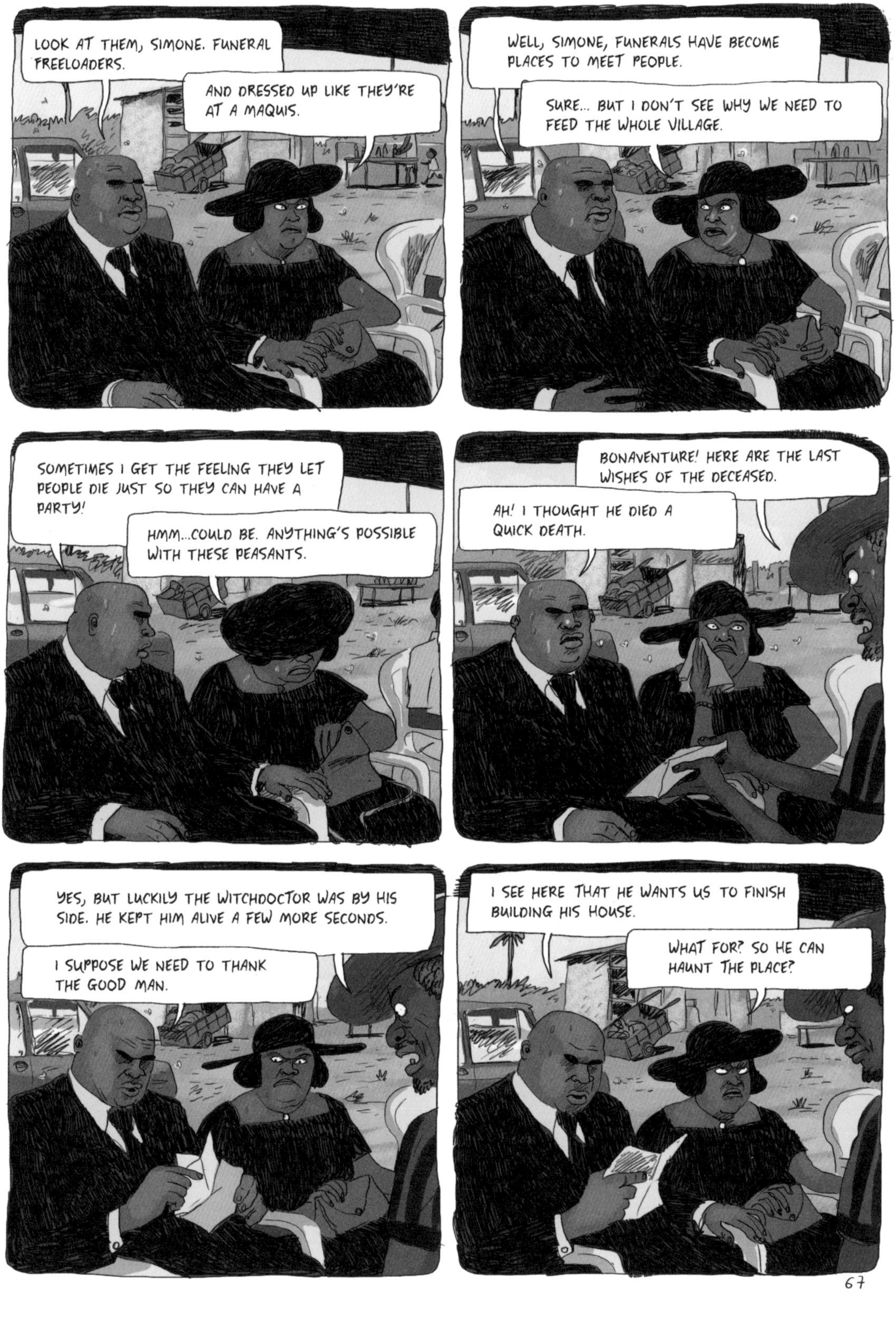
LOOK AT THEM, SIMONE. FUNERAL FREELOADERS.
AND DRESSED UP LIKE THEY'RE AT A MAQUIS.
WELL, SIMONE, FUNERALS HAVE BECOME PLACES TO MEET PEOPLE.
SURE... BUT I DON'T SEE WHY WE NEED TO FEED THE WHOLE VILLAGE.
SOMETIMES I GET THE FEELING THEY LET PEOPLE DIE JUST SO THEY CAN HAVE A PARTY!
HMM...COULD BE. ANYTHING'S POSSIBLE WITH THESE PEASANTS.
BONAVENTURE! HERE ARE THE LAST WISHES OF THE DECEASED.
AH! I THOUGHT HE DIED A QUICK DEATH.
YES, BUT LUCKILY THE WITCHDOCTOR WAS BY HIS SIDE. HE KEPT HIM ALIVE A FEW MORE SECONDS.
I SUPPOSE WE NEED TO THANK THE GOOD MAN.
I SEE HERE THAT HE WANTS US TO FINISH BUILDING HIS HOUSE.
WHAT FOR? SO HE CAN HAUNT THE PLACE?

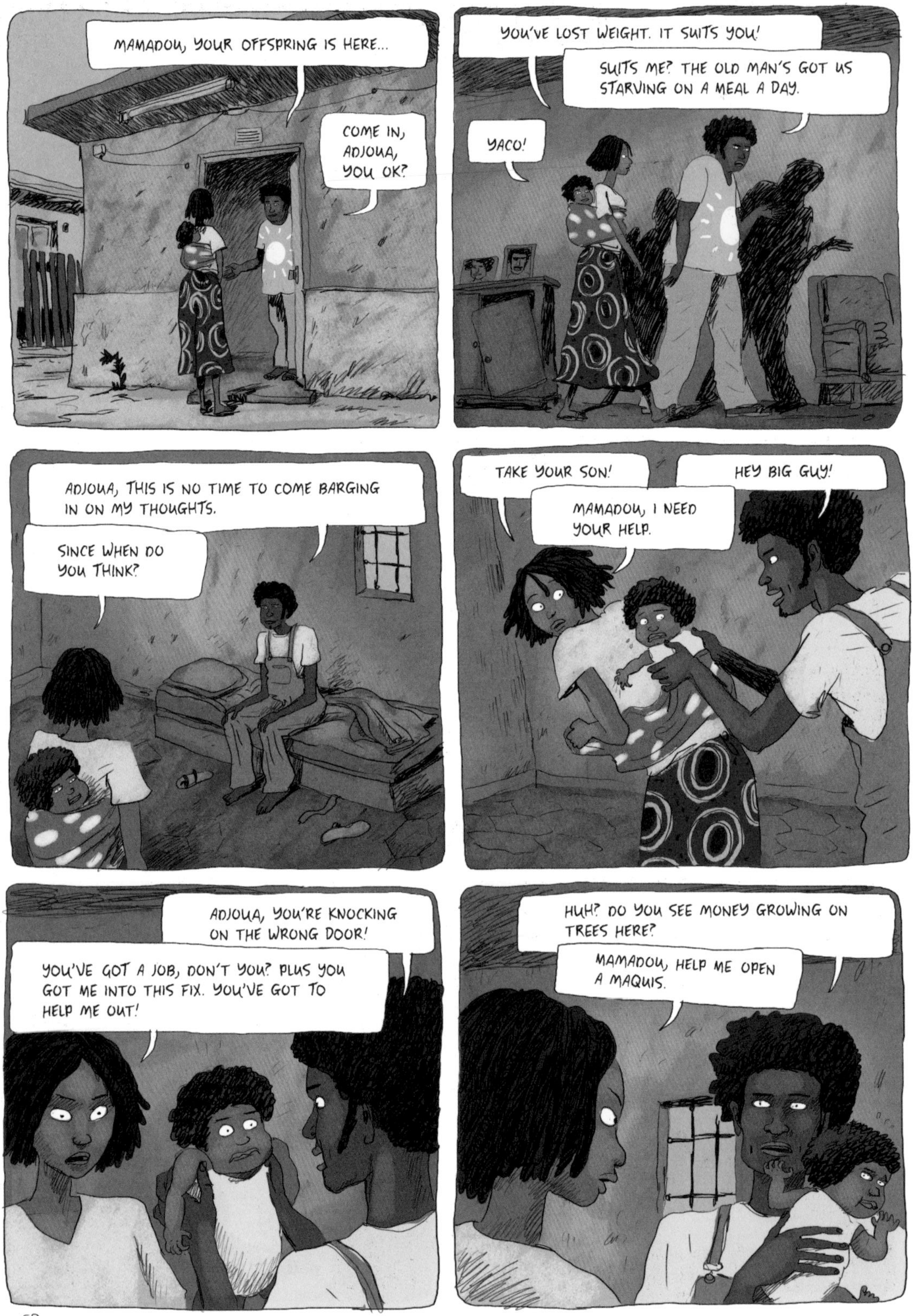
MAMADOU, YOUR OFFSPRING IS HERE...
COME IN, ADJOUA, YOU OK?
YOU'VE LOST WEIGHT. IT SUITS YOU!
SUITS ME? THE OLD MAN'S GOT US STARVING ON A MEAL A DAY.
YACO!
ADJOUA, THIS IS NO TIME TO COME BARGING IN ON MY THOUGHTS.
SINCE WHEN DO YOU THINK?
TAKE YOUR SON!
MAMADOU, I NEED YOUR HELP.
HEY BIG GUY!
ADJOUA, YOU'RE KNOCKING ON THE WRONG DOOR!
YOU'VE GOT A JOB, DON'T YOU? PLUS YOU GOT ME INTO THIS FIX. YOU'VE GOT TO HELP ME OUT!
HUH? DO YOU SEE MONEY GROWING ON TREES HERE?
MAMADOU, HELP ME OPEN A MAQUIS.

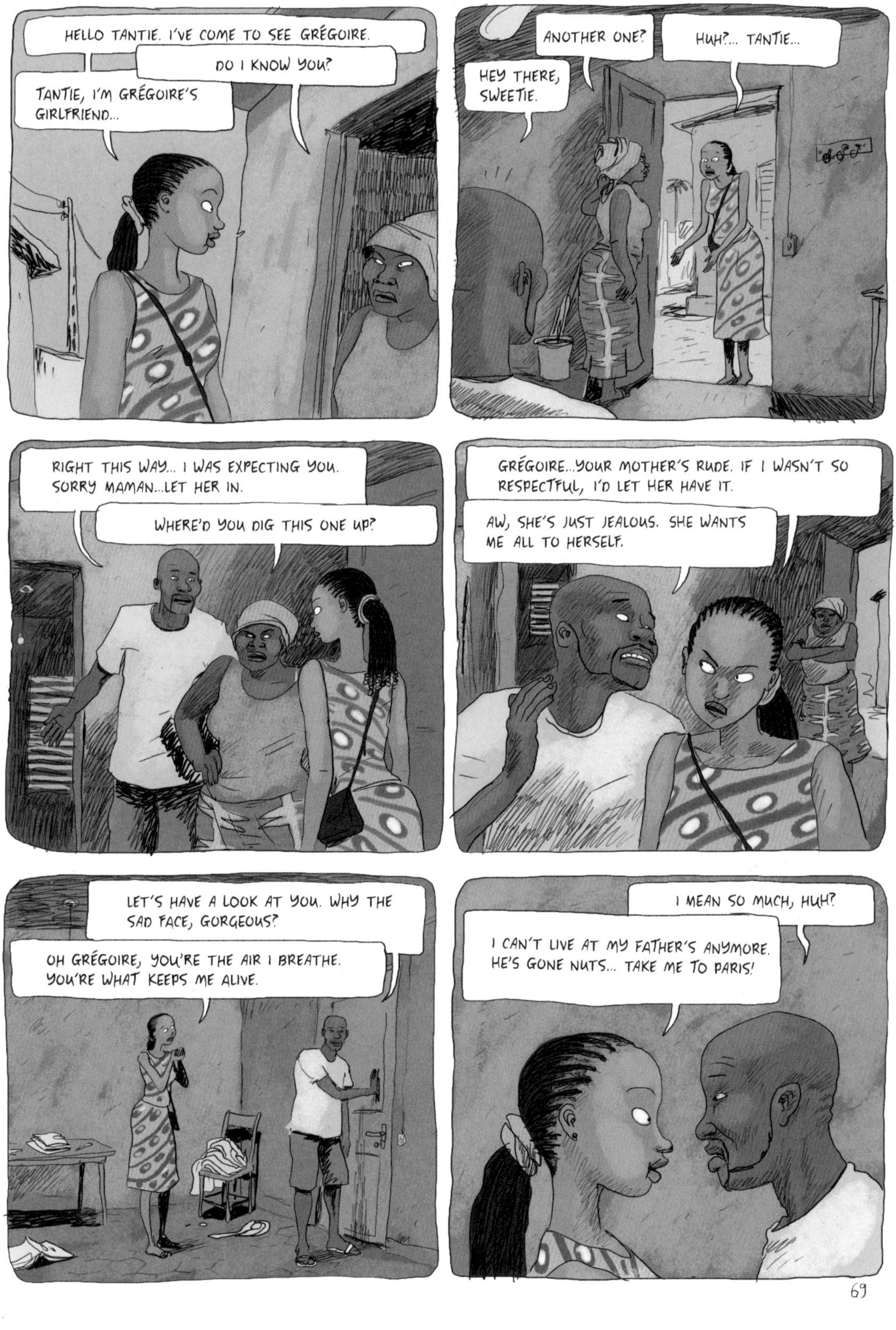
HELLO TANTIE. I'VE COME TO SEE GRÉGOIRE.
DO I KNOW YOU?
TANTIE, I'M GRÉGOIRE'S GIRLFRIEND...
HEY THERE, SWEETIE.
ANOTHER ONE?
HUH?... TANTIE...
RIGHT THIS WAY... I WAS EXPECTING YOU. SORRY MAMAN...LET HER IN.
WHERE'D YOU DIG THIS ONE UP?
GRÉGOIRE...YOUR MOTHER'S RUDE. IF I WASN'T SO RESPECTFUL, I'D LET HER HAVE IT.
AW, SHE'S JUST JEALOUS. SHE WANTS ME ALL TO HERSELF.
LET'S HAVE A LOOK AT YOU. WHY THE SAD FACE, GORGEOUS?
OH GRÉGOIRE, YOU'RE THE AIR I BREATHE. YOU'RE WHAT KEEPS ME ALIVE.
I MEAN SO MUCH, HUH?
I CAN'T LIVE AT MY FATHER'S ANYMORE. HE'S GONE NUTS... TAKE ME TO PARIS!

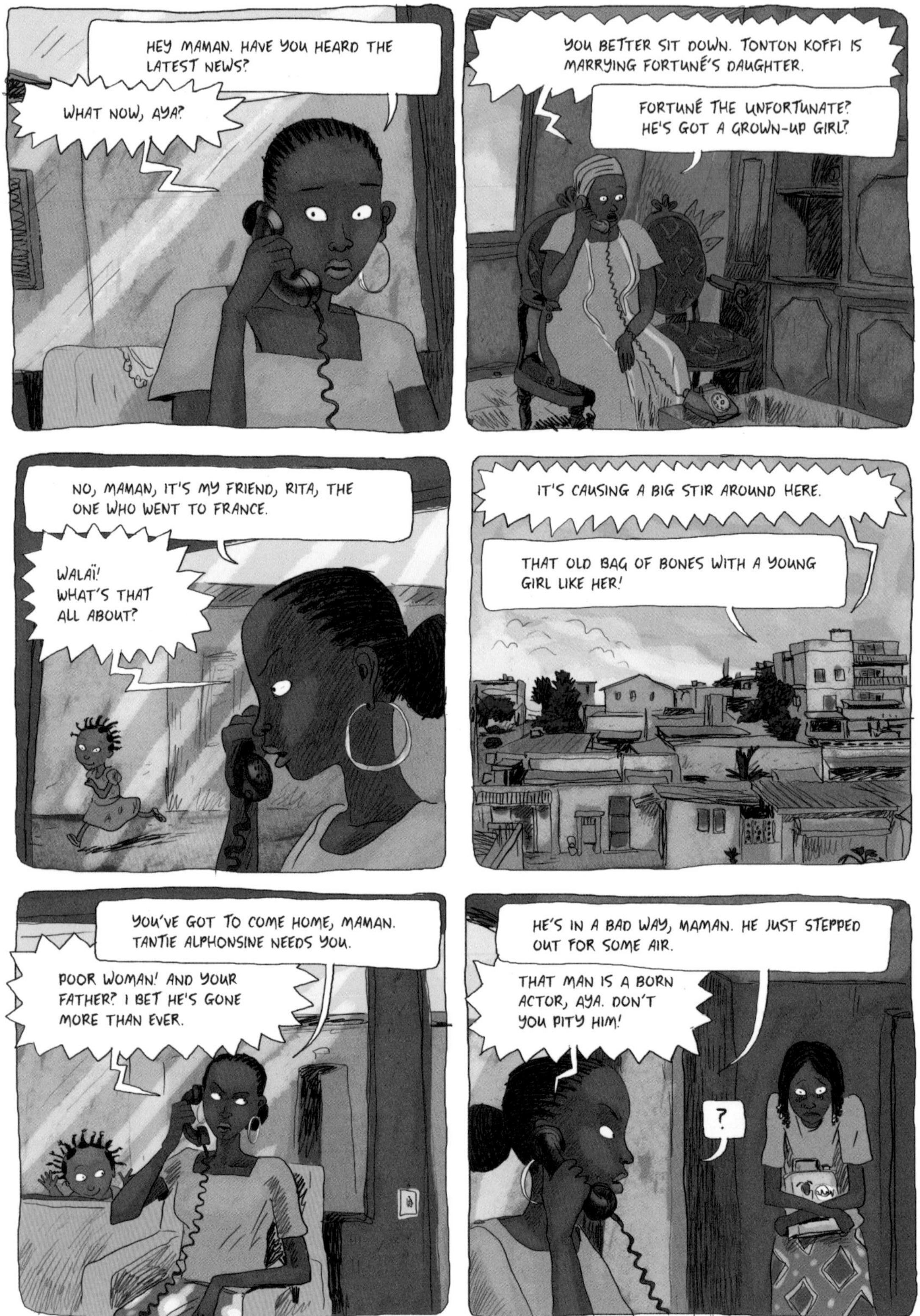
HEY MAMAN. HAVE YOU HEARD THE LATEST NEWS?
WHAT NOW, AYA?
YOU BETTER SIT DOWN. TONTON KOFFI IS MARRYING FORTUNÉ'S DAUGHTER.
FORTUNÉ THE UNFORTUNATE? HE'S GOT A GROWN-UP GIRL?
NO, MAMAN, IT'S MY FRIEND, RITA, THE ONE WHO WENT TO FRANCE.
WALAÏ! WHAT'S THAT ALL ABOUT?
IT'S CAUSING A BIG STIR AROUND HERE.
THAT OLD BAG OF BONES WITH A YOUNG GIRL LIKE HER!
YOU'VE GOT TO COME HOME, MAMAN. TANTIE ALPHONSINE NEEDS YOU.
POOR WOMAN! AND YOUR FATHER? I BET HE'S GONE MORE THAN EVER.
HE'S IN A BAD WAY, MAMAN. HE JUST STEPPED OUT FOR SOME AIR.
THAT MAN IS A BORN ACTOR, AYA. DON'T YOU PITY HIM!
?

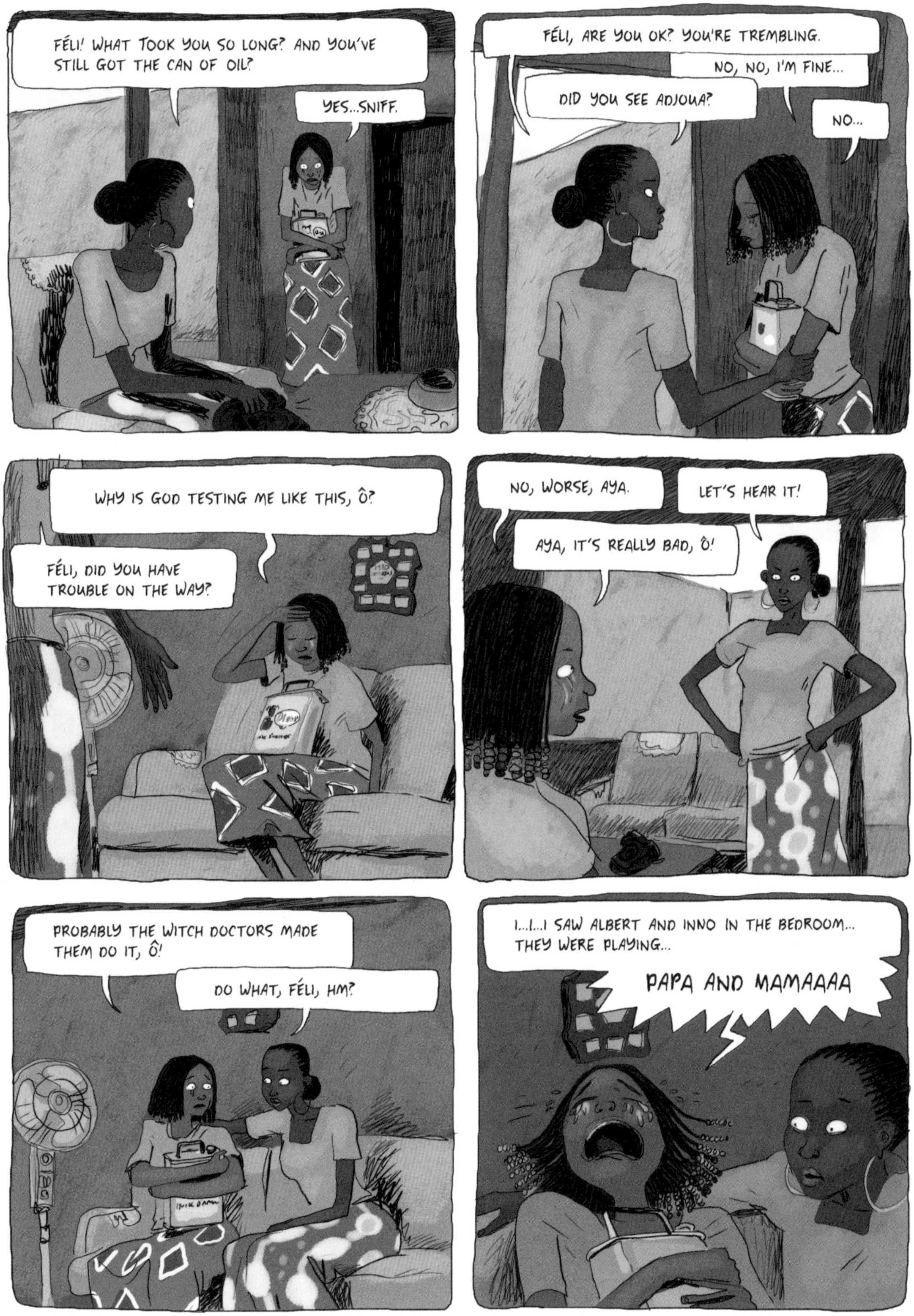
FÉLI! WHAT TOOK YOU SO LONG? AND YOU'VE STILL GOT THE CAN OF OIL?
YES...SNIFF.
FÉLI, ARE YOU OK? YOU'RE TREMBLING.
NO, NO, I'M FINE...
DID YOU SEE ADJOUA?
NO...
WHY IS GOD TESTING ME LIKE THIS, Ô?
FÉLI, DID YOU HAVE TROUBLE ON THE WAY?
NO, WORSE, AYA.
LET'S HEAR IT!
AYA, IT'S REALLY BAD, Ô!
PROBABLY THE WITCH DOCTORS MADE THEM DO IT, Ô!
DO WHAT, FÉLI, HM?
I...I...I SAW ALBERT AND INNO IN THE BEDROOM... THEY WERE PLAYING...
PAPA AND MAMAAAA

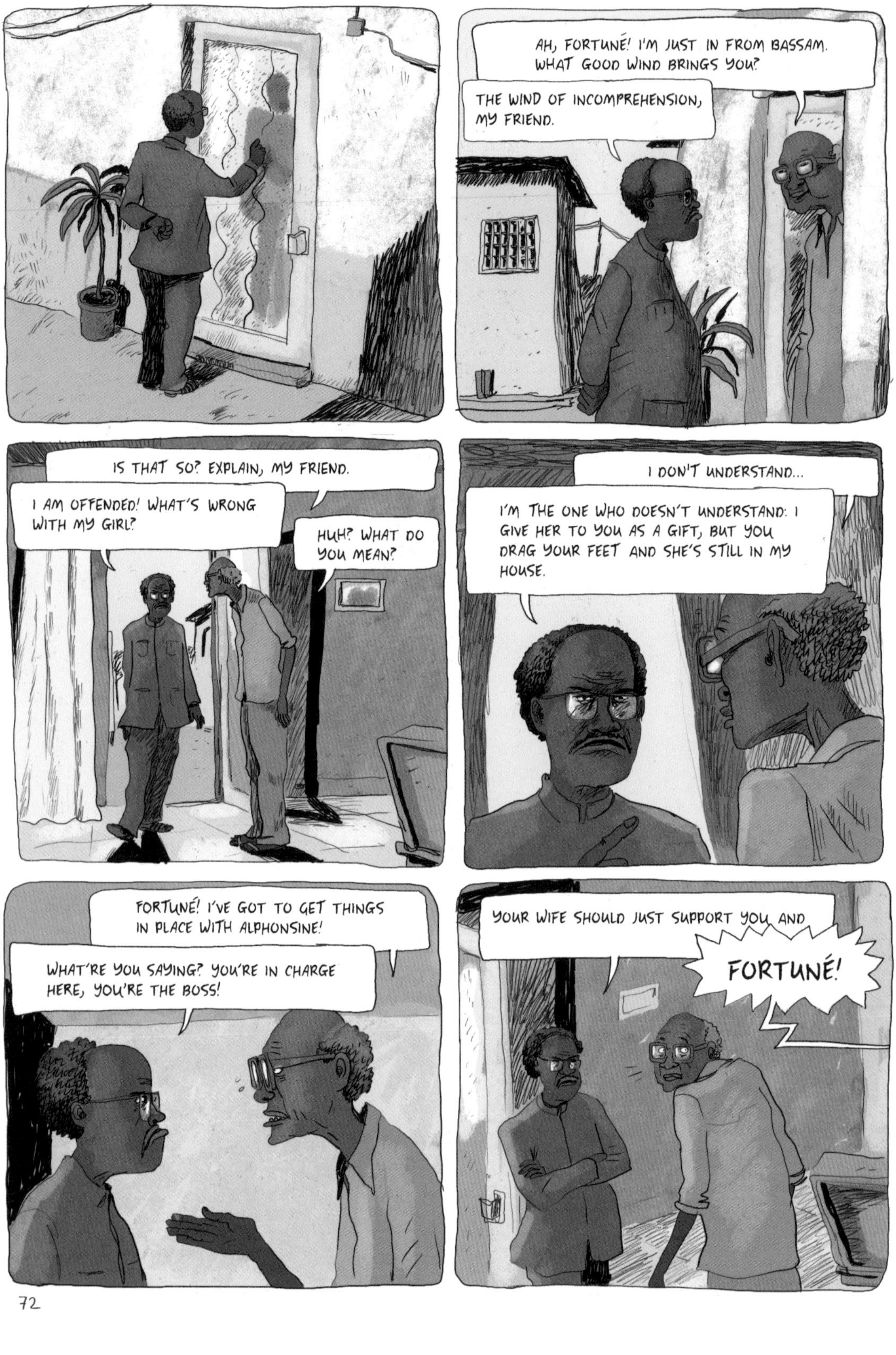
AH, FORTUNÉ! I'M JUST IN FROM BASSAM. WHAT GOOD WIND BRINGS YOU?
THE WIND OF INCOMPREHENSION, MY FRIEND.
IS THAT SO? EXPLAIN, MY FRIEND.
I AM OFFENDED! WHAT'S WRONG WITH MY GIRL?
HUH? WHAT DO YOU MEAN?
I DON'T UNDERSTAND...
I'M THE ONE WHO DOESN'T UNDERSTAND: I GIVE HER TO YOU AS A GIFT, BUT YOU DRAG YOUR FEET AND SHE'S STILL IN MY HOUSE.
FORTUNÉ! I'VE GOT TO GET THINGS IN PLACE WITH ALPHONSINE!
WHAT'RE YOU SAYING? YOU'RE IN CHARGE HERE, YOU'RE THE BOSS!
YOUR WIFE SHOULD JUST SUPPORT YOU AND
FORTUNÉ!

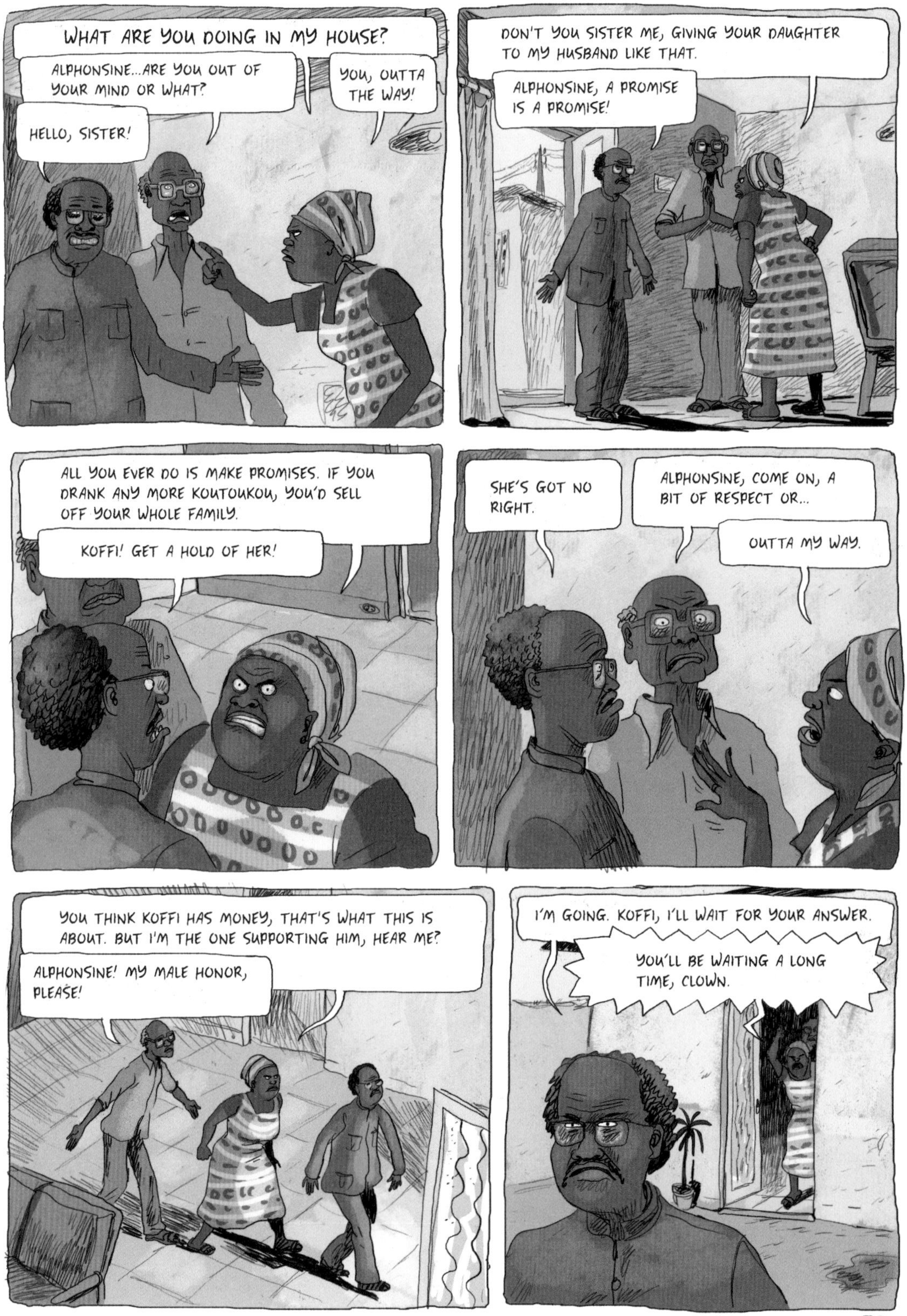
WHAT ARE YOU DOING IN MY HOUSE?
ALPHONSINE...ARE YOU OUT OF YOUR MIND OR WHAT?
YOU, OUTTA THE WAY!
HELLO, SISTER!
DON'T YOU SISTER ME, GIVING YOUR DAUGHTER TO MY HUSBAND LIKE THAT.
ALPHONSINE, A PROMISE IS A PROMISE!
ALL YOU EVER DO IS MAKE PROMISES. IF YOU DRANK ANY MORE KOUTOUKOU, YOU'D SELL OFF YOUR WHOLE FAMILY.
KOFFI! GET A HOLD OF HER!
SHE'S GOT NO RIGHT.
ALPHONSINE, COME ON, A BIT OF RESPECT OR...
OUTTA MY WAY.
YOU THINK KOFFI HAS MONEY, THAT'S WHAT THIS IS ABOUT. BUT I'M THE ONE SUPPORTING HIM, HEAR ME?
ALPHONSINE! MY MALE HONOR, PLEASE!
I'M GOING. KOFFI, I'LL WAIT FOR YOUR ANSWER.
YOU'LL BE WAITING A LONG TIME, CLOWN.

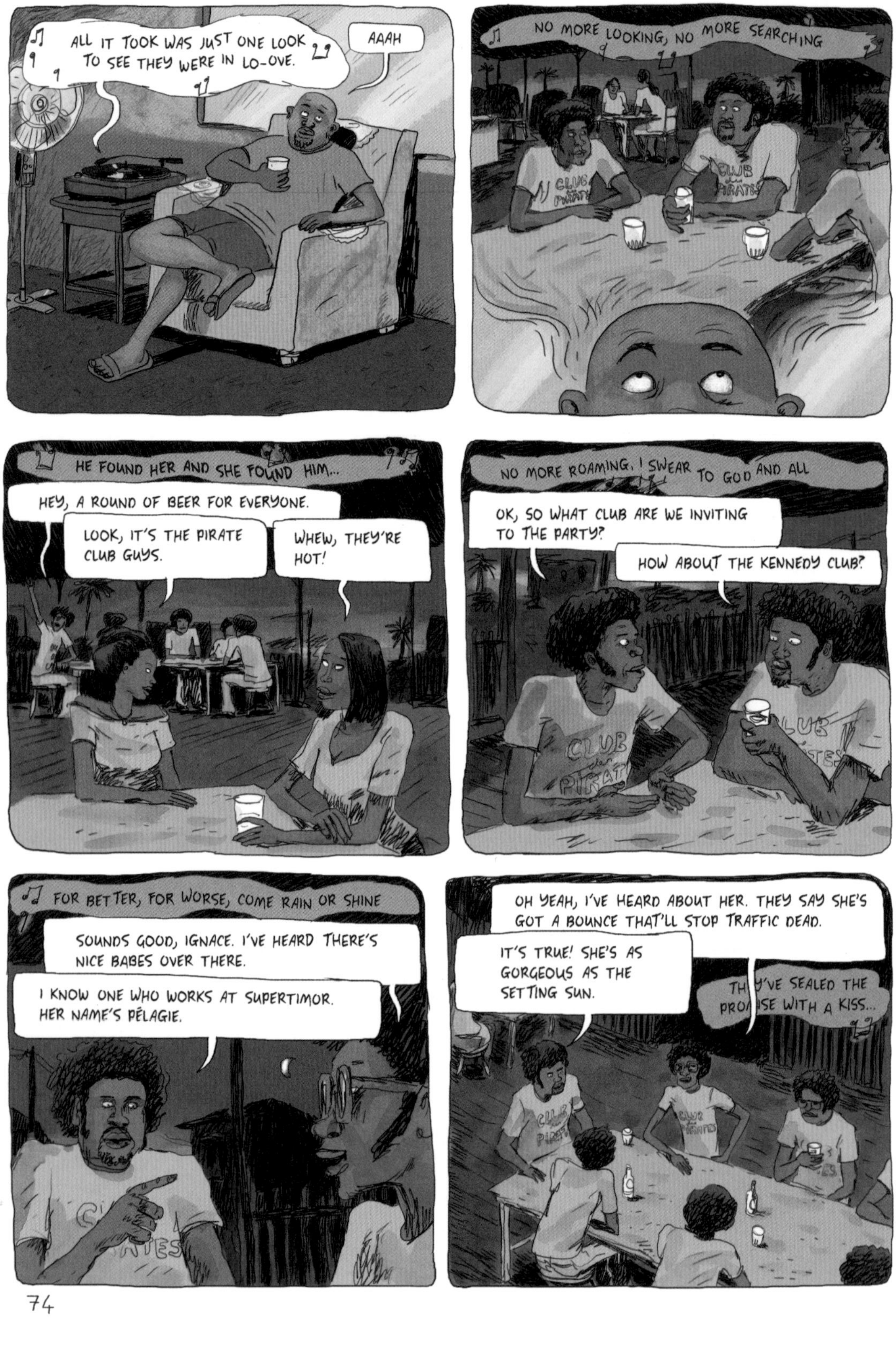
ALL IT TOOK WAS JUST ONE LOOK TO SEE THEY WERE IN LO-OVE.
AAAH
NO MORE LOOKING, NO MORE SEARCHING
CLUB PIRATES
HE FOUND HER AND SHE FOUND HIM...
HEY, A ROUND OF BEER FOR EVERYONE.
LOOK, IT'S THE PIRATE CLUB GUYS.
WHEW, THEY'RE HOT!
NO MORE ROAMING, I SWEAR TO GOD AND ALL
OK, SO WHAT CLUB ARE WE INVITING TO THE PARTY?
HOW ABOUT THE KENNEDY CLUB?
FOR BETTER, FOR WORSE, COME RAIN OR SHINE
SOUNDS GOOD, IGNACE. I'VE HEARD THERE'S NICE BABES OVER THERE.
I KNOW ONE WHO WORKS AT SUPERTIMOR. HER NAME'S PÉLAGIE.
OH YEAH, I'VE HEARD ABOUT HER. THEY SAY SHE'S GOT A BOUNCE THAT'LL STOP TRAFFIC DEAD.
IT'S TRUE! SHE'S AS GORGEOUS AS THE SETTING SUN.
THEY'VE SEALED THE PROMISE WITH A KISS...

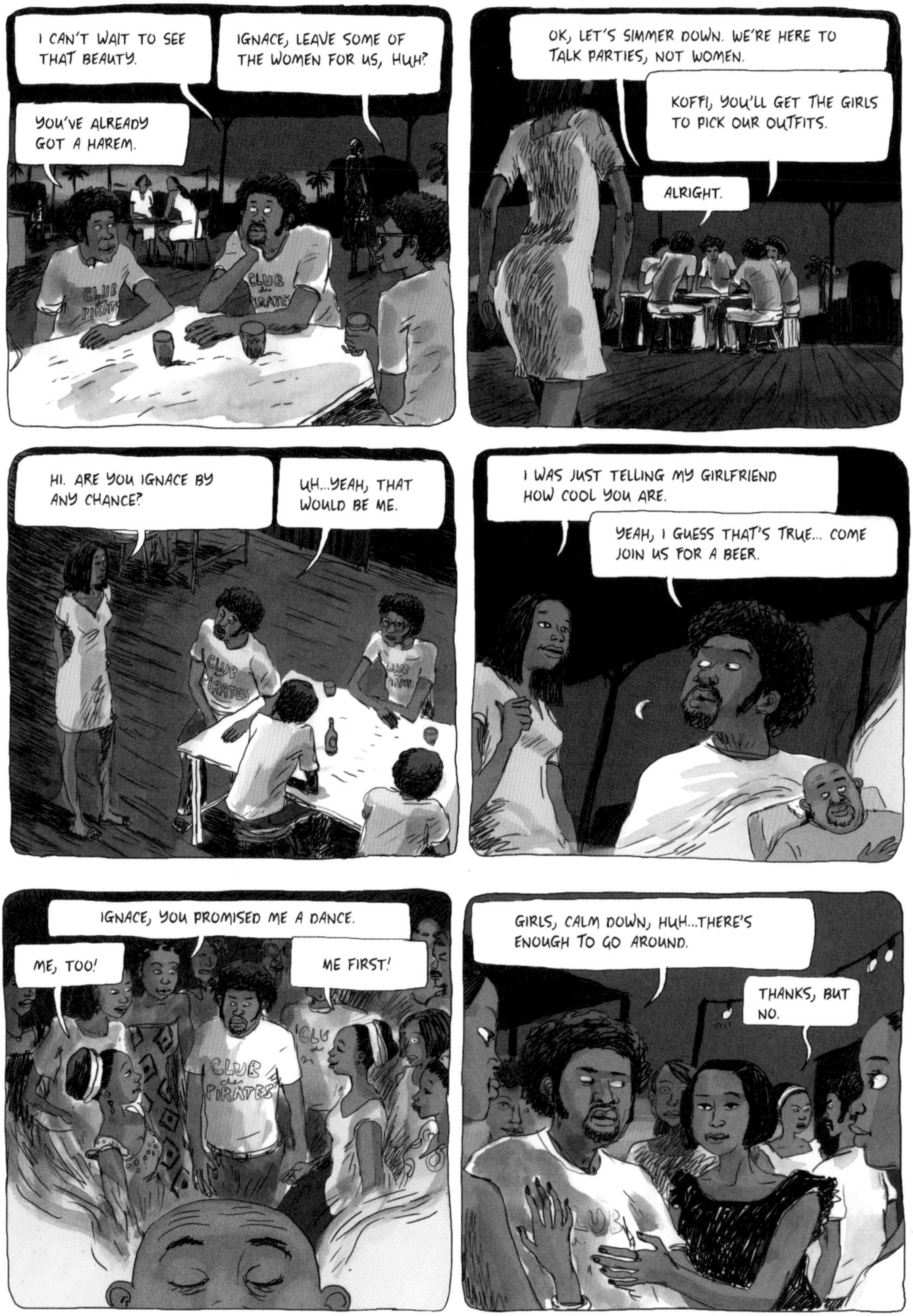
I CAN'T WAIT TO SEE THAT BEAUTY.
YOU'VE ALREADY GOT A HAREM.
IGNACE, LEAVE SOME OF THE WOMEN FOR US, HUH?
OK, LET'S SIMMER DOWN. WE'RE HERE TO TALK PARTIES, NOT WOMEN.
KOFFI, YOU'LL GET THE GIRLS TO PICK OUR OUTFITS.
ALRIGHT.
HI. ARE YOU IGNACE BY ANY CHANCE?
UH...YEAH, THAT WOULD BE ME.
I WAS JUST TELLING MY GIRLFRIEND HOW COOL YOU ARE.
YEAH, I GUESS THAT'S TRUE... COME JOIN US FOR A BEER.
IGNACE, YOU PROMISED ME A DANCE.
ME, TOO!
ME FIRST!
GIRLS, CALM DOWN, HUH...THERE'S ENOUGH TO GO AROUND.
THANKS, BUT NO.

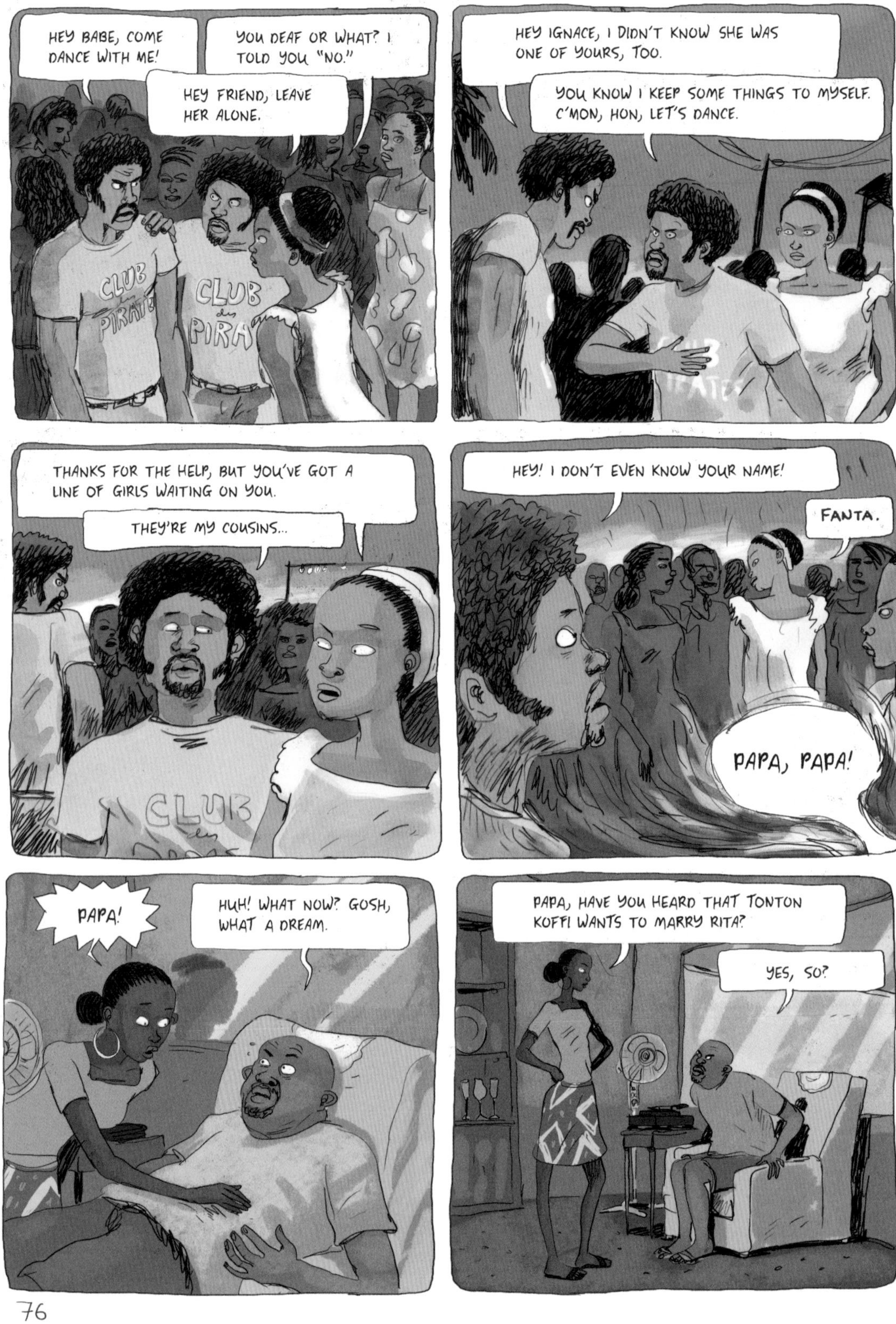
HEY BABE, COME DANCE WITH ME!
YOU DEAF OR WHAT? I TOLD YOU "NO."
HEY FRIEND, LEAVE HER ALONE.
CLUB des PIRATES
HEY IGNACE, I DIDN'T KNOW SHE WAS ONE OF YOURS, TOO.
YOU KNOW I KEEP SOME THINGS TO MYSELF. C'MON, HON, LET'S DANCE.
THANKS FOR THE HELP, BUT YOU'VE GOT A LINE OF GIRLS WAITING ON YOU.
THEY'RE MY COUSINS...
HEY! I DON'T EVEN KNOW YOUR NAME!
FANTA.
PAPA, PAPA!
PAPA!
HUH! WHAT NOW? GOSH, WHAT A DREAM.
PAPA, HAVE YOU HEARD THAT TONTON KOFFI WANTS TO MARRY RITA?
YES, SO?

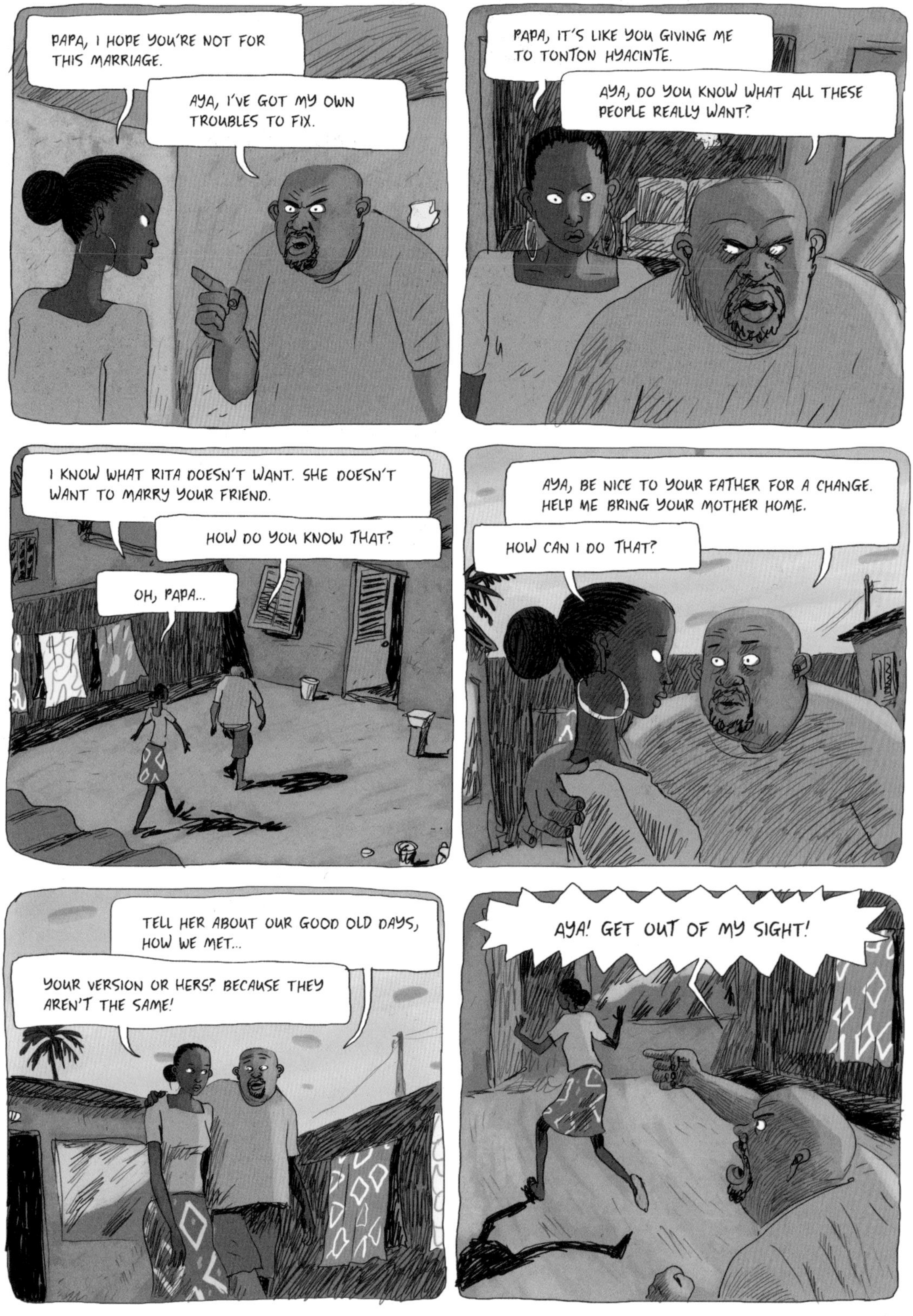
PAPA, I HOPE YOU'RE NOT FOR THIS MARRIAGE.
AYA, I'VE GOT MY OWN TROUBLES TO FIX.
PAPA, IT'S LIKE YOU GIVING ME TO TONTON HYACINTE.
AYA, DO YOU KNOW WHAT ALL THESE PEOPLE REALLY WANT?
I KNOW WHAT RITA DOESN'T WANT. SHE DOESN'T WANT TO MARRY YOUR FRIEND.
HOW DO YOU KNOW THAT?
OH, PAPA...
AYA, BE NICE TO YOUR FATHER FOR A CHANGE. HELP ME BRING YOUR MOTHER HOME.
HOW CAN I DO THAT?
TELL HER ABOUT OUR GOOD OLD DAYS, HOW WE MET...
YOUR VERSION OR HERS? BECAUSE THEY AREN'T THE SAME!
AYA! GET OUT OF MY SIGHT!

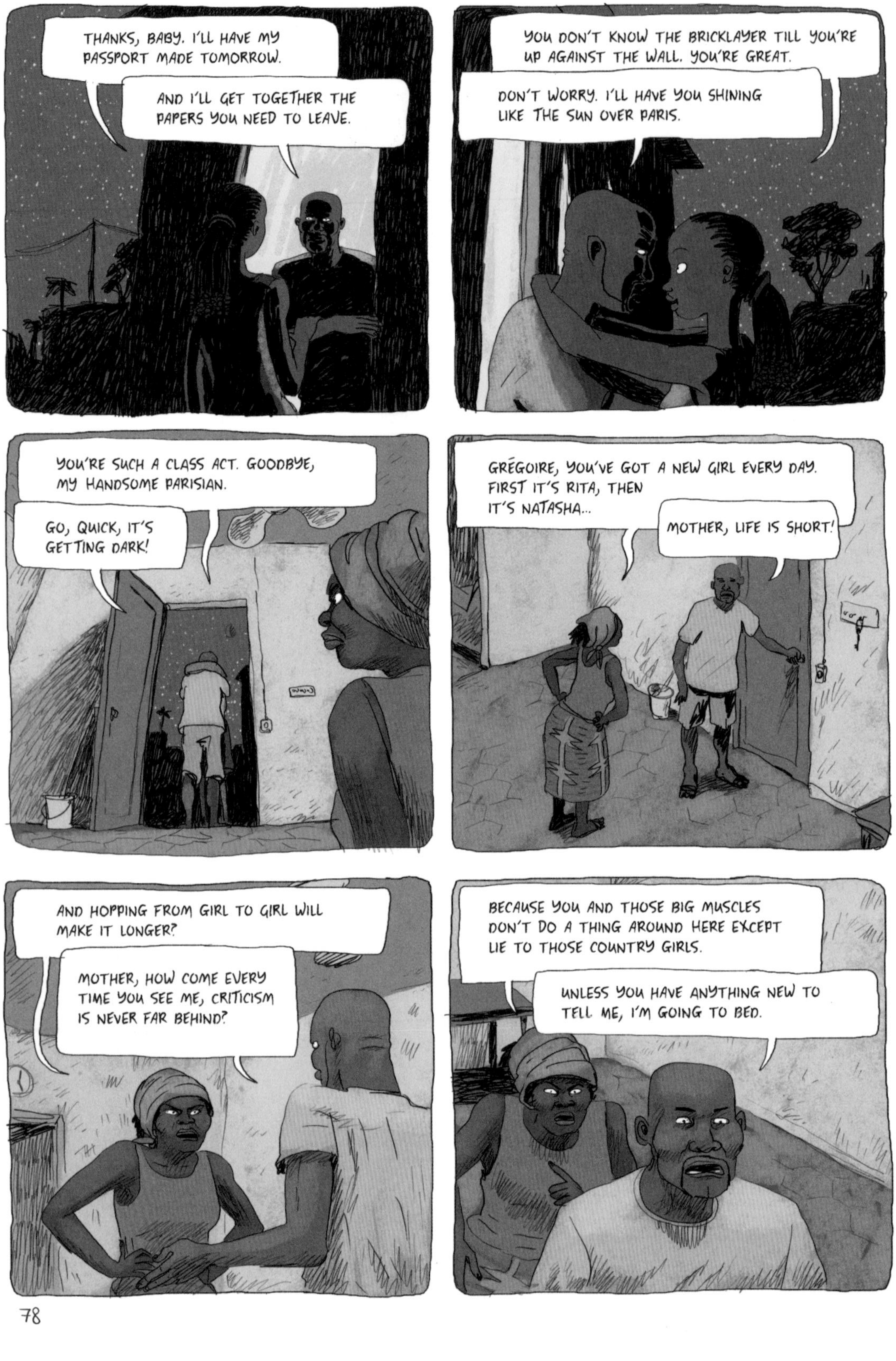
THANKS, BABY. I'LL HAVE MY PASSPORT MADE TOMORROW.
AND I'LL GET TOGETHER THE PAPERS YOU NEED TO LEAVE.
YOU DON'T KNOW THE BRICKLAYER TILL YOU'RE UP AGAINST THE WALL. YOU'RE GREAT.
DON'T WORRY. I'LL HAVE YOU SHINING LIKE THE SUN OVER PARIS.
YOU'RE SUCH A CLASS ACT. GOODBYE, MY HANDSOME PARISIAN.
GO, QUICK, IT'S GETTING DARK!
GRÉGOIRE, YOU'VE GOT A NEW GIRL EVERY DAY. FIRST IT'S RITA, THEN IT'S NATASHA...
MOTHER, LIFE IS SHORT!
AND HOPPING FROM GIRL TO GIRL WILL MAKE IT LONGER?
MOTHER, HOW COME EVERY TIME YOU SEE ME, CRITICISM IS NEVER FAR BEHIND?
BECAUSE YOU AND THOSE BIG MUSCLES DON'T DO A THING AROUND HERE EXCEPT LIE TO THOSE COUNTRY GIRLS.
UNLESS YOU HAVE ANYTHING NEW TO TELL ME, I'M GOING TO BED.

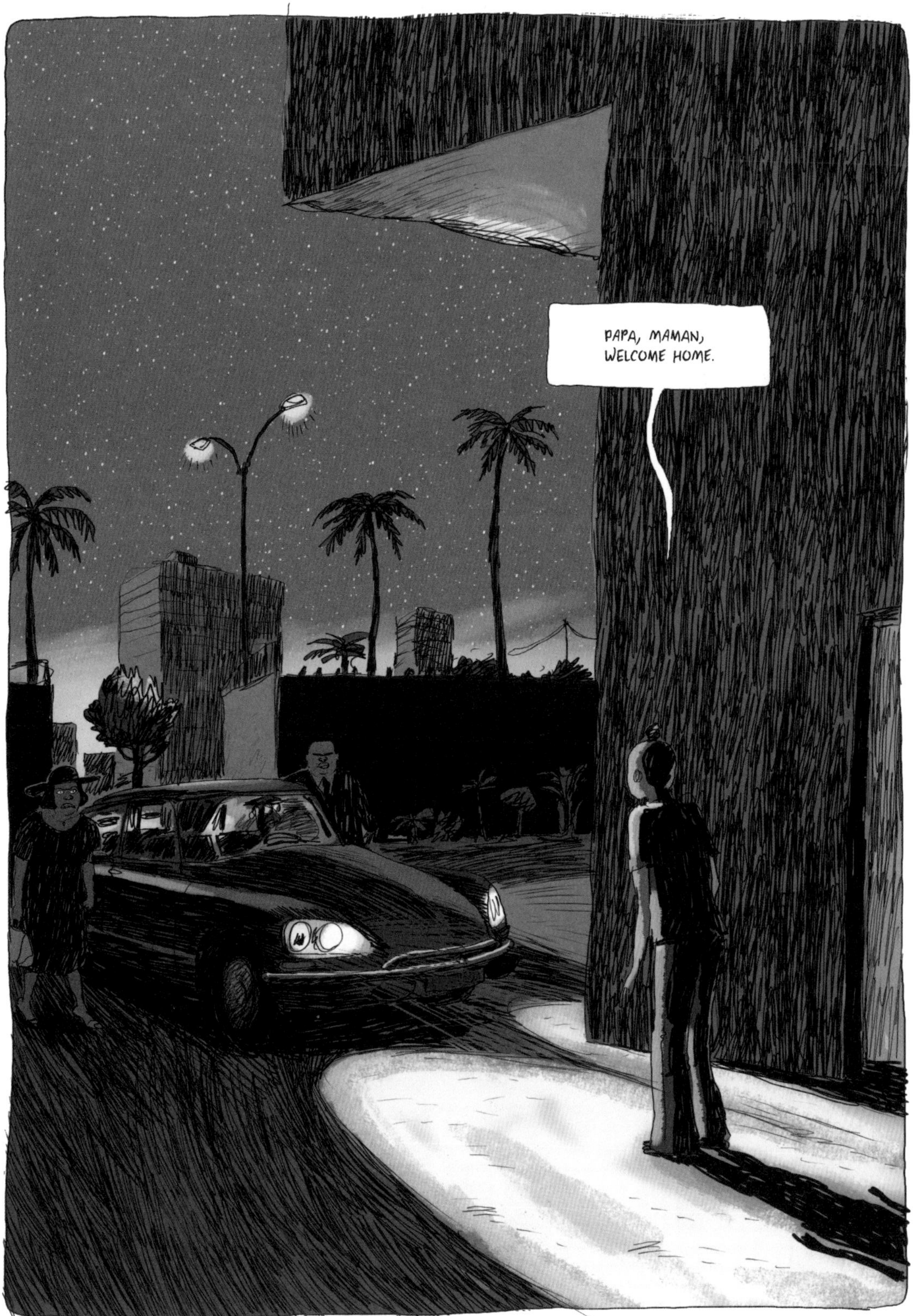
PAPA, MAMAN, WELCOME HOME.

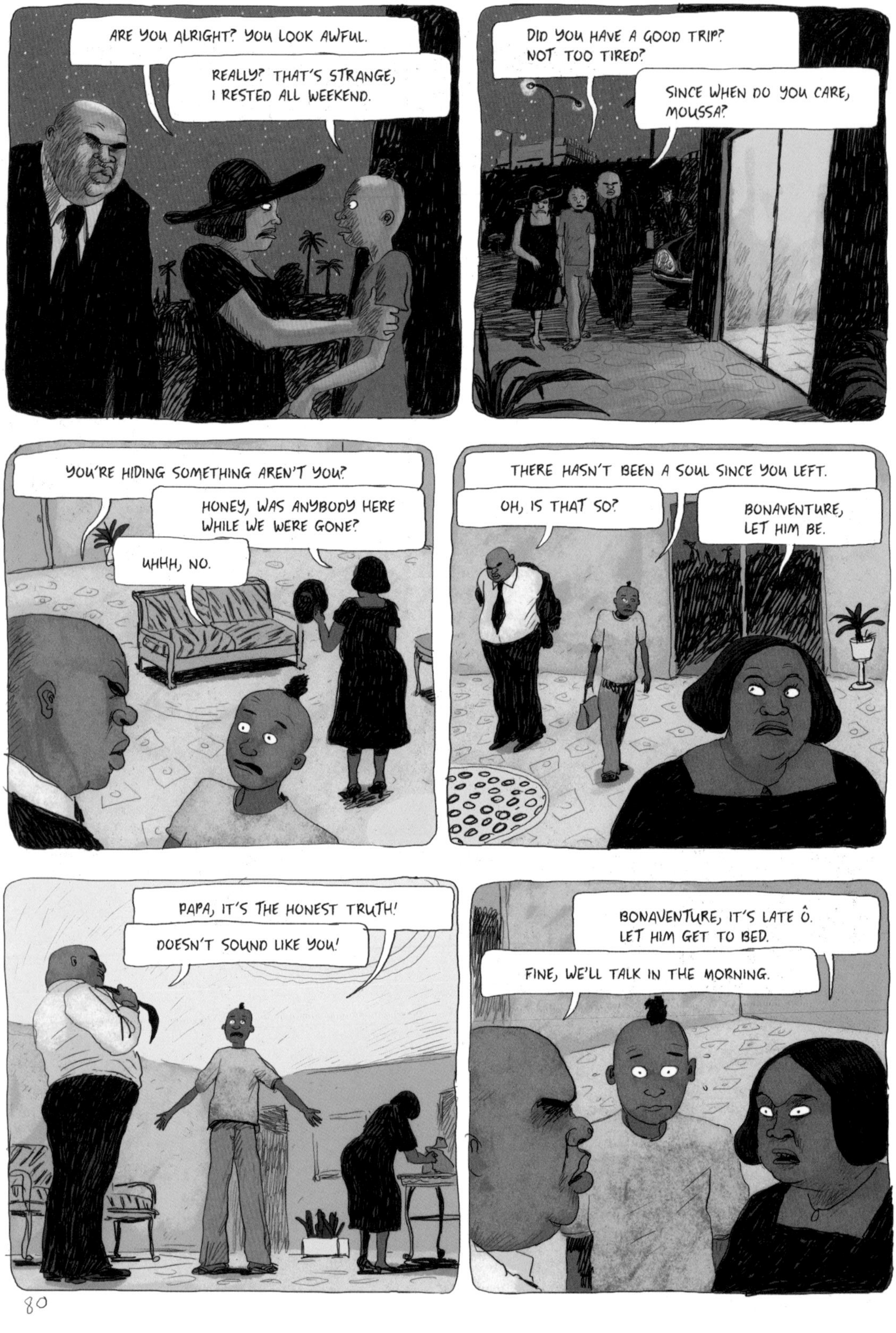

ARE YOU ALRIGHT? YOU LOOK AWFUL.
REALLY? THAT'S STRANGE, I RESTED ALL WEEKEND.
DID YOU HAVE A GOOD TRIP? NOT TOO TIRED?
SINCE WHEN DO YOU CARE, MOUSSA?
YOU'RE HIDING SOMETHING AREN'T YOU?
HONEY, WAS ANYBODY HERE WHILE WE WERE GONE?
UHHH, NO.
THERE HASN'T BEEN A SOUL SINCE YOU LEFT.
OH, IS THAT SO?
BONAVENTURE, LET HIM BE.
PAPA, IT'S THE HONEST TRUTH!
DOESN'T SOUND LIKE YOU!
BONAVENTURE, IT'S LATE Ô. LET HIM GET TO BED.
FINE, WE'LL TALK IN THE MORNING.

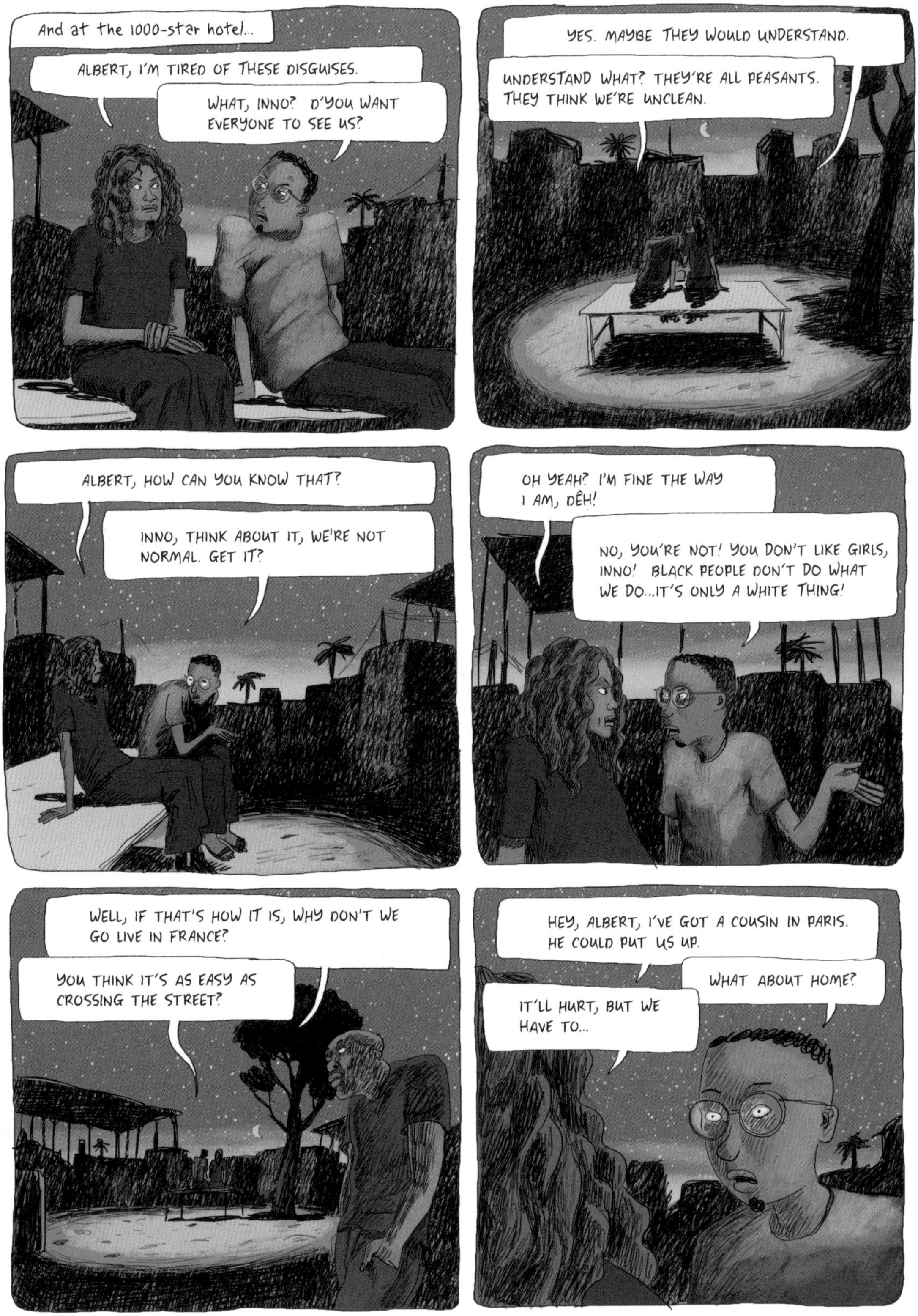
And at the 1000-star hotel...
ALBERT, I'M TIRED OF THESE DISGUISES.
WHAT, INNO? D'YOU WANT EVERYONE TO SEE US?
YES. MAYBE THEY WOULD UNDERSTAND.
UNDERSTAND WHAT? THEY'RE ALL PEASANTS. THEY THINK WE'RE UNCLEAN.
ALBERT, HOW CAN YOU KNOW THAT?
INNO, THINK ABOUT IT, WE'RE NOT NORMAL. GET IT?
OH YEAH? I'M FINE THE WAY I AM, DÊH!
NO, YOU'RE NOT! YOU DON'T LIKE GIRLS, INNO! BLACK PEOPLE DON'T DO WHAT WE DO...IT'S ONLY A WHITE THING!
WELL, IF THAT'S HOW IT IS, WHY DON'T WE GO LIVE IN FRANCE?
YOU THINK IT'S AS EASY AS CROSSING THE STREET?
HEY, ALBERT, I'VE GOT A COUSIN IN PARIS. HE COULD PUT US UP.
WHAT ABOUT HOME?
IT'LL HURT, BUT WE HAVE TO...

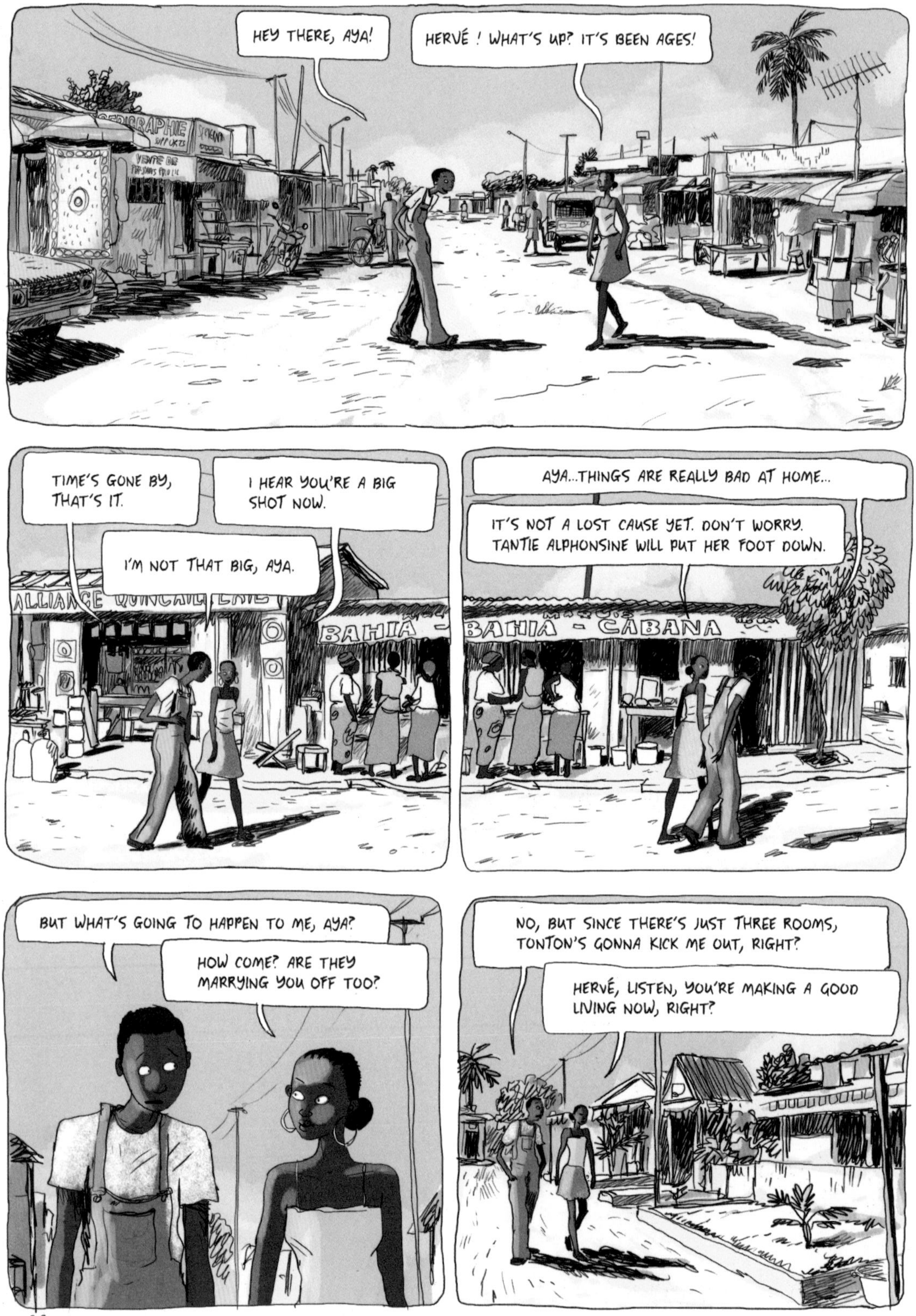
HEY THERE, AYA!
HERVÉ ! WHAT'S UP? IT'S BEEN AGES!
TIME'S GONE BY, THAT'S IT.
I HEAR YOU'RE A BIG SHOT NOW.
I'M NOT THAT BIG, AYA.
BAHIA
AYA...THINGS ARE REALLY BAD AT HOME...
IT'S NOT A LOST CAUSE YET. DON'T WORRY. TANTIE ALPHONSINE WILL PUT HER FOOT DOWN.
BAHIA - CABANA
BUT WHAT'S GOING TO HAPPEN TO ME, AYA?
HOW COME? ARE THEY MARRYING YOU OFF TOO?
NO, BUT SINCE THERE'S JUST THREE ROOMS, TONTON'S GONNA KICK ME OUT, RIGHT?
HERVÉ, LISTEN, YOU'RE MAKING A GOOD LIVING NOW, RIGHT?

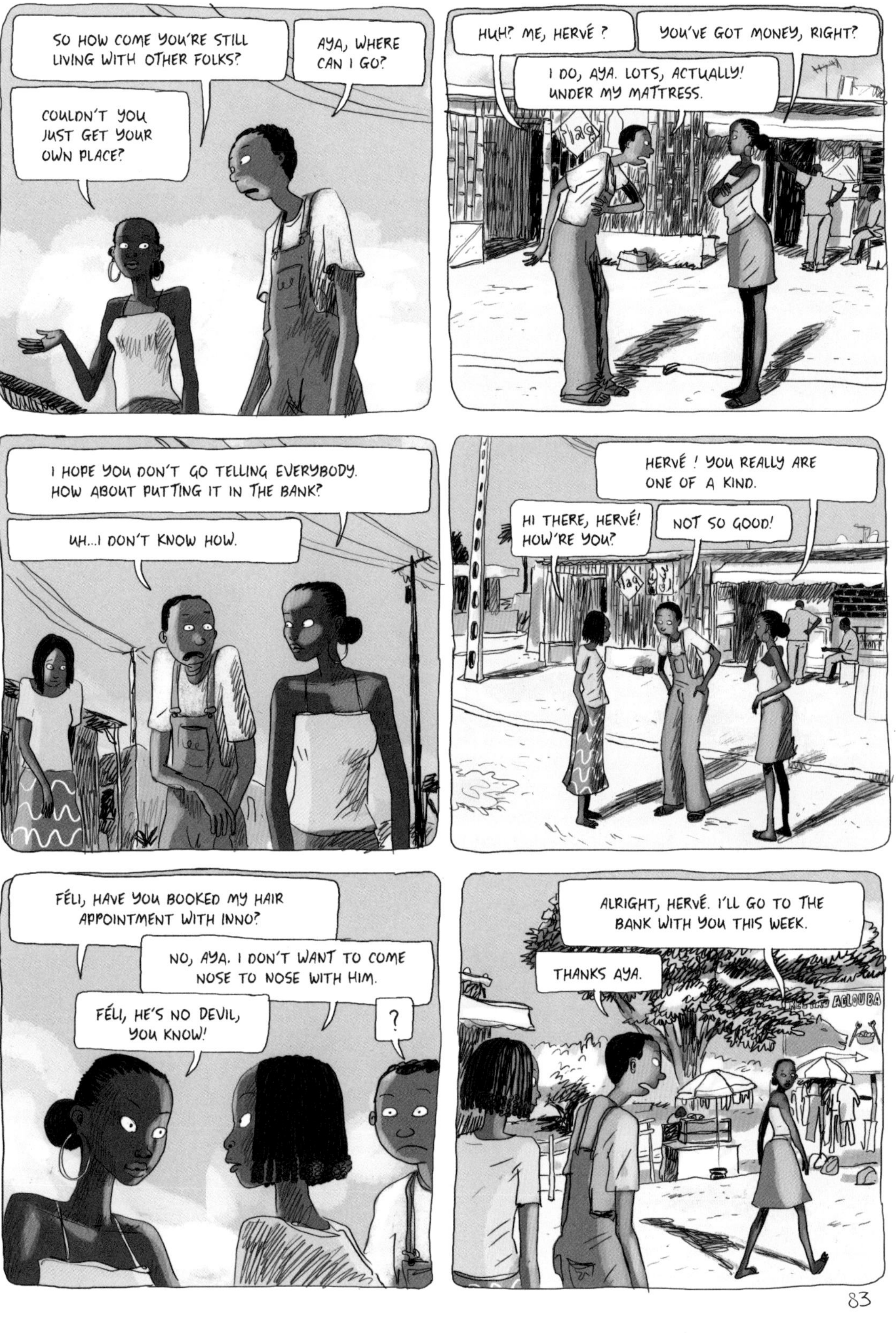
SO HOW COME YOU'RE STILL LIVING WITH OTHER FOLKS?
COULDN'T YOU JUST GET YOUR OWN PLACE?
AYA, WHERE CAN I GO?
HUH? ME, HERVÉ ?
YOU'VE GOT MONEY, RIGHT?
I DO, AYA. LOTS, ACTUALLY! UNDER MY MATTRESS.
I HOPE YOU DON'T GO TELLING EVERYBODY. HOW ABOUT PUTTING IT IN THE BANK?
UH...I DON'T KNOW HOW.
HI THERE, HERVÉ! HOW'RE YOU?
NOT SO GOOD!
HERVÉ ! YOU REALLY ARE ONE OF A KIND.
FÉLI, HAVE YOU BOOKED MY HAIR APPOINTMENT WITH INNO?
NO, AYA. I DON'T WANT TO COME NOSE TO NOSE WITH HIM.
FÉLI, HE'S NO DEVIL, YOU KNOW!
?
ALRIGHT, HERVÉ. I'LL GO TO THE BANK WITH YOU THIS WEEK.
THANKS AYA.
AGLOUBA

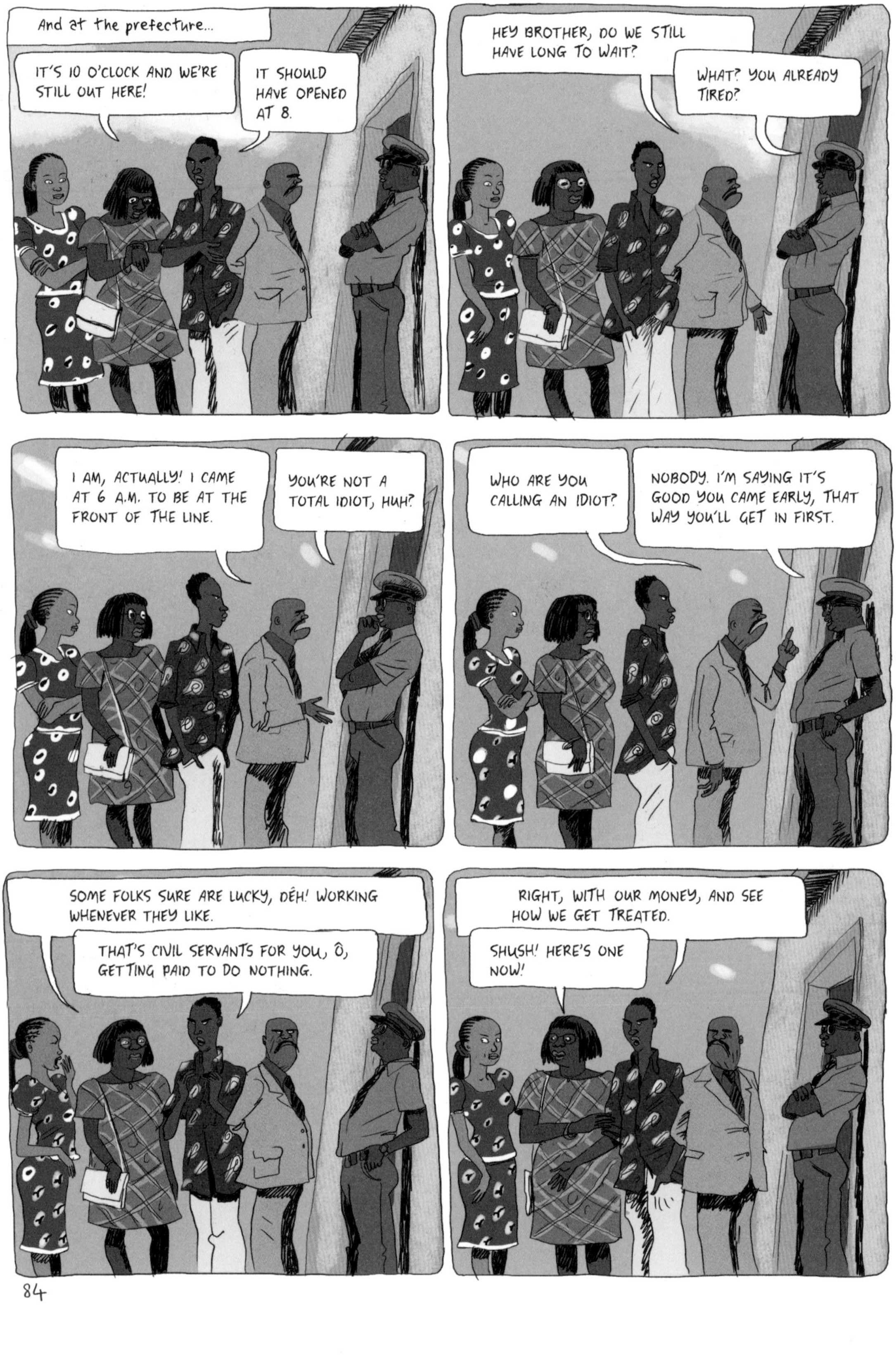
And at the prefecture...
IT'S 10 O'CLOCK AND WE'RE STILL OUT HERE!
IT SHOULD HAVE OPENED AT 8.
HEY BROTHER, DO WE STILL HAVE LONG TO WAIT?
WHAT? YOU ALREADY TIRED?
I AM, ACTUALLY! I CAME AT 6 A.M. TO BE AT THE FRONT OF THE LINE.
YOU'RE NOT A TOTAL IDIOT, HUH?
WHO ARE YOU CALLING AN IDIOT?
NOBODY. I'M SAYING IT'S GOOD YOU CAME EARLY, THAT WAY YOU'LL GET IN FIRST.
SOME FOLKS SURE ARE LUCKY, DÉH! WORKING WHENEVER THEY LIKE.
THAT'S CIVIL SERVANTS FOR YOU, Ô, GETTING PAID TO DO NOTHING.
RIGHT, WITH OUR MONEY, AND SEE HOW WE GET TREATED.
SHUSH! HERE'S ONE NOW!

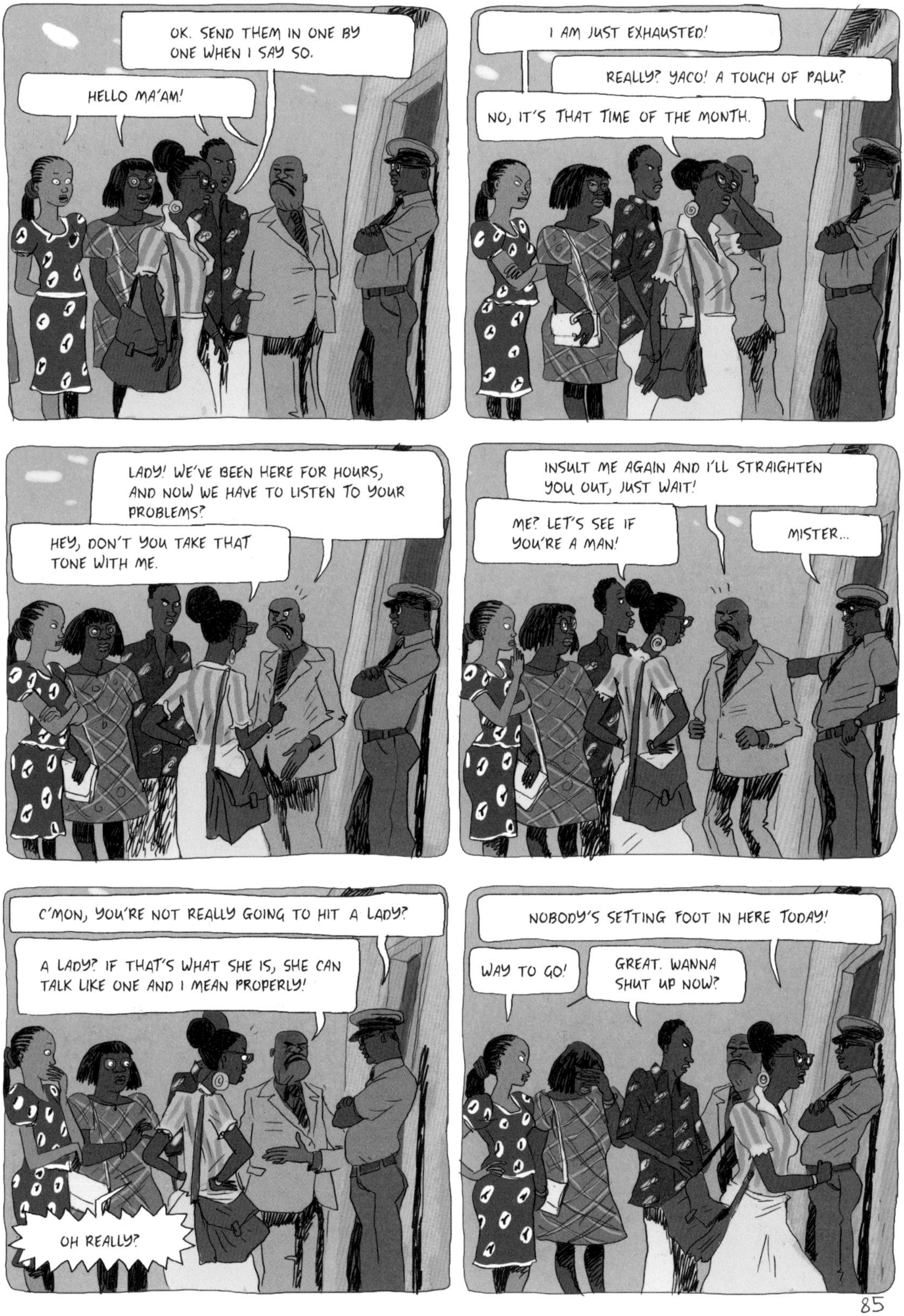
OK. SEND THEM IN ONE BY ONE WHEN I SAY SO.
HELLO MA'AM!
I AM JUST EXHAUSTED!
REALLY? YACO! A TOUCH OF PALU?
NO, IT'S THAT TIME OF THE MONTH.
LADY! WE'VE BEEN HERE FOR HOURS, AND NOW WE HAVE TO LISTEN TO YOUR PROBLEMS?
HEY, DON'T YOU TAKE THAT TONE WITH ME.
INSULT ME AGAIN AND I'LL STRAIGHTEN YOU OUT, JUST WAIT!
ME? LET'S SEE IF YOU'RE A MAN!
MISTER...
C'MON, YOU'RE NOT REALLY GOING TO HIT A LADY?
A LADY? IF THAT'S WHAT SHE IS, SHE CAN TALK LIKE ONE AND I MEAN PROPERLY!
OH REALLY?
NOBODY'S SETTING FOOT IN HERE TODAY!
WAY TO GO!
GREAT. WANNA SHUT UP NOW?

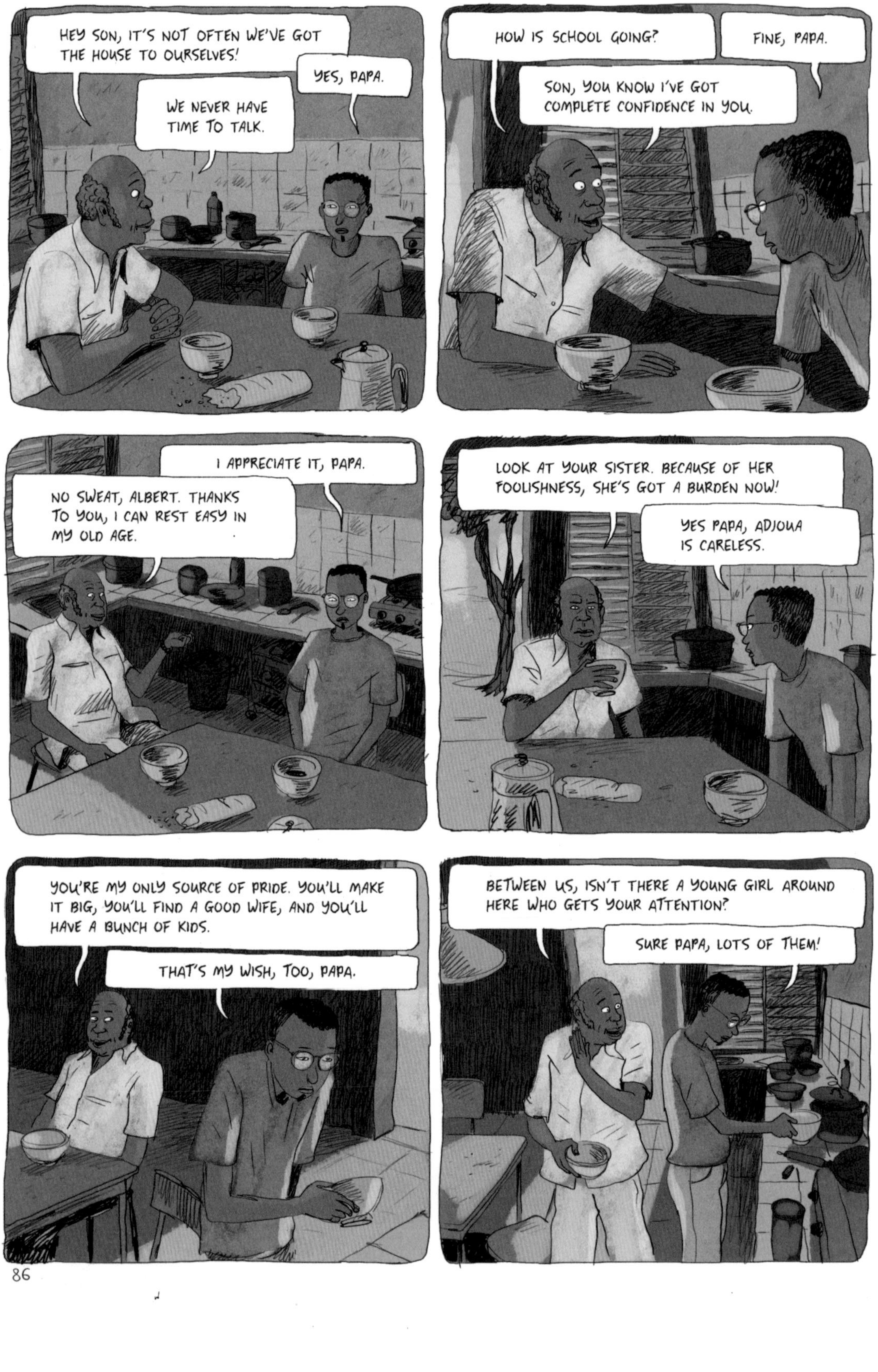
HEY SON, IT'S NOT OFTEN WE'VE GOT THE HOUSE TO OURSELVES!
WE NEVER HAVE TIME TO TALK.
YES, PAPA.
HOW IS SCHOOL GOING?
FINE, PAPA.
SON, YOU KNOW I'VE GOT COMPLETE CONFIDENCE IN YOU.
NO SWEAT, ALBERT. THANKS TO YOU, I CAN REST EASY IN MY OLD AGE.
I APPRECIATE IT, PAPA.
LOOK AT YOUR SISTER. BECAUSE OF HER FOOLISHNESS, SHE'S GOT A BURDEN NOW!
YES PAPA, ADJOUA IS CARELESS.
YOU'RE MY ONLY SOURCE OF PRIDE. YOU'LL MAKE IT BIG, YOU'LL FIND A GOOD WIFE, AND YOU'LL HAVE A BUNCH OF KIDS.
THAT'S MY WISH, TOO, PAPA.
BETWEEN US, ISN'T THERE A YOUNG GIRL AROUND HERE WHO GETS YOUR ATTENTION?
SURE PAPA, LOTS OF THEM!

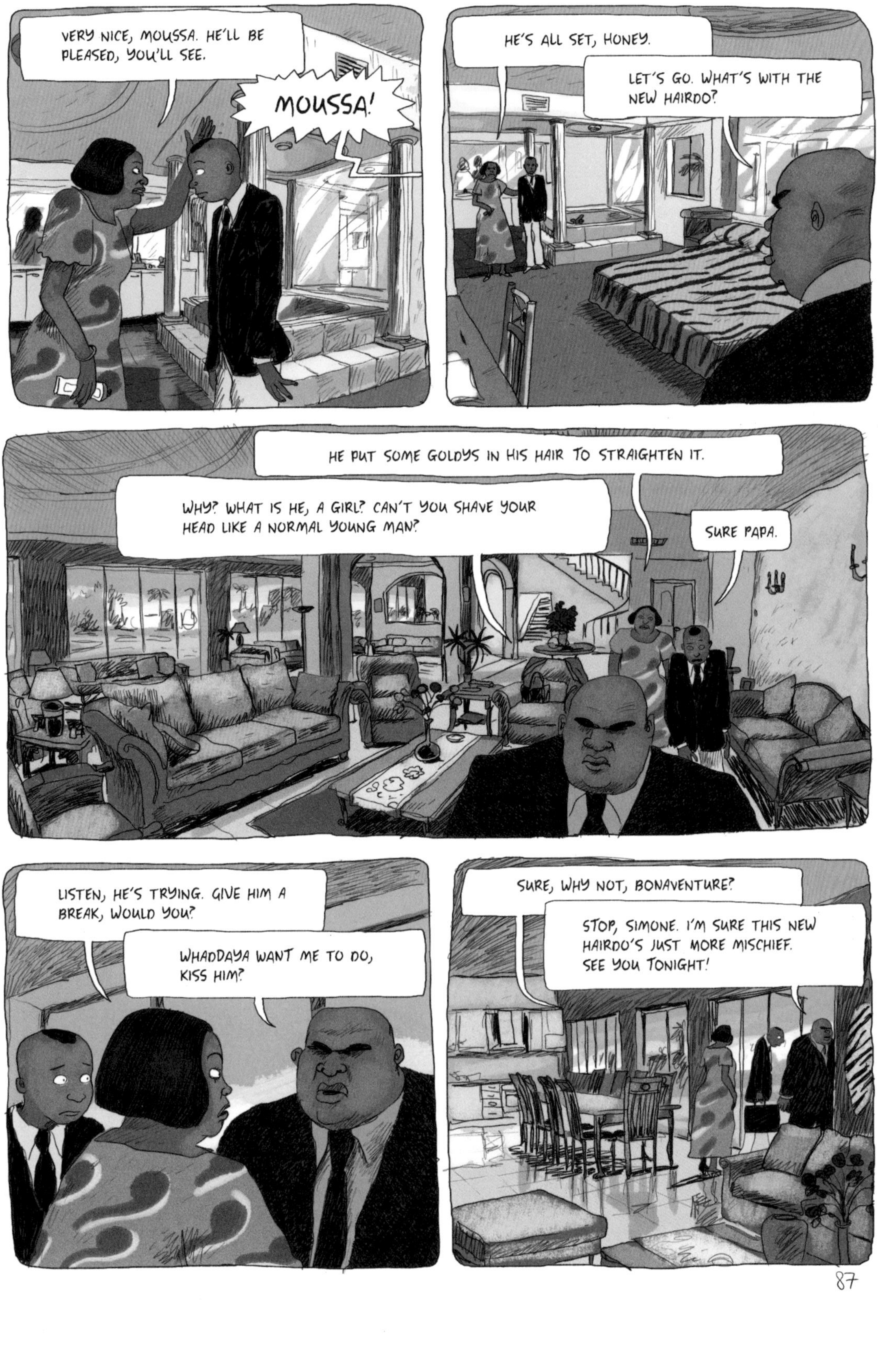
VERY NICE, MOUSSA. HE'LL BE PLEASED, YOU'LL SEE.
MOUSSA!
HE'S ALL SET, HONEY.
LET'S GO. WHAT'S WITH THE NEW HAIRDO?
HE PUT SOME GOLDYS IN HIS HAIR TO STRAIGHTEN IT.
WHY? WHAT IS HE, A GIRL? CAN'T YOU SHAVE YOUR HEAD LIKE A NORMAL YOUNG MAN?
SURE PAPA.
LISTEN, HE'S TRYING. GIVE HIM A BREAK, WOULD YOU?
WHADDAYA WANT ME TO DO, KISS HIM?
SURE, WHY NOT, BONAVENTURE?
STOP, SIMONE. I'M SURE THIS NEW HAIRDO'S JUST MORE MISCHIEF. SEE YOU TONIGHT!

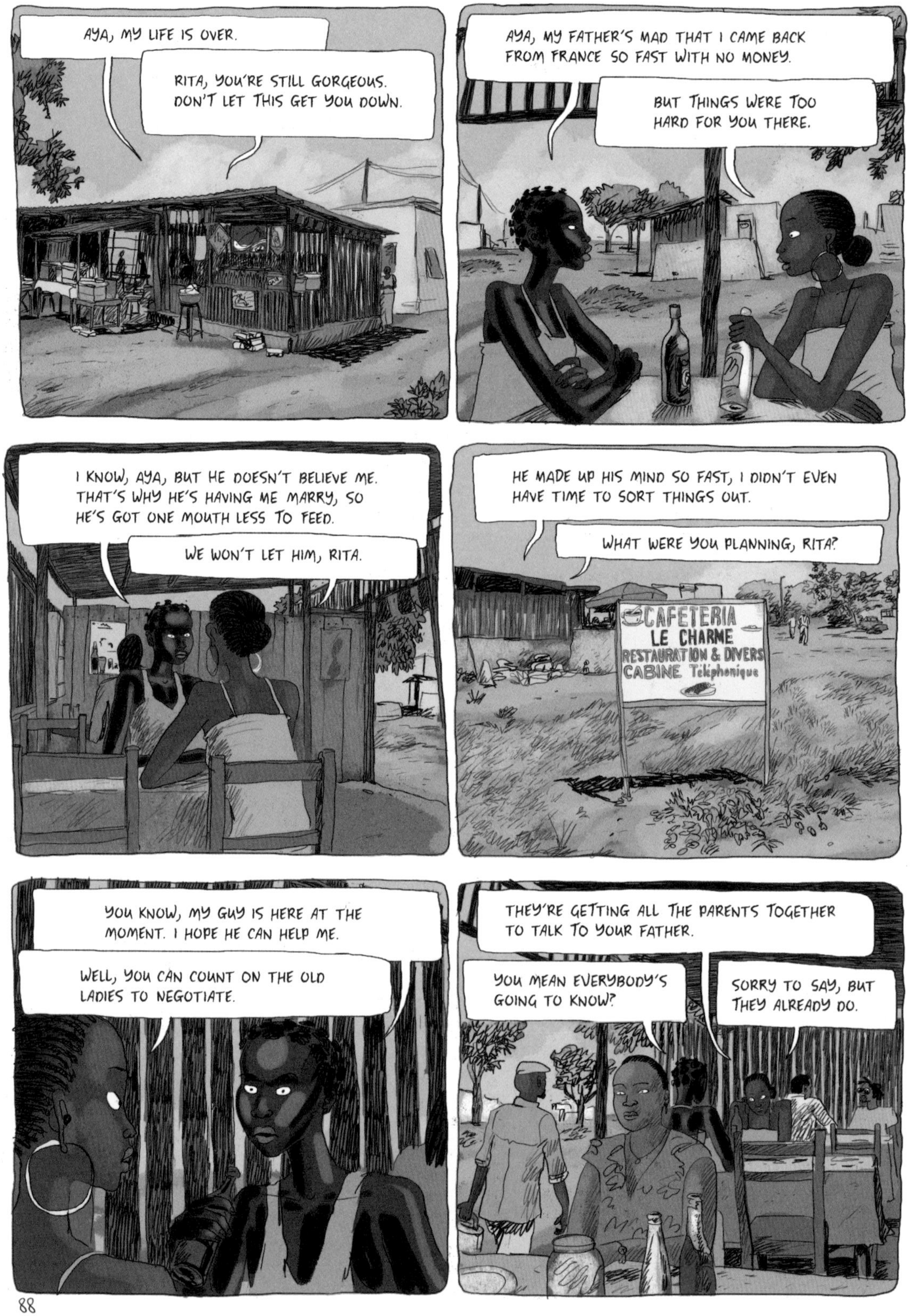
AYA, MY LIFE IS OVER.
RITA, YOU'RE STILL GORGEOUS. DON'T LET THIS GET YOU DOWN.
AYA, MY FATHER'S MAD THAT I CAME BACK FROM FRANCE SO FAST WITH NO MONEY.
BUT THINGS WERE TOO HARD FOR YOU THERE.
I KNOW, AYA, BUT HE DOESN'T BELIEVE ME. THAT'S WHY HE'S HAVING ME MARRY, SO HE'S GOT ONE MOUTH LESS TO FEED.
WE WON'T LET HIM, RITA.
HE MADE UP HIS MIND SO FAST, I DIDN'T EVEN HAVE TIME TO SORT THINGS OUT.
WHAT WERE YOU PLANNING, RITA?
CAFETERIA
LE CHARME
RESTAURATION & DIVERS
CABINE Téléphonique
YOU KNOW, MY GUY IS HERE AT THE MOMENT. I HOPE HE CAN HELP ME.
WELL, YOU CAN COUNT ON THE OLD LADIES TO NEGOTIATE.
THEY'RE GETTING ALL THE PARENTS TOGETHER TO TALK TO YOUR FATHER.
YOU MEAN EVERYBODY'S GOING TO KNOW?
SORRY TO SAY, BUT THEY ALREADY DO.

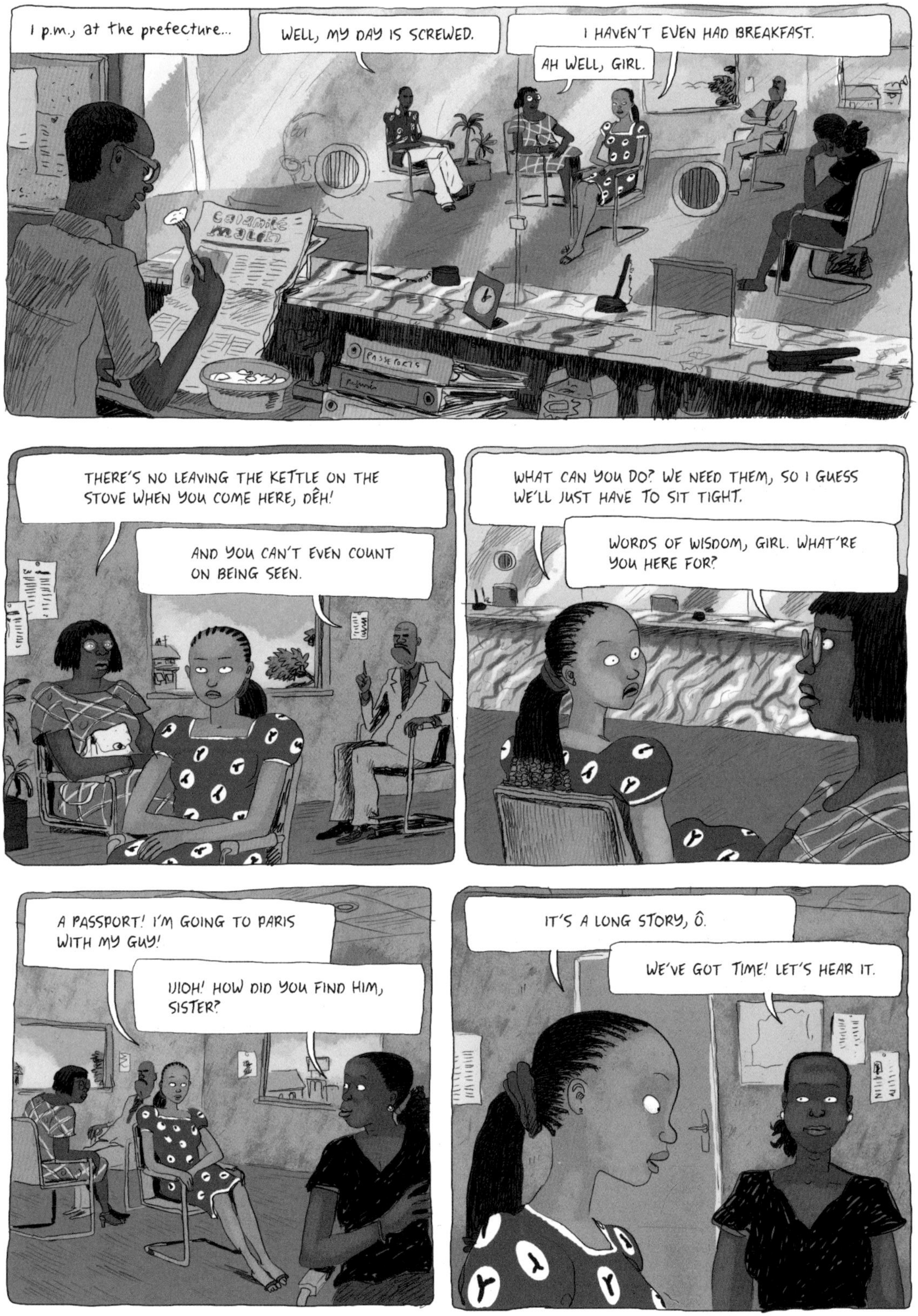
I p.m., at the prefecture...
WELL, MY DAY IS SCREWED.
I HAVEN'T EVEN HAD BREAKFAST.
AH WELL, GIRL.
THERE'S NO LEAVING THE KETTLE ON THE STOVE WHEN YOU COME HERE, DÊH!
AND YOU CAN'T EVEN COUNT ON BEING SEEN.
WHAT CAN YOU DO? WE NEED THEM, SO I GUESS WE'LL JUST HAVE TO SIT TIGHT.
WORDS OF WISDOM, GIRL. WHAT'RE YOU HERE FOR?
A PASSPORT! I'M GOING TO PARIS WITH MY GUY!
WOH! HOW DID YOU FIND HIM, SISTER?
IT'S A LONG STORY, Ô.
WE'VE GOT TIME! LET'S HEAR IT.

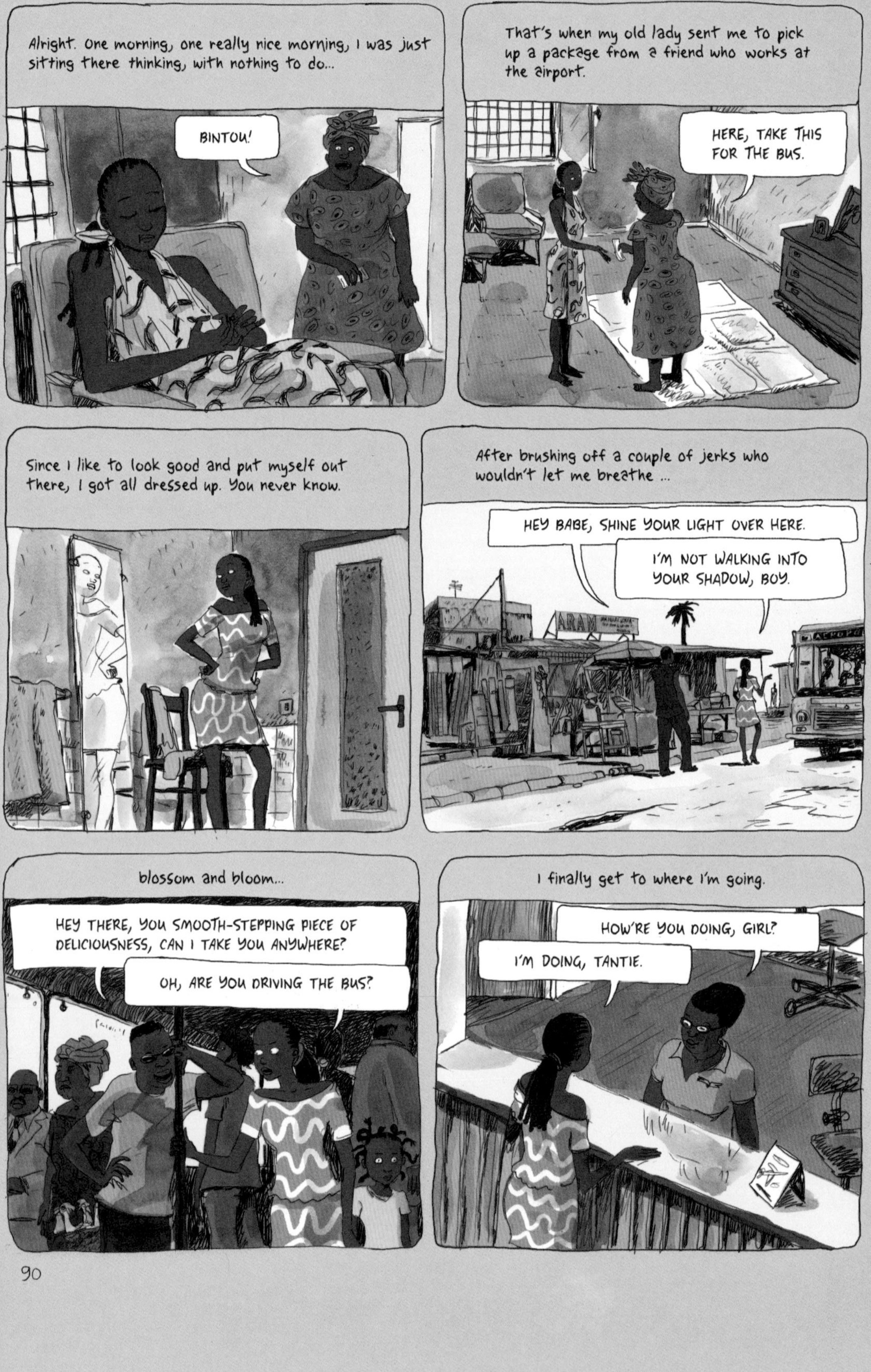
Alright. One morning, one really nice morning, I was just sitting there thinking, with nothing to do...
BINTOU!
That's when my old lady sent me to pick up a package from a friend who works at the airport.
HERE, TAKE THIS FOR THE BUS.
Since I like to look good and put myself out there, I got all dressed up. You never know.
After brushing off a couple of jerks who wouldn't let me breathe ...
HEY BABE, SHINE YOUR LIGHT OVER HERE.
I'M NOT WALKING INTO YOUR SHADOW, BOY.
ARAM
blossom and bloom...
HEY THERE, YOU SMOOTH-STEPPING PIECE OF DELICIOUSNESS, CAN I TAKE YOU ANYWHERE?
OH, ARE YOU DRIVING THE BUS?
I finally get to where I'm going.
HOW'RE YOU DOING, GIRL?
I'M DOING, TANTIE.

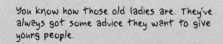
You know how those old ladies are. They've always got some advice they want to give young people.

AH GIRL, LIFE IS HARD, Ô. CHIN UP, YOU'LL FIND A GOOD MAN!

YES TANTIE.

And since good advice never killed anybody, I listened patiently.

JUST DON'T THINK YOU CAN TRUST MEN, Ô. ONCE THEY SAY HELLO, THE REST IS ALL LIES.

YES TANTIE.

That's when I hear a voice, a real sweet melody, behind me.

BONJOURRR, BEAUTIFUL, DO YOU WORK IN THIS AIRPORT?

I turn around and I'm looking at this elegant, handsome guy, real cool, dressed to the nines, with a French accent to top it off.

NO. CAN I HELP YOU?

HOW CAN A PERSON FIND A TAXI AROUND HERE?

He was fresh out of France!

JUST FOLLOW ME. I'M BINTOU, AND YOU?

MADEMOISELLE BINTOU!

YOUR TURN, PLEASE!

I'M COMING, Ô!

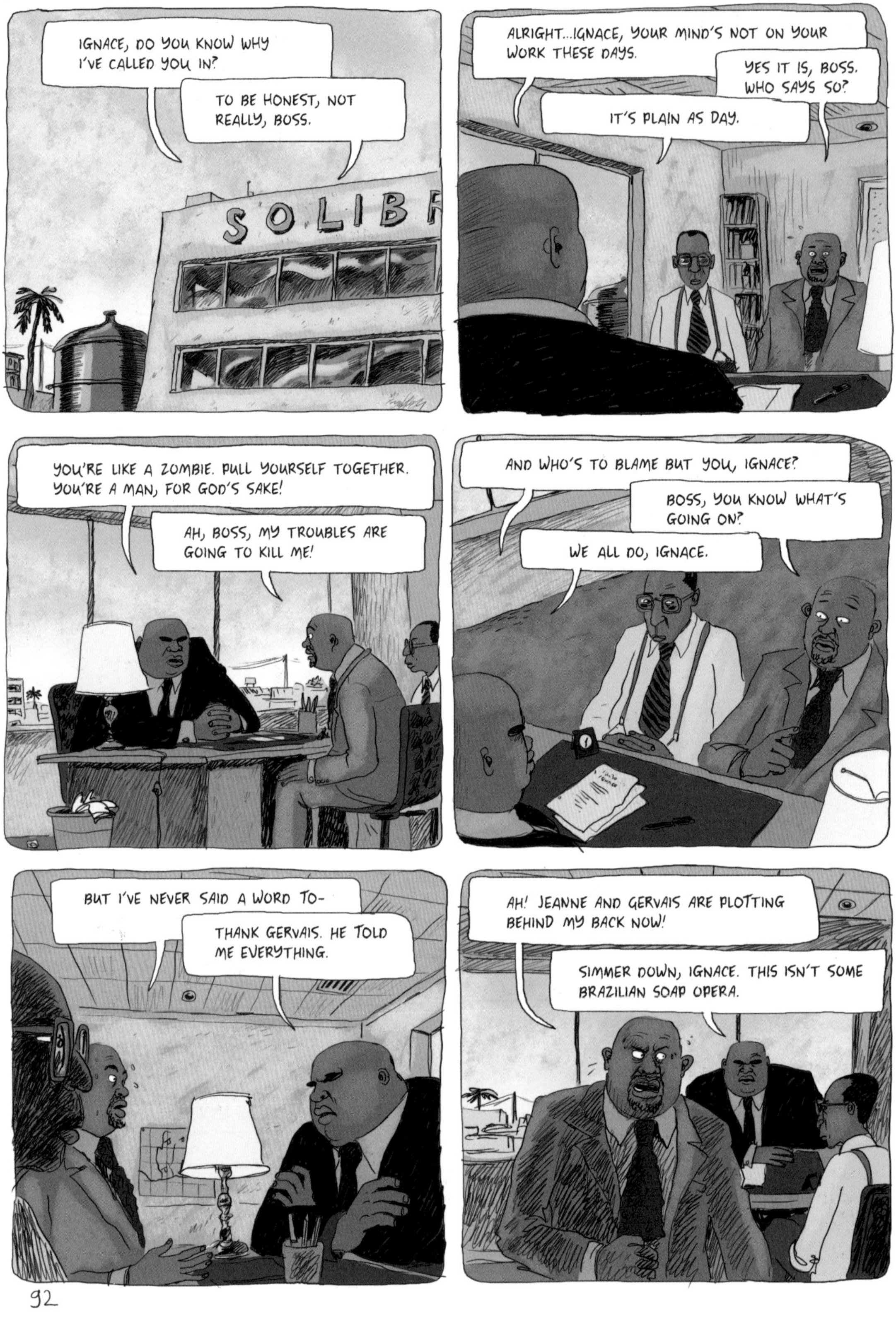

IGNACE, DO YOU KNOW WHY I'VE CALLED YOU IN?
TO BE HONEST, NOT REALLY, BOSS.
SOLIB
ALRIGHT...IGNACE, YOUR MIND'S NOT ON YOUR WORK THESE DAYS.
YES IT IS, BOSS. WHO SAYS SO?
IT'S PLAIN AS DAY.
YOU'RE LIKE A ZOMBIE. PULL YOURSELF TOGETHER. YOU'RE A MAN, FOR GOD'S SAKE!
AH, BOSS, MY TROUBLES ARE GOING TO KILL ME!
AND WHO'S TO BLAME BUT YOU, IGNACE?
BOSS, YOU KNOW WHAT'S GOING ON?
WE ALL DO, IGNACE.
BUT I'VE NEVER SAID A WORD TO-
THANK GERVAIS. HE TOLD ME EVERYTHING.
AH! JEANNE AND GERVAIS ARE PLOTTING BEHIND MY BACK NOW!
SIMMER DOWN, IGNACE. THIS ISN'T SOME BRAZILIAN SOAP OPERA.

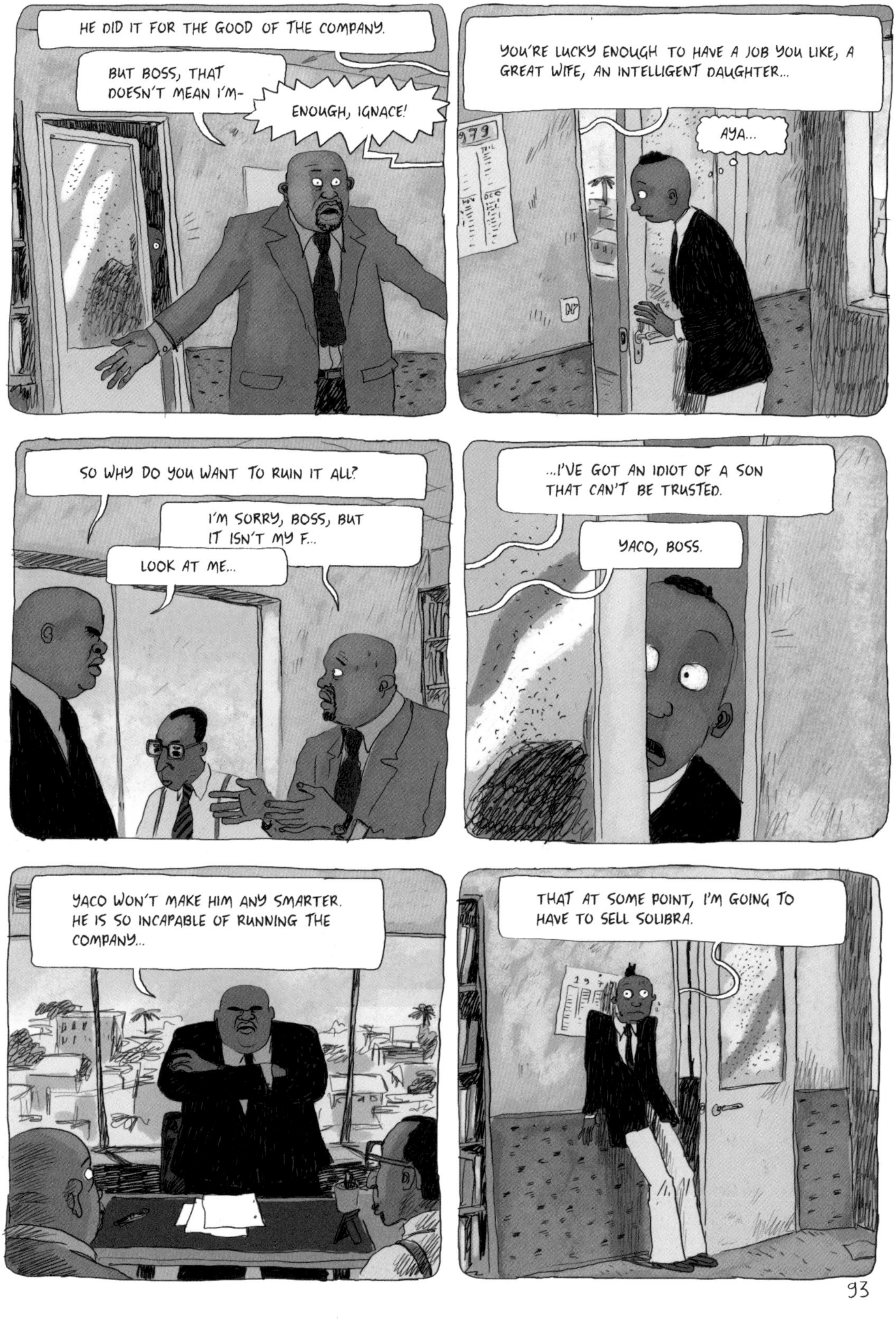
HE DID IT FOR THE GOOD OF THE COMPANY.
BUT BOSS, THAT DOESN'T MEAN I'M-
ENOUGH, IGNACE!
YOU'RE LUCKY ENOUGH TO HAVE A JOB YOU LIKE, A GREAT WIFE, AN INTELLIGENT DAUGHTER...
AYA...
SO WHY DO YOU WANT TO RUIN IT ALL?
I'M SORRY, BOSS, BUT IT ISN'T MY F...
LOOK AT ME...
...I'VE GOT AN IDIOT OF A SON THAT CAN'T BE TRUSTED.
YACO, BOSS.
YACO WON'T MAKE HIM ANY SMARTER. HE IS SO INCAPABLE OF RUNNING THE COMPANY...
THAT AT SOME POINT, I'M GOING TO HAVE TO SELL SOLIBRA.

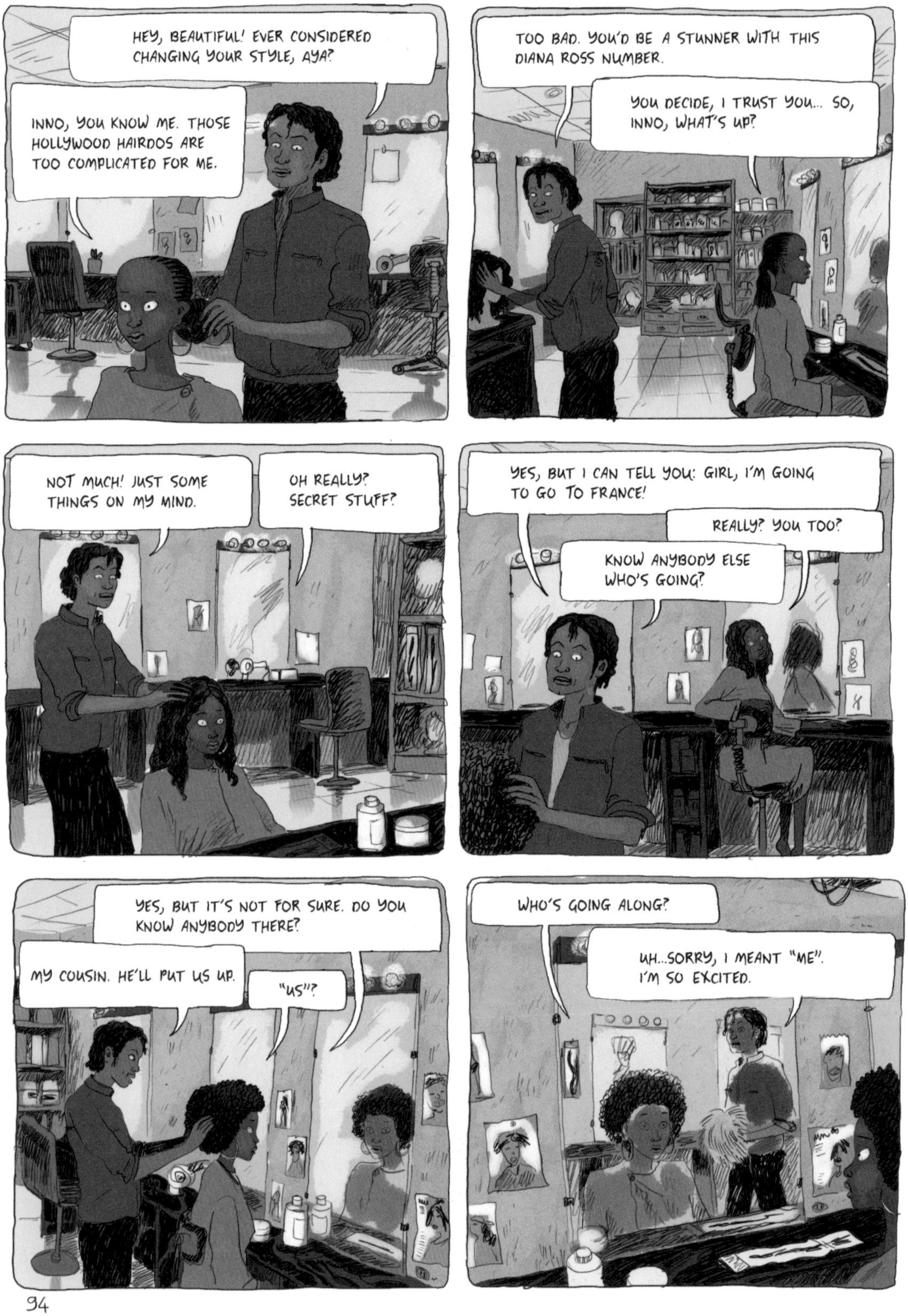
HEY, BEAUTIFUL! EVER CONSIDERED CHANGING YOUR STYLE, AYA?
INNO, YOU KNOW ME. THOSE HOLLYWOOD HAIRDOS ARE TOO COMPLICATED FOR ME.
TOO BAD. YOU'D BE A STUNNER WITH THIS DIANA ROSS NUMBER.
YOU DECIDE, I TRUST YOU... SO, INNO, WHAT'S UP?
NOT MUCH! JUST SOME THINGS ON MY MIND.
OH REALLY? SECRET STUFF?
YES, BUT I CAN TELL YOU: GIRL, I'M GOING TO GO TO FRANCE!
REALLY? YOU TOO?
KNOW ANYBODY ELSE WHO'S GOING?
YES, BUT IT'S NOT FOR SURE. DO YOU KNOW ANYBODY THERE?
MY COUSIN. HE'LL PUT US UP.
"US"?
WHO'S GOING ALONG?
UH...SORRY, I MEANT "ME". I'M SO EXCITED.

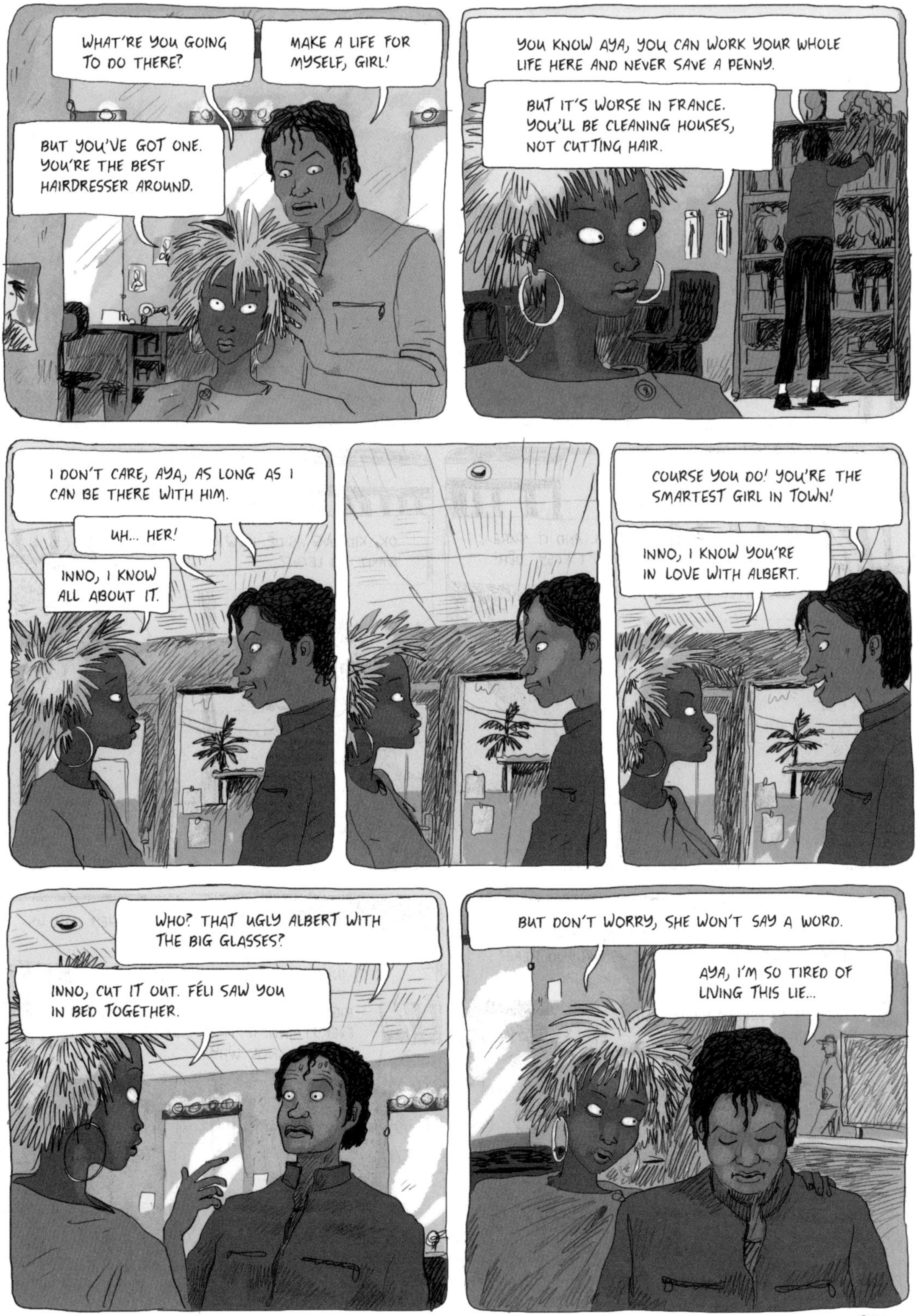
WHAT'RE YOU GOING TO DO THERE?
MAKE A LIFE FOR MYSELF, GIRL!
BUT YOU'VE GOT ONE. YOU'RE THE BEST HAIRDRESSER AROUND.
YOU KNOW AYA, YOU CAN WORK YOUR WHOLE LIFE HERE AND NEVER SAVE A PENNY.
BUT IT'S WORSE IN FRANCE. YOU'LL BE CLEANING HOUSES, NOT CUTTING HAIR.
I DON'T CARE, AYA, AS LONG AS I CAN BE THERE WITH HIM.
UH... HER!
INNO, I KNOW ALL ABOUT IT.
COURSE YOU DO! YOU'RE THE SMARTEST GIRL IN TOWN!
INNO, I KNOW YOU'RE IN LOVE WITH ALBERT.
WHO? THAT UGLY ALBERT WITH THE BIG GLASSES?
INNO, CUT IT OUT. FÉLI SAW YOU IN BED TOGETHER.
BUT DON'T WORRY, SHE WON'T SAY A WORD.
AYA, I'M SO TIRED OF LIVING THIS LIE...

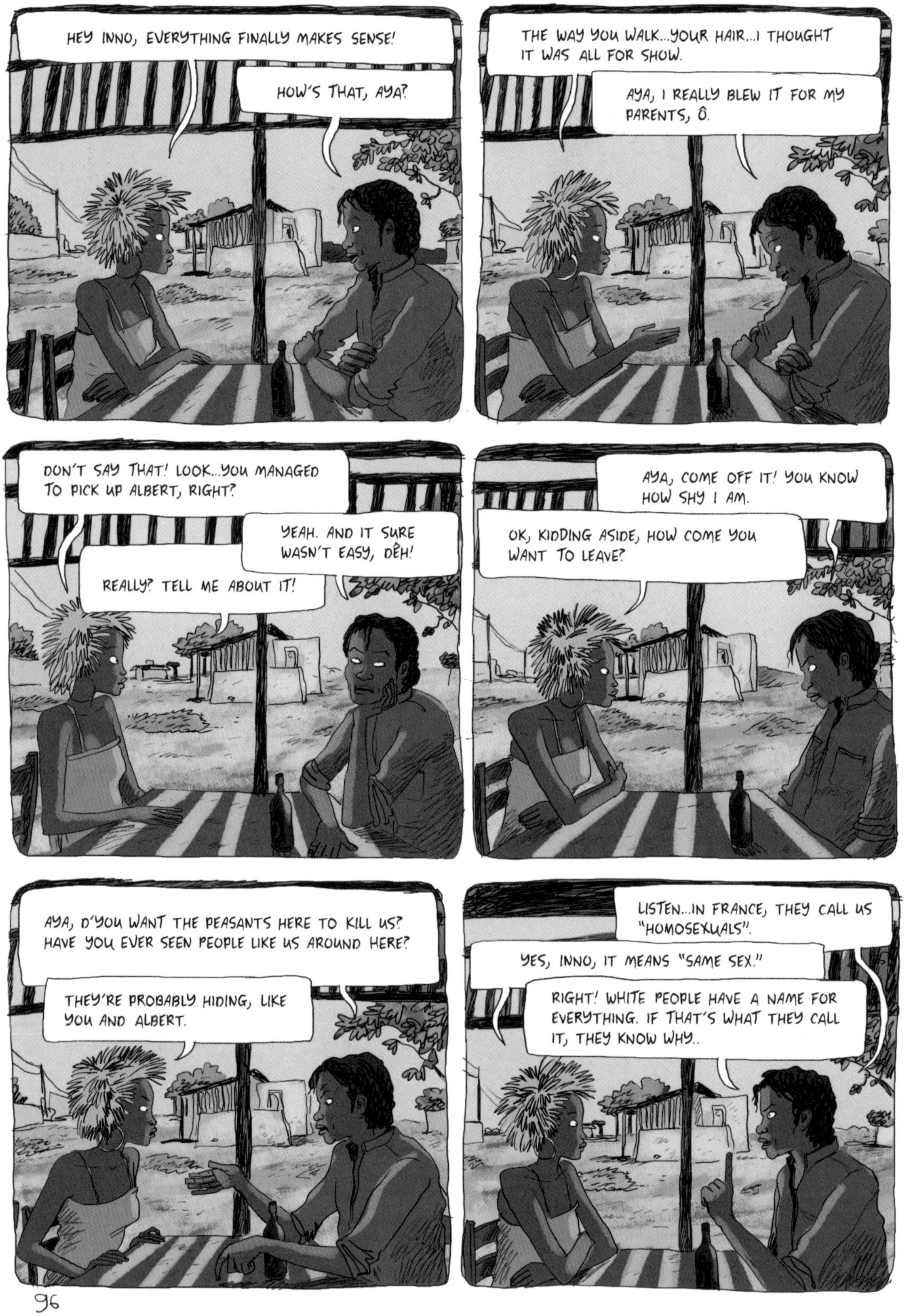
HEY INNO, EVERYTHING FINALLY MAKES SENSE!
HOW'S THAT, AYA?
THE WAY YOU WALK...YOUR HAIR...I THOUGHT IT WAS ALL FOR SHOW.
AYA, I REALLY BLEW IT FOR MY PARENTS, Ô.
DON'T SAY THAT! LOOK...YOU MANAGED TO PICK UP ALBERT, RIGHT?
YEAH. AND IT SURE WASN'T EASY, DÊH!
REALLY? TELL ME ABOUT IT!
AYA, COME OFF IT! YOU KNOW HOW SHY I AM.
OK, KIDDING ASIDE, HOW COME YOU WANT TO LEAVE?
AYA, D'YOU WANT THE PEASANTS HERE TO KILL US? HAVE YOU EVER SEEN PEOPLE LIKE US AROUND HERE?
THEY'RE PROBABLY HIDING, LIKE YOU AND ALBERT.
LISTEN...IN FRANCE, THEY CALL US "HOMOSEXUALS".
YES, INNO, IT MEANS "SAME SEX."
RIGHT! WHITE PEOPLE HAVE A NAME FOR EVERYTHING. IF THAT'S WHAT THEY CALL IT, THEY KNOW WHY..

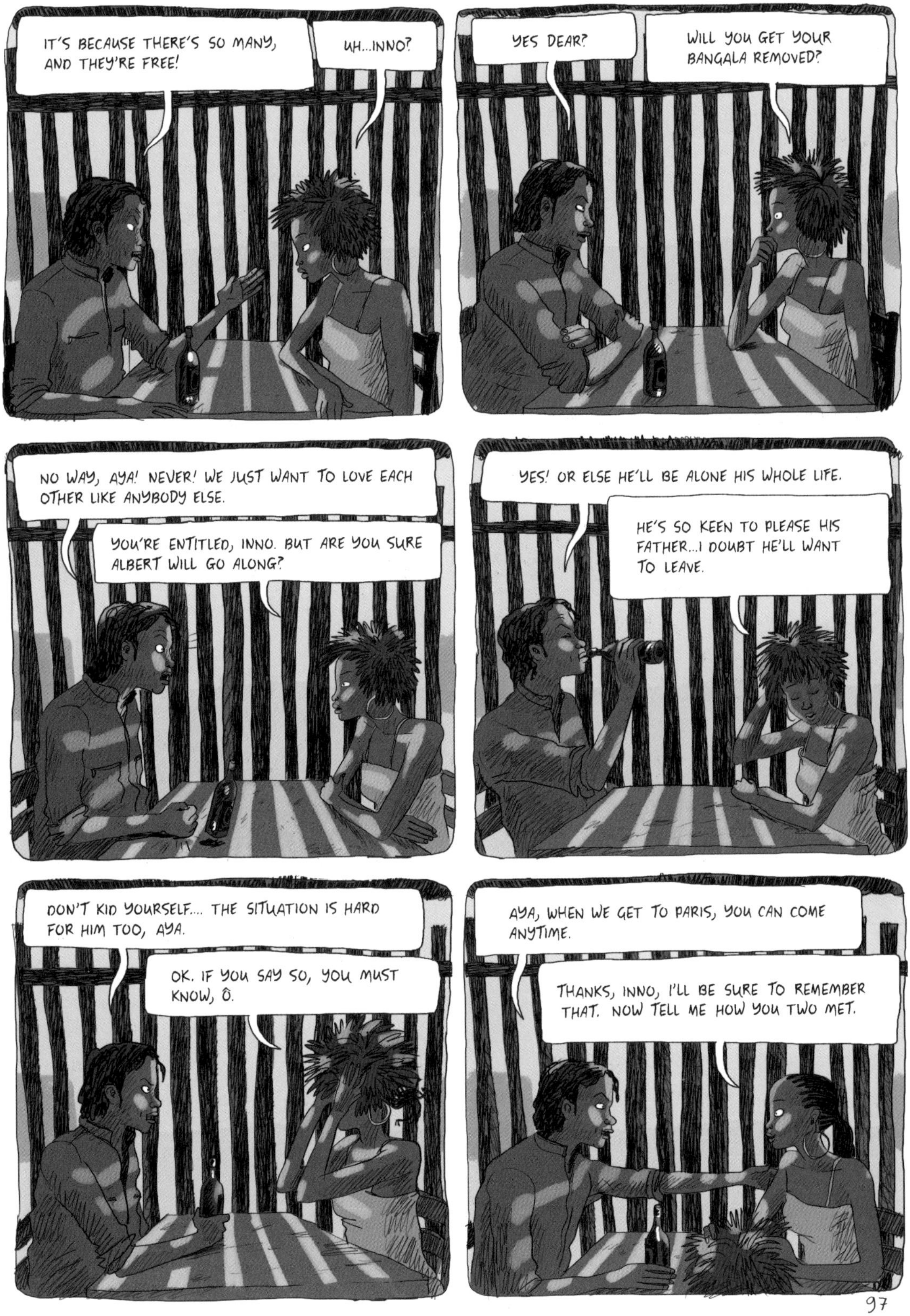
IT'S BECAUSE THERE'S SO MANY, AND THEY'RE FREE!
UH...INNO?
YES DEAR?
WILL YOU GET YOUR BANGALA REMOVED?
NO WAY, AYA! NEVER! WE JUST WANT TO LOVE EACH OTHER LIKE ANYBODY ELSE.
YOU'RE ENTITLED, INNO. BUT ARE YOU SURE ALBERT WILL GO ALONG?
YES! OR ELSE HE'LL BE ALONE HIS WHOLE LIFE.
HE'S SO KEEN TO PLEASE HIS FATHER...I DOUBT HE'LL WANT TO LEAVE.
DON'T KID YOURSELF.... THE SITUATION IS HARD FOR HIM TOO, AYA.
OK. IF YOU SAY SO, YOU MUST KNOW, Ô.
AYA, WHEN WE GET TO PARIS, YOU CAN COME ANYTIME.
THANKS, INNO, I'LL BE SURE TO REMEMBER THAT. NOW TELL ME HOW YOU TWO MET.

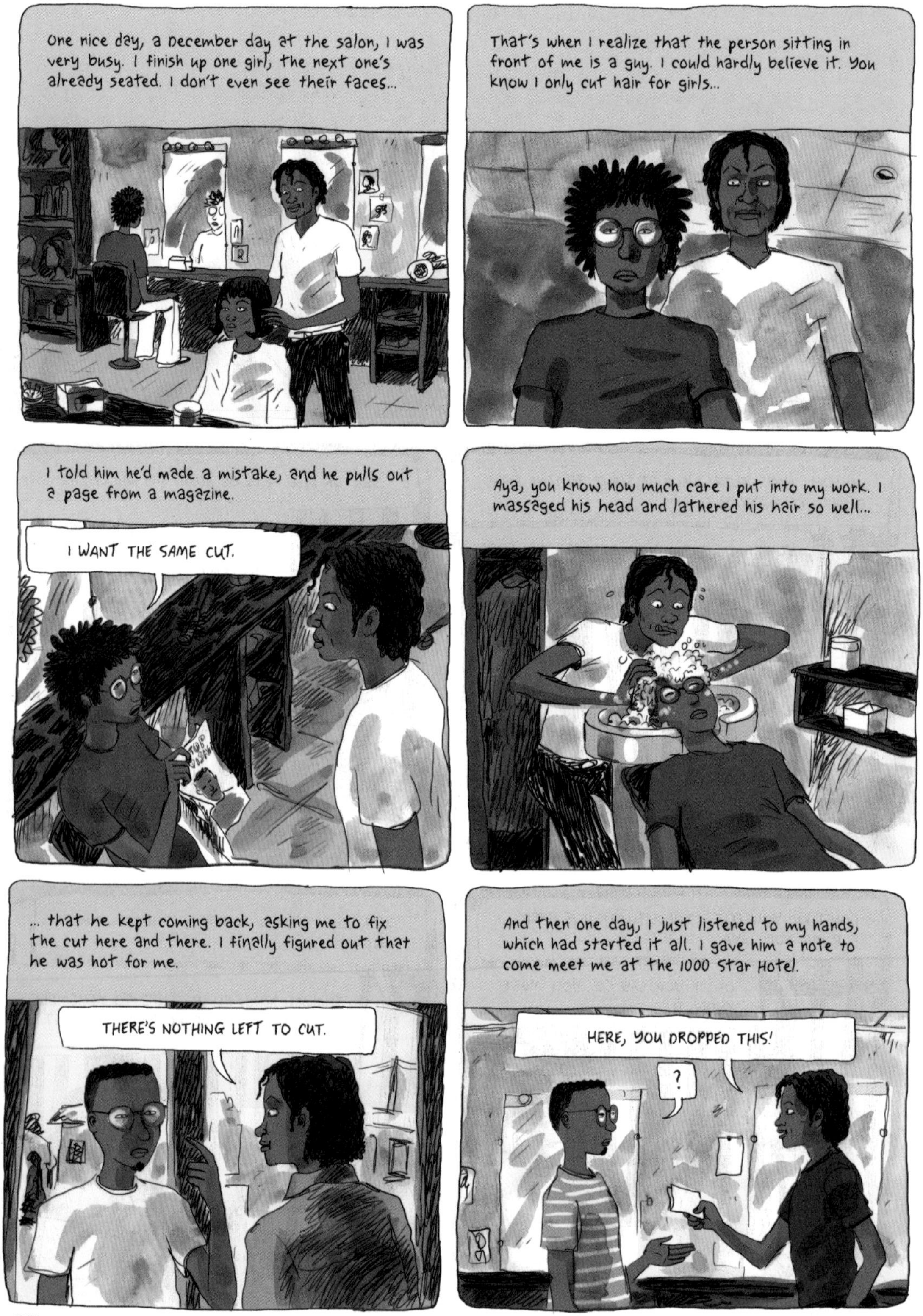
One nice day, a December day at the salon, I was very busy. I finish up one girl, the next one's already seated. I don't even see their faces...
That's when I realize that the person sitting in front of me is a guy. I could hardly believe it. You know I only cut hair for girls...
I told him he'd made a mistake, and he pulls out a page from a magazine.
I WANT THE SAME CUT.
Aya, you know how much care I put into my work. I massaged his head and lathered his hair so well...
... that he kept coming back, asking me to fix the cut here and there. I finally figured out that he was hot for me.
THERE'S NOTHING LEFT TO CUT.
And then one day, I just listened to my hands, which had started it all. I gave him a note to come meet me at the 1000 Star Hotel.
HERE, YOU DROPPED THIS!
?

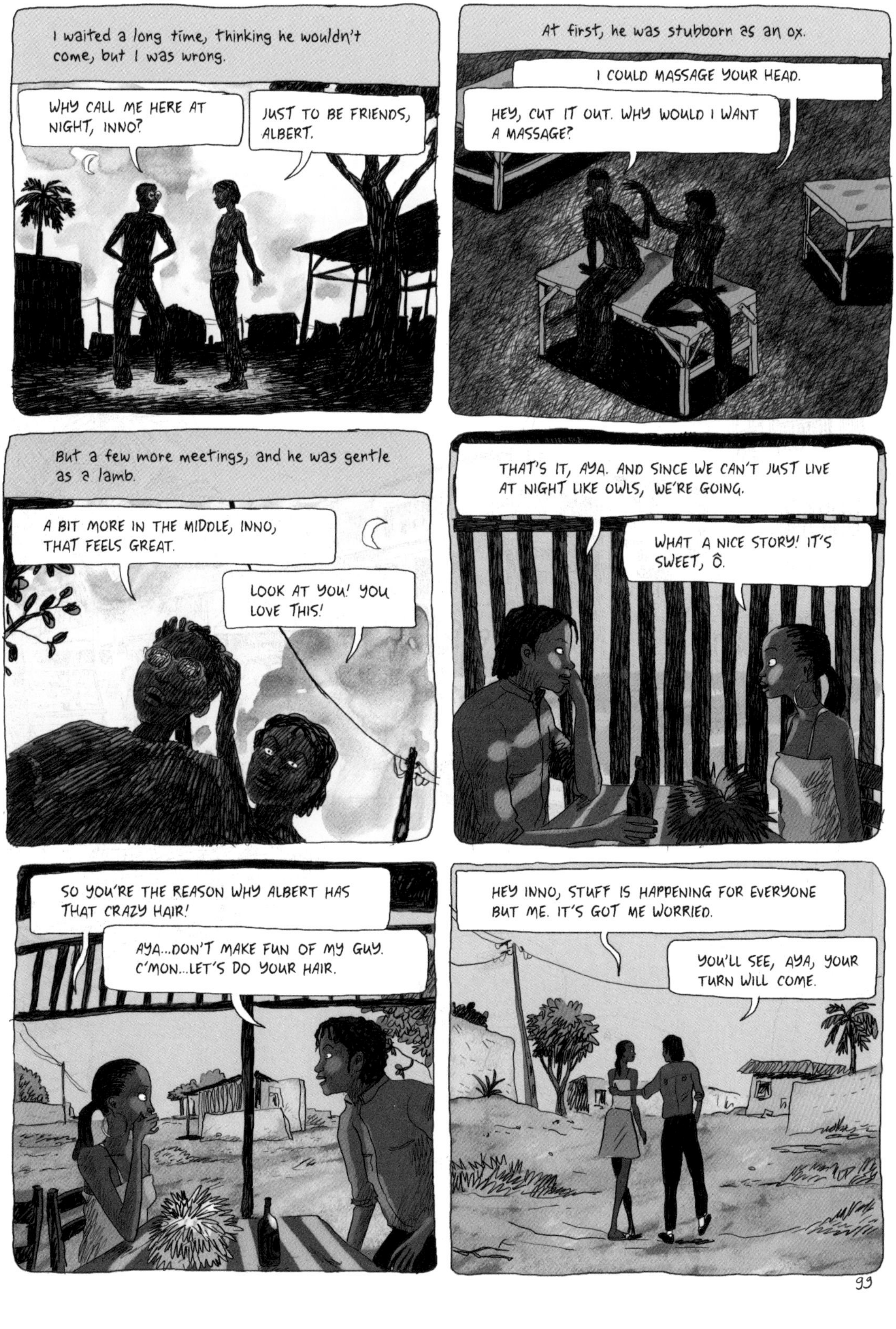

I waited a long time, thinking he wouldn't come, but I was wrong.
WHY CALL ME HERE AT NIGHT, INNO?
JUST TO BE FRIENDS, ALBERT.
At first, he was stubborn as an ox.
I COULD MASSAGE YOUR HEAD.
HEY, CUT IT OUT. WHY WOULD I WANT A MASSAGE?
But a few more meetings, and he was gentle as a lamb.
A BIT MORE IN THE MIDDLE, INNO, THAT FEELS GREAT.
LOOK AT YOU! YOU LOVE THIS!
THAT'S IT, AYA. AND SINCE WE CAN'T JUST LIVE AT NIGHT LIKE OWLS, WE'RE GOING.
WHAT A NICE STORY! IT'S SWEET, Ô.
SO YOU'RE THE REASON WHY ALBERT HAS THAT CRAZY HAIR!
AYA...DON'T MAKE FUN OF MY GUY. C'MON...LET'S DO YOUR HAIR.
HEY INNO, STUFF IS HAPPENING FOR EVERYONE BUT ME. IT'S GOT ME WORRIED.
YOU'LL SEE, AYA, YOUR TURN WILL COME.

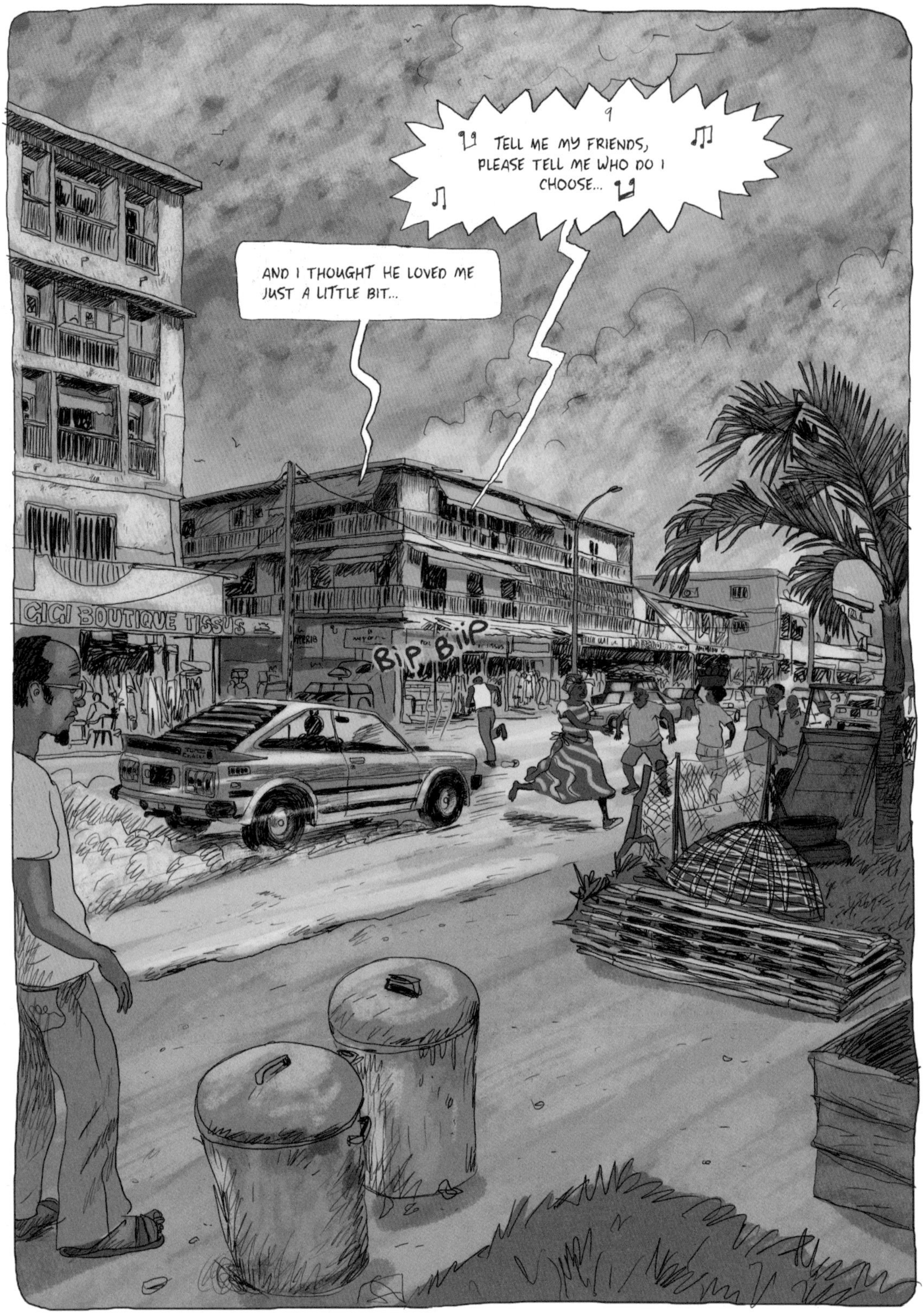
TELL ME MY FRIENDS, PLEASE TELL ME WHO DO I CHOOSE...
AND I THOUGHT HE LOVED ME JUST A LITTLE BIT...
GIGI BOUTIQUE TISSUS
BIP BIIP

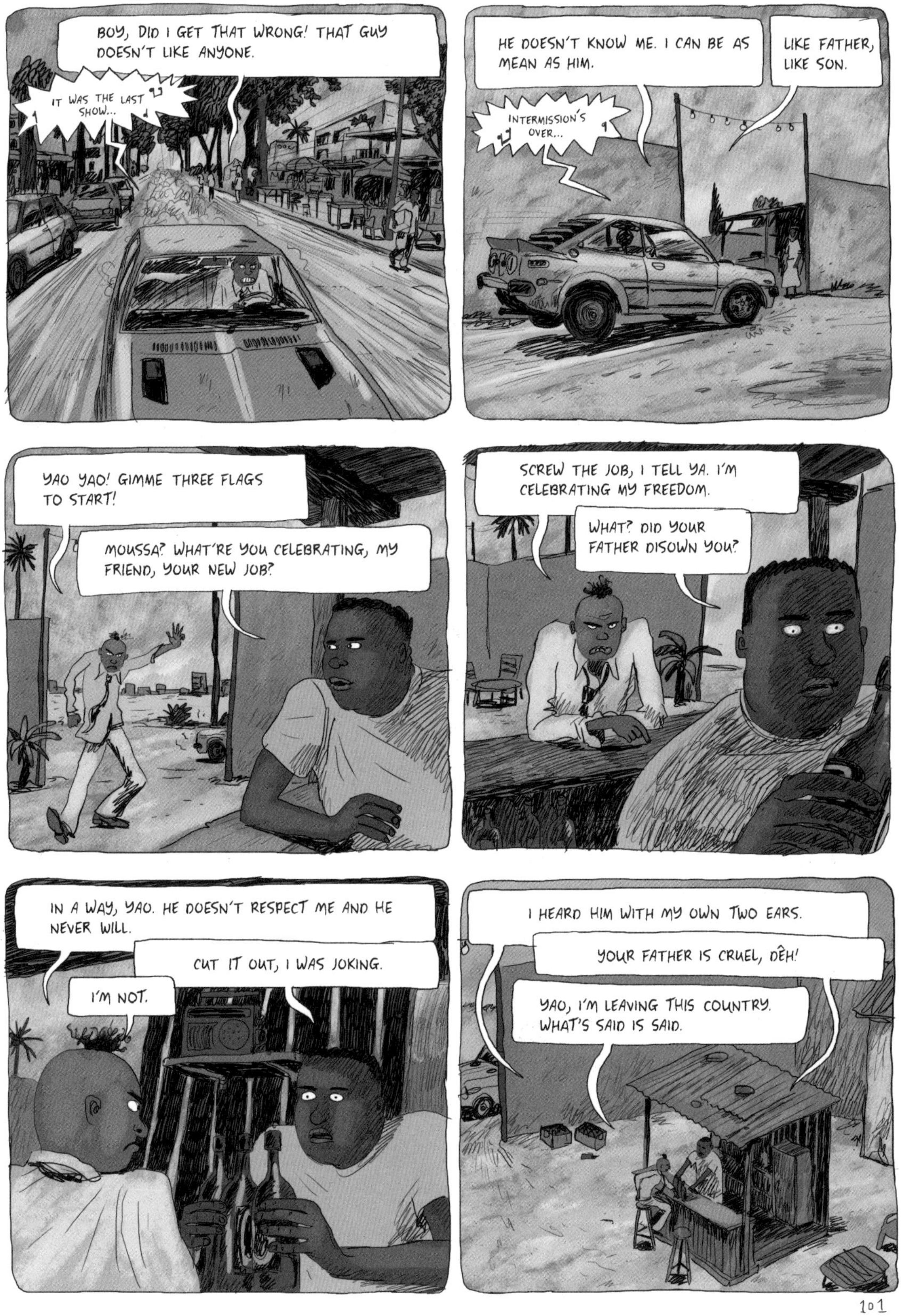
BOY, DID I GET THAT WRONG! THAT GUY DOESN'T LIKE ANYONE.
IT WAS THE LAST SHOW...
HE DOESN'T KNOW ME. I CAN BE AS MEAN AS HIM.
LIKE FATHER, LIKE SON.
INTERMISSION'S OVER...
YAO YAO! GIMME THREE FLAGS TO START!
MOUSSA? WHAT'RE YOU CELEBRATING, MY FRIEND, YOUR NEW JOB?
SCREW THE JOB, I TELL YA. I'M CELEBRATING MY FREEDOM.
WHAT? DID YOUR FATHER DISOWN YOU?
IN A WAY, YAO. HE DOESN'T RESPECT ME AND HE NEVER WILL.
CUT IT OUT, I WAS JOKING.
I'M NOT.
I HEARD HIM WITH MY OWN TWO EARS.
YOUR FATHER IS CRUEL, DÊH!
YAO, I'M LEAVING THIS COUNTRY. WHAT'S SAID IS SAID.

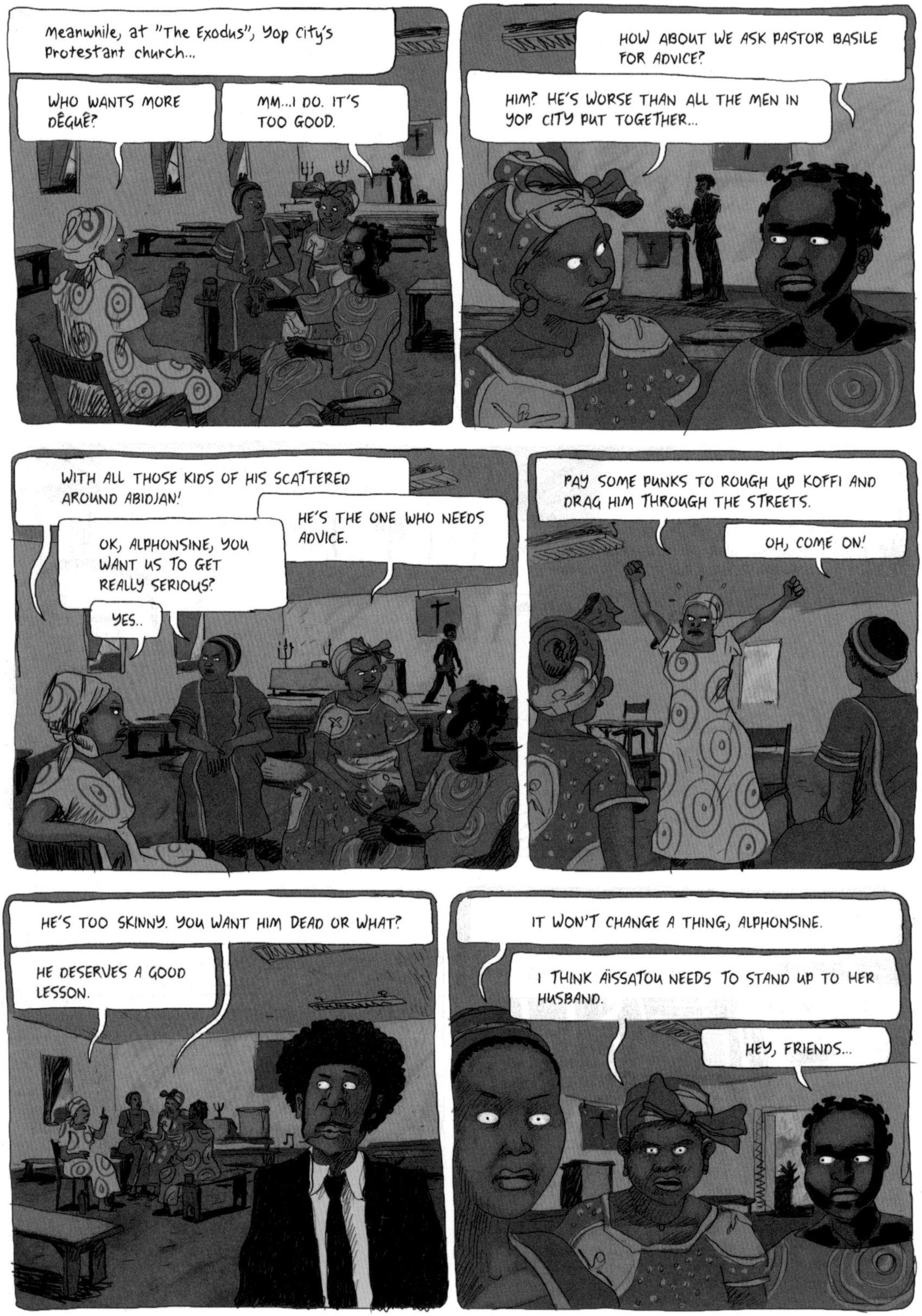
Meanwhile, at "The Exodus", Yop City's protestant church...
WHO WANTS MORE DÊGUÊ?
MM...I DO. IT'S TOO GOOD.
HOW ABOUT WE ASK PASTOR BASILE FOR ADVICE?
HIM? HE'S WORSE THAN ALL THE MEN IN YOP CITY PUT TOGETHER...
WITH ALL THOSE KIDS OF HIS SCATTERED AROUND ABIDJAN!
HE'S THE ONE WHO NEEDS ADVICE.
OK, ALPHONSINE, YOU WANT US TO GET REALLY SERIOUS?
YES..
PAY SOME PUNKS TO ROUGH UP KOFFI AND DRAG HIM THROUGH THE STREETS.
OH, COME ON!
HE'S TOO SKINNY. YOU WANT HIM DEAD OR WHAT?
HE DESERVES A GOOD LESSON.
IT WON'T CHANGE A THING, ALPHONSINE.
I THINK AÏSSATOU NEEDS TO STAND UP TO HER HUSBAND.
HEY, FRIENDS...

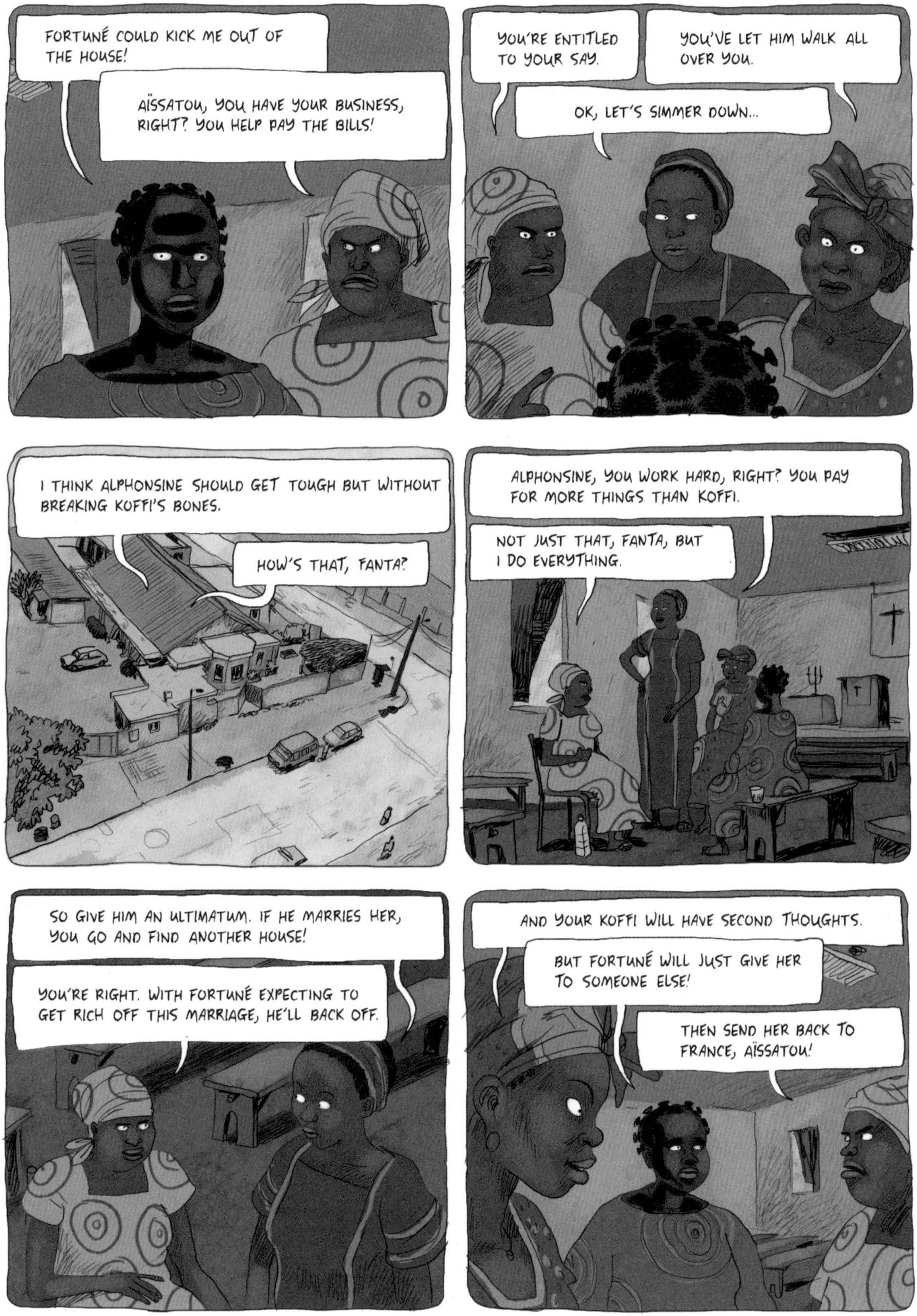
FORTUNÉ COULD KICK ME OUT OF THE HOUSE!
AÏSSATOU, YOU HAVE YOUR BUSINESS, RIGHT? YOU HELP PAY THE BILLS!
YOU'RE ENTITLED TO YOUR SAY.
YOU'VE LET HIM WALK ALL OVER YOU.
OK, LET'S SIMMER DOWN...
I THINK ALPHONSINE SHOULD GET TOUGH BUT WITHOUT BREAKING KOFFI'S BONES.
HOW'S THAT, FANTA?
ALPHONSINE, YOU WORK HARD, RIGHT? YOU PAY FOR MORE THINGS THAN KOFFI.
NOT JUST THAT, FANTA, BUT I DO EVERYTHING.
SO GIVE HIM AN ULTIMATUM. IF HE MARRIES HER, YOU GO AND FIND ANOTHER HOUSE!
YOU'RE RIGHT. WITH FORTUNÉ EXPECTING TO GET RICH OFF THIS MARRIAGE, HE'LL BACK OFF.
AND YOUR KOFFI WILL HAVE SECOND THOUGHTS.
BUT FORTUNÉ WILL JUST GIVE HER TO SOMEONE ELSE!
THEN SEND HER BACK TO FRANCE, AÏSSATOU!

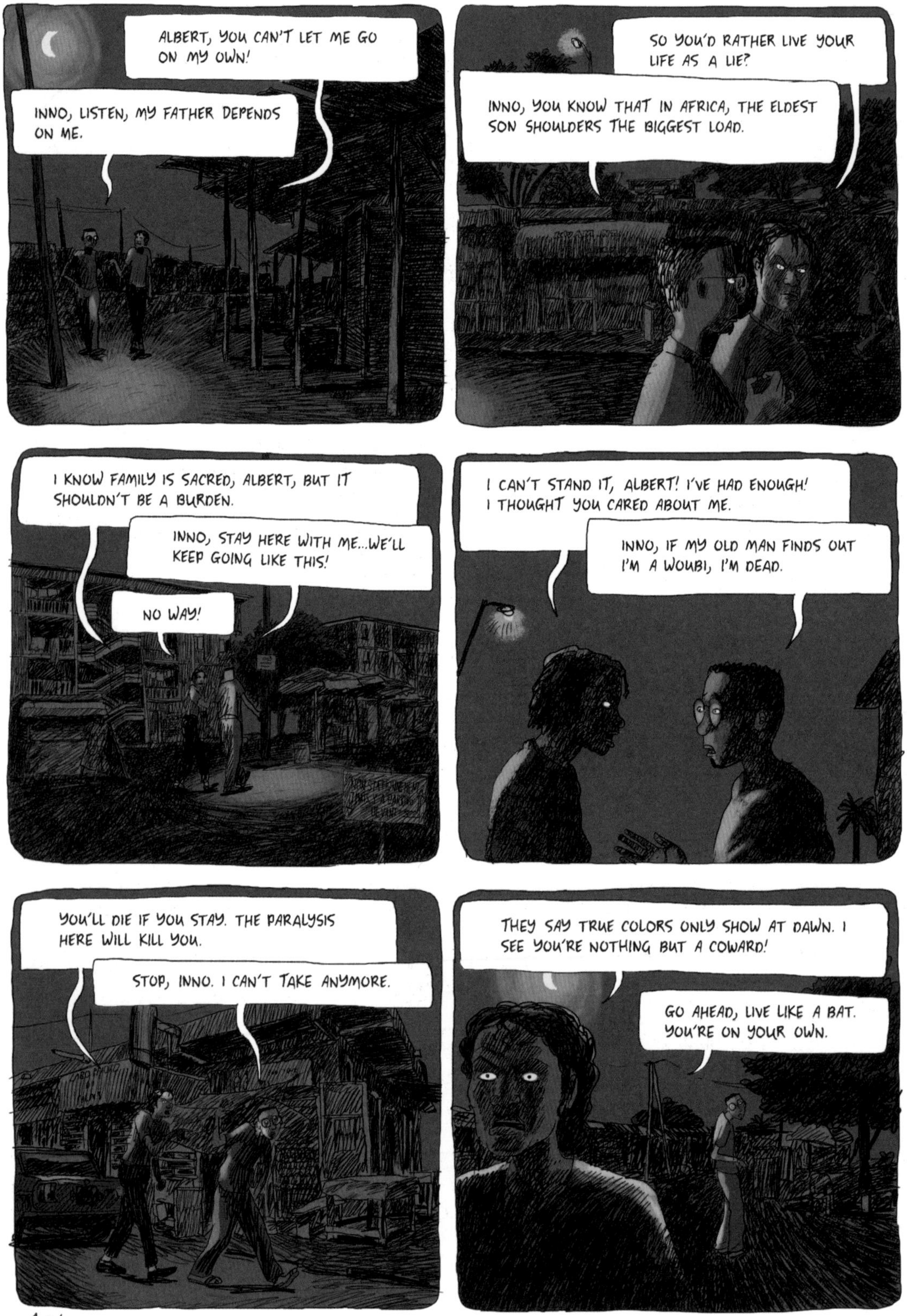
ALBERT, YOU CAN'T LET ME GO ON MY OWN!
INNO, LISTEN, MY FATHER DEPENDS ON ME.
SO YOU'D RATHER LIVE YOUR LIFE AS A LIE?
INNO, YOU KNOW THAT IN AFRICA, THE ELDEST SON SHOULDERS THE BIGGEST LOAD.
I KNOW FAMILY IS SACRED, ALBERT, BUT IT SHOULDN'T BE A BURDEN.
INNO, STAY HERE WITH ME...WE'LL KEEP GOING LIKE THIS!
NO WAY!
I CAN'T STAND IT, ALBERT! I'VE HAD ENOUGH! I THOUGHT YOU CARED ABOUT ME.
INNO, IF MY OLD MAN FINDS OUT I'M A WOUBI, I'M DEAD.
YOU'LL DIE IF YOU STAY. THE PARALYSIS HERE WILL KILL YOU.
STOP, INNO. I CAN'T TAKE ANYMORE.
THEY SAY TRUE COLORS ONLY SHOW AT DAWN. I SEE YOU'RE NOTHING BUT A COWARD!
GO AHEAD, LIVE LIKE A BAT. YOU'RE ON YOUR OWN.

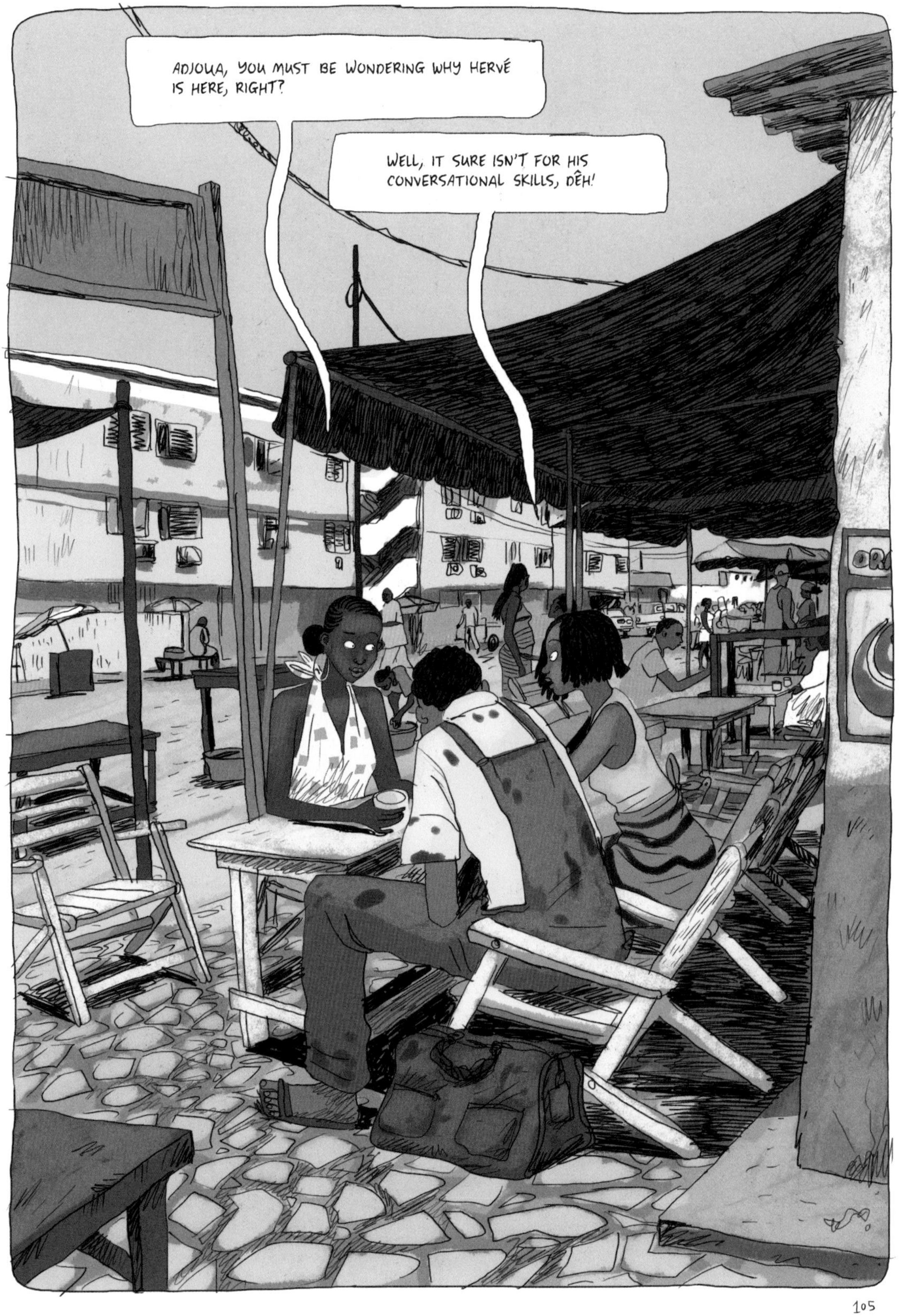
ADJOUA, YOU MUST BE WONDERING WHY HERVÉ IS HERE, RIGHT?
WELL, IT SURE ISN'T FOR HIS CONVERSATIONAL SKILLS, DÊH!

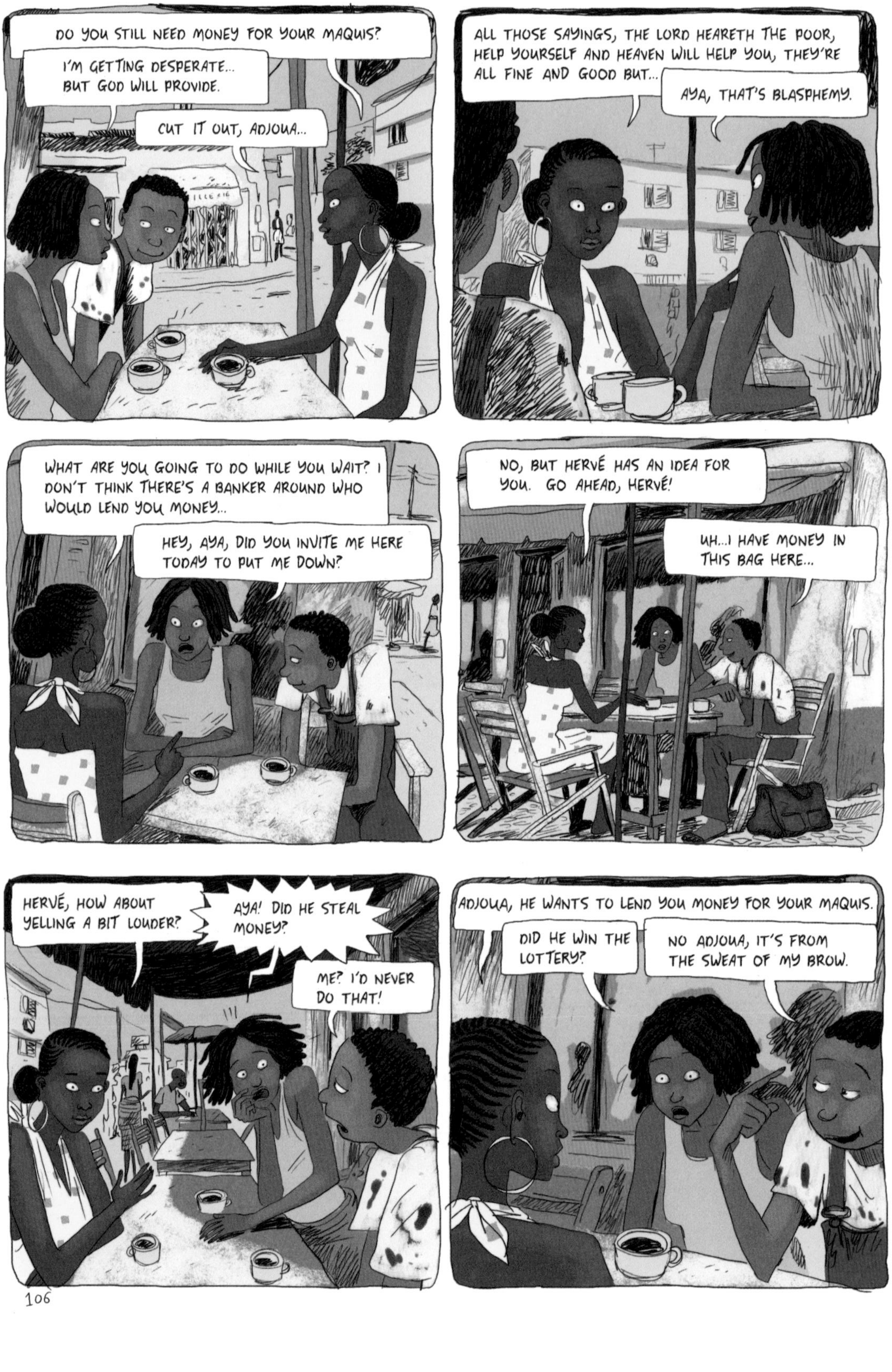
DO YOU STILL NEED MONEY FOR YOUR MAQUIS?
I'M GETTING DESPERATE... BUT GOD WILL PROVIDE.
CUT IT OUT, ADJOUA...
ALL THOSE SAYINGS, THE LORD HEARETH THE POOR, HELP YOURSELF AND HEAVEN WILL HELP YOU, THEY'RE ALL FINE AND GOOD BUT...
AYA, THAT'S BLASPHEMY.
WHAT ARE YOU GOING TO DO WHILE YOU WAIT? I DON'T THINK THERE'S A BANKER AROUND WHO WOULD LEND YOU MONEY...
HEY, AYA, DID YOU INVITE ME HERE TODAY TO PUT ME DOWN?
NO, BUT HERVÉ HAS AN IDEA FOR YOU. GO AHEAD, HERVÉ!
UH...I HAVE MONEY IN THIS BAG HERE...
HERVÉ, HOW ABOUT YELLING A BIT LOUDER?
AYA! DID HE STEAL MONEY?
ME? I'D NEVER DO THAT!
ADJOUA, HE WANTS TO LEND YOU MONEY FOR YOUR MAQUIS.
DID HE WIN THE LOTTERY?
NO ADJOUA, IT'S FROM THE SWEAT OF MY BROW.

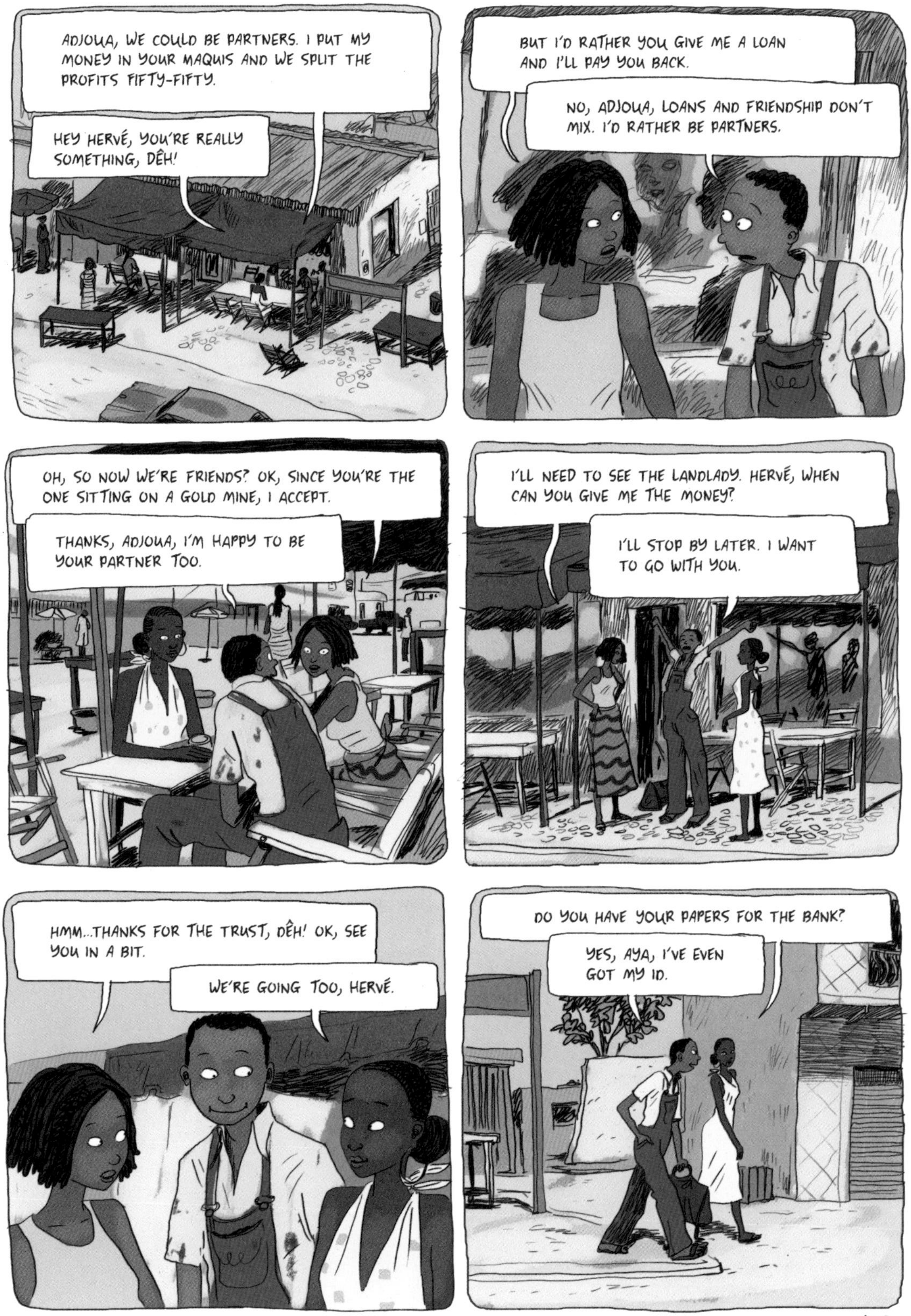
ADJOUA, WE COULD BE PARTNERS. I PUT MY MONEY IN YOUR MAQUIS AND WE SPLIT THE PROFITS FIFTY-FIFTY.
HEY HERVÉ, YOU'RE REALLY SOMETHING, DÊH!
BUT I'D RATHER YOU GIVE ME A LOAN AND I'LL PAY YOU BACK.
NO, ADJOUA, LOANS AND FRIENDSHIP DON'T MIX. I'D RATHER BE PARTNERS.
OH, SO NOW WE'RE FRIENDS? OK, SINCE YOU'RE THE ONE SITTING ON A GOLD MINE, I ACCEPT.
THANKS, ADJOUA, I'M HAPPY TO BE YOUR PARTNER TOO.
I'LL NEED TO SEE THE LANDLADY. HERVÉ, WHEN CAN YOU GIVE ME THE MONEY?
I'LL STOP BY LATER. I WANT TO GO WITH YOU.
HMM...THANKS FOR THE TRUST, DÊH! OK, SEE YOU IN A BIT.
WE'RE GOING TOO, HERVÉ.
DO YOU HAVE YOUR PAPERS FOR THE BANK?
YES, AYA, I'VE EVEN GOT MY ID.

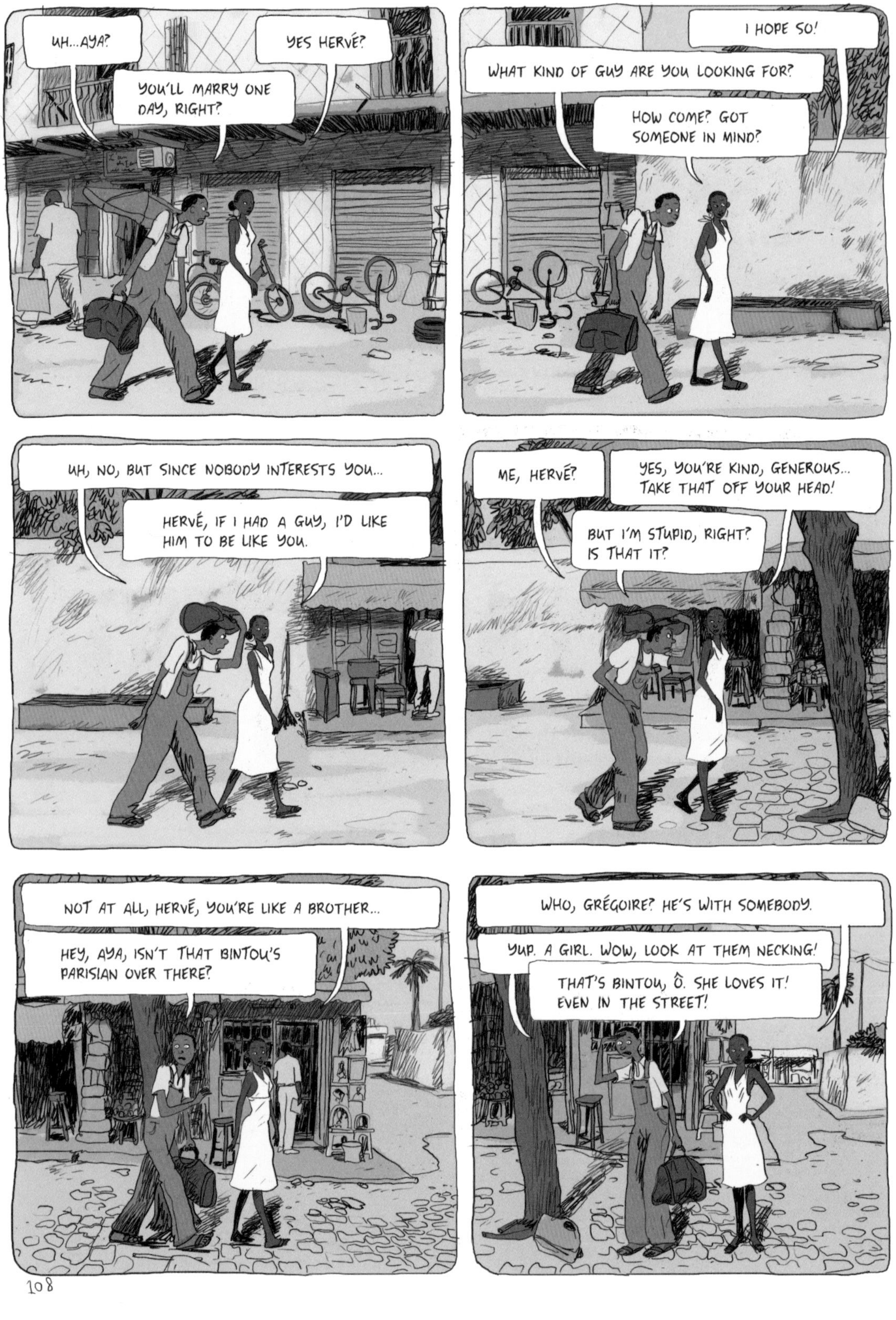
UH...AYA?
YOU'LL MARRY ONE DAY, RIGHT?
YES HERVÉ?
WHAT KIND OF GUY ARE YOU LOOKING FOR?
HOW COME? GOT SOMEONE IN MIND?
I HOPE SO!
UH, NO, BUT SINCE NOBODY INTERESTS YOU...
HERVÉ, IF I HAD A GUY, I'D LIKE HIM TO BE LIKE YOU.
ME, HERVÉ?
BUT I'M STUPID, RIGHT? IS THAT IT?
YES, YOU'RE KIND, GENEROUS... TAKE THAT OFF YOUR HEAD!
NOT AT ALL, HERVÉ, YOU'RE LIKE A BROTHER...
HEY, AYA, ISN'T THAT BINTOU'S PARISIAN OVER THERE?
WHO, GRÉGOIRE? HE'S WITH SOMEBODY.
YUP. A GIRL. WOW, LOOK AT THEM NECKING!
THAT'S BINTOU, Ô. SHE LOVES IT! EVEN IN THE STREET!

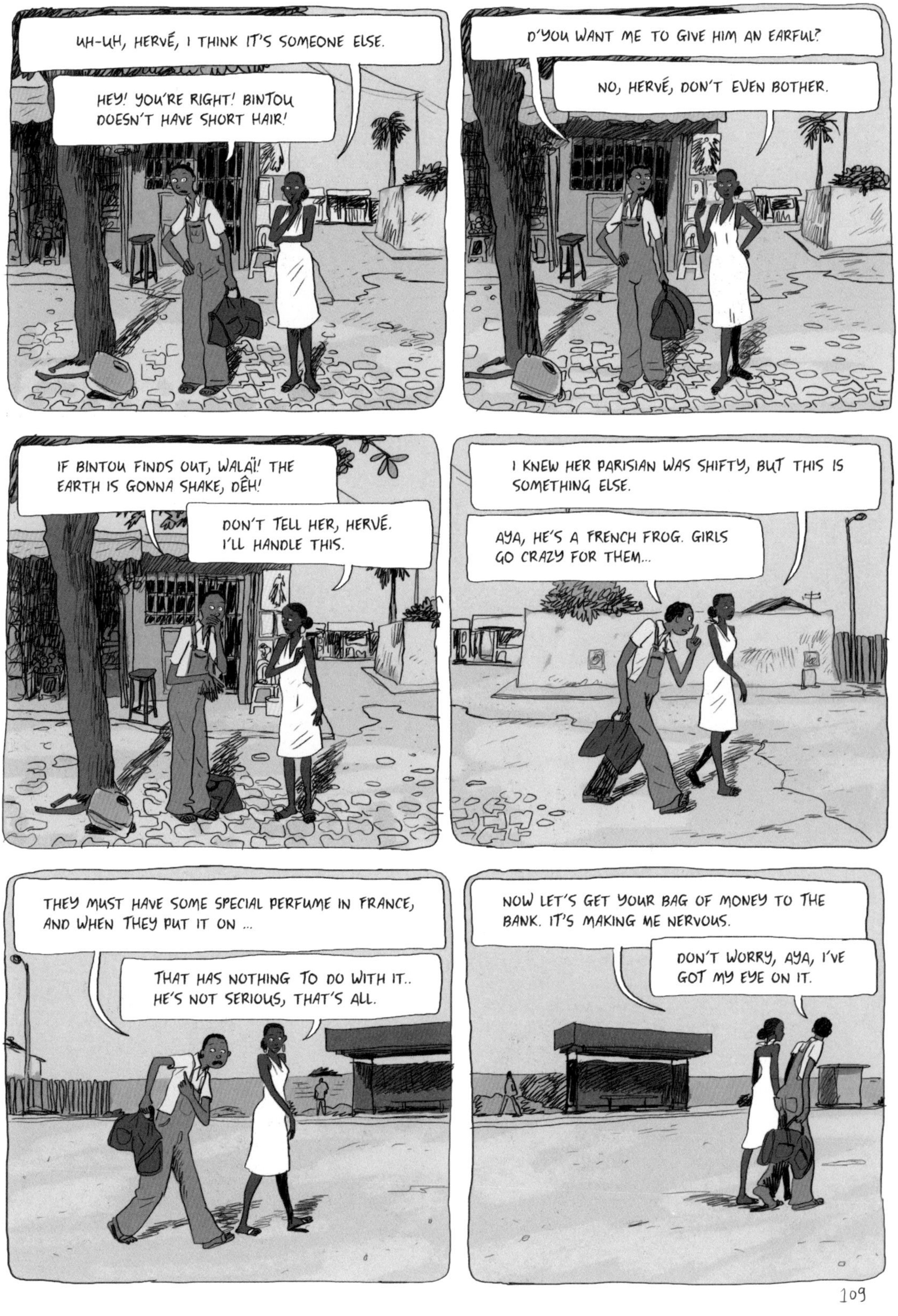
UH-UH, HERVÉ, I THINK IT'S SOMEONE ELSE.
HEY! YOU'RE RIGHT! BINTOU DOESN'T HAVE SHORT HAIR!
D'YOU WANT ME TO GIVE HIM AN EARFUL?
NO, HERVÉ, DON'T EVEN BOTHER.
IF BINTOU FINDS OUT, WALAÏ! THE EARTH IS GONNA SHAKE, DÊH!
DON'T TELL HER, HERVÉ. I'LL HANDLE THIS.
I KNEW HER PARISIAN WAS SHIFTY, BUT THIS IS SOMETHING ELSE.
AYA, HE'S A FRENCH FROG. GIRLS GO CRAZY FOR THEM...
THEY MUST HAVE SOME SPECIAL PERFUME IN FRANCE, AND WHEN THEY PUT IT ON ...
THAT HAS NOTHING TO DO WITH IT.. HE'S NOT SERIOUS, THAT'S ALL.
NOW LET'S GET YOUR BAG OF MONEY TO THE BANK. IT'S MAKING ME NERVOUS.
DON'T WORRY, AYA, I'VE GOT MY EYE ON IT.

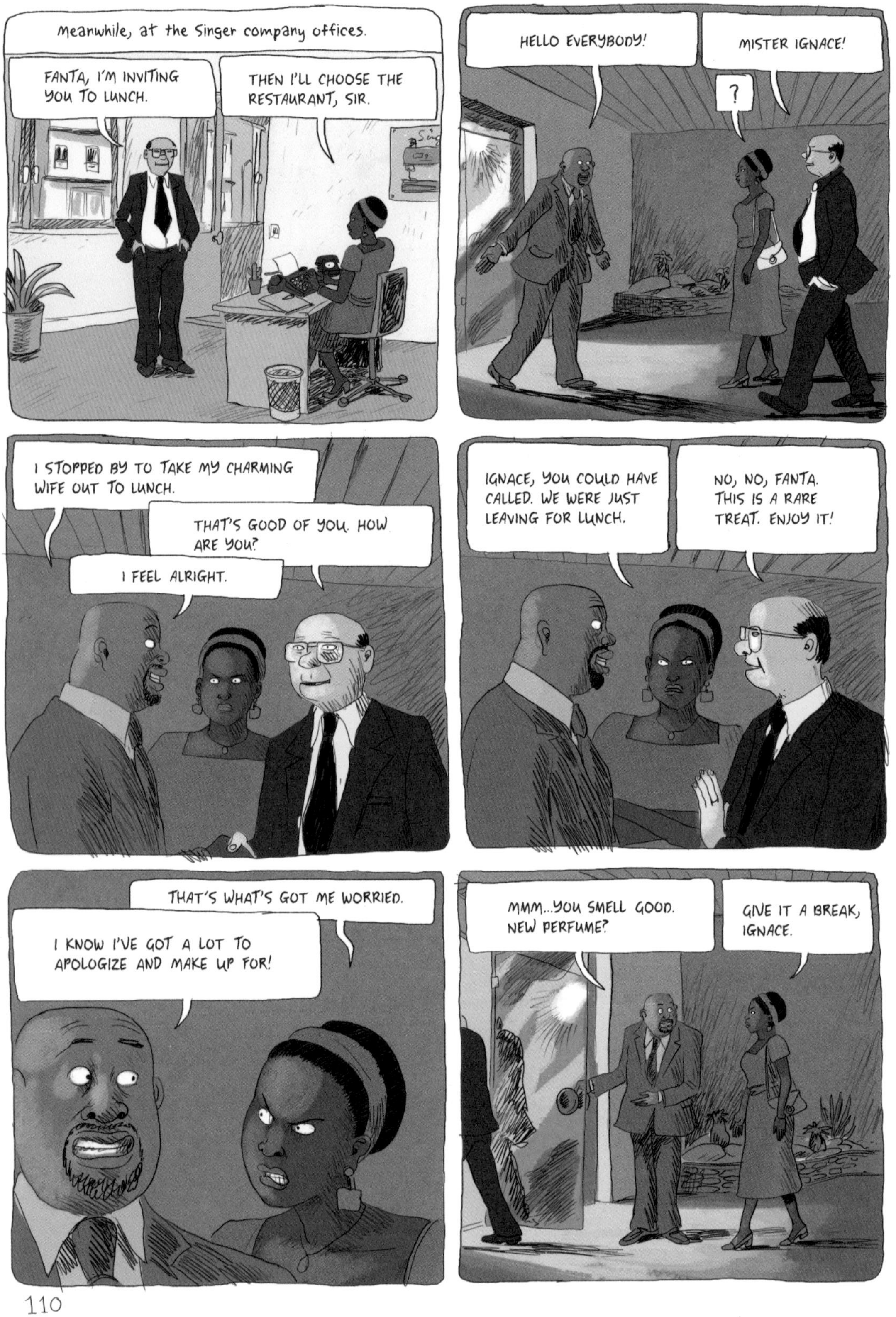

Meanwhile, at the Singer company offices.
FANTA, I'M INVITING YOU TO LUNCH.
THEN I'LL CHOOSE THE RESTAURANT, SIR.
HELLO EVERYBODY!
MISTER IGNACE!
?
I STOPPED BY TO TAKE MY CHARMING WIFE OUT TO LUNCH.
THAT'S GOOD OF YOU. HOW ARE YOU?
I FEEL ALRIGHT.
IGNACE, YOU COULD HAVE CALLED. WE WERE JUST LEAVING FOR LUNCH.
NO, NO, FANTA. THIS IS A RARE TREAT. ENJOY IT!
I KNOW I'VE GOT A LOT TO APOLOGIZE AND MAKE UP FOR!
THAT'S WHAT'S GOT ME WORRIED.
MMM...YOU SMELL GOOD. NEW PERFUME?
GIVE IT A BREAK, IGNACE.

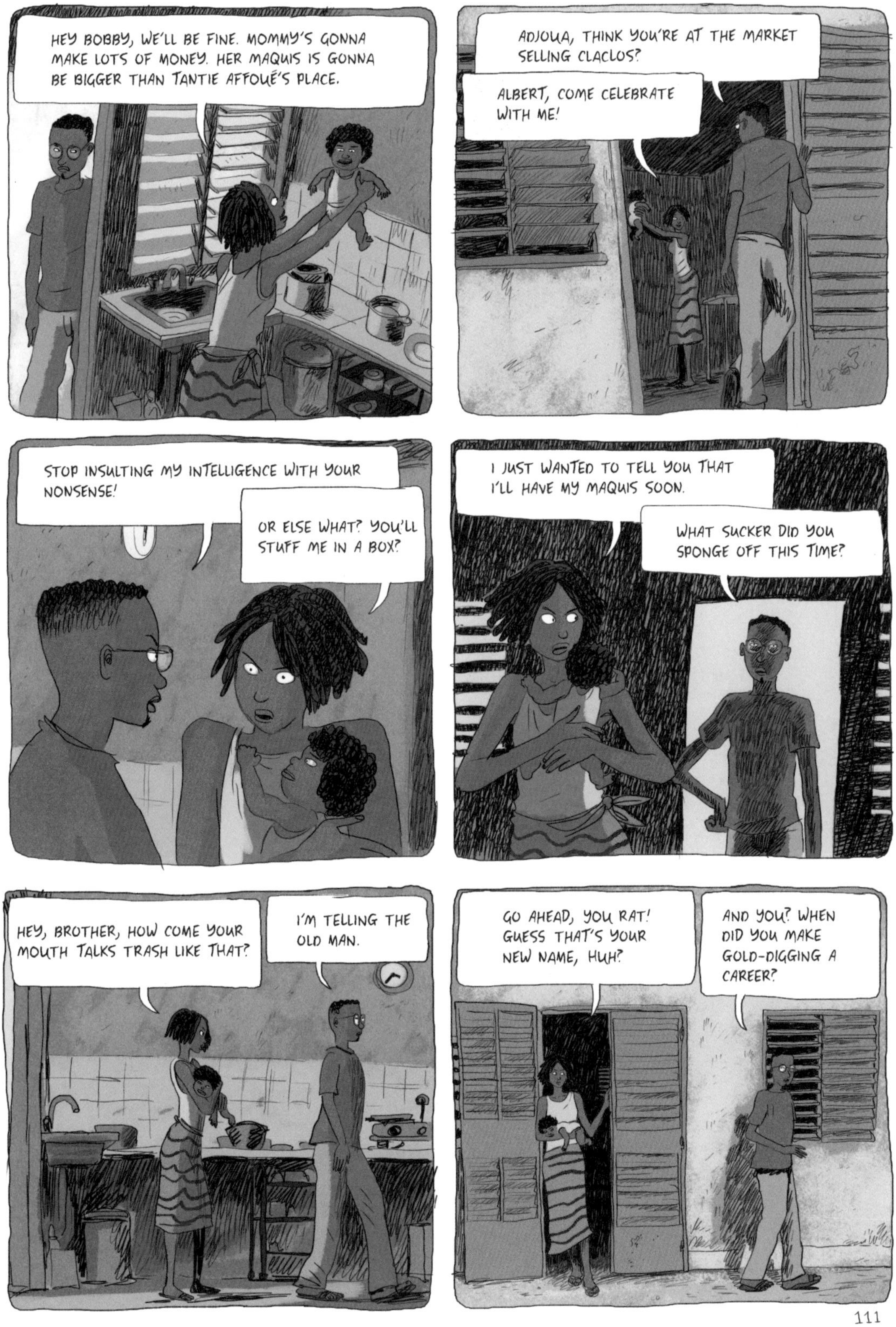
HEY BOBBY, WE'LL BE FINE. MOMMY'S GONNA MAKE LOTS OF MONEY. HER MAQUIS IS GONNA BE BIGGER THAN TANTIE AFFOUÉ'S PLACE.
ADJOUA, THINK YOU'RE AT THE MARKET SELLING CLACLOS?
ALBERT, COME CELEBRATE WITH ME!
STOP INSULTING MY INTELLIGENCE WITH YOUR NONSENSE!
OR ELSE WHAT? YOU'LL STUFF ME IN A BOX?
I JUST WANTED TO TELL YOU THAT I'LL HAVE MY MAQUIS SOON.
WHAT SUCKER DID YOU SPONGE OFF THIS TIME?
HEY, BROTHER, HOW COME YOUR MOUTH TALKS TRASH LIKE THAT?
I'M TELLING THE OLD MAN.
GO AHEAD, YOU RAT! GUESS THAT'S YOUR NEW NAME, HUH?
AND YOU? WHEN DID YOU MAKE GOLD-DIGGING A CAREER?

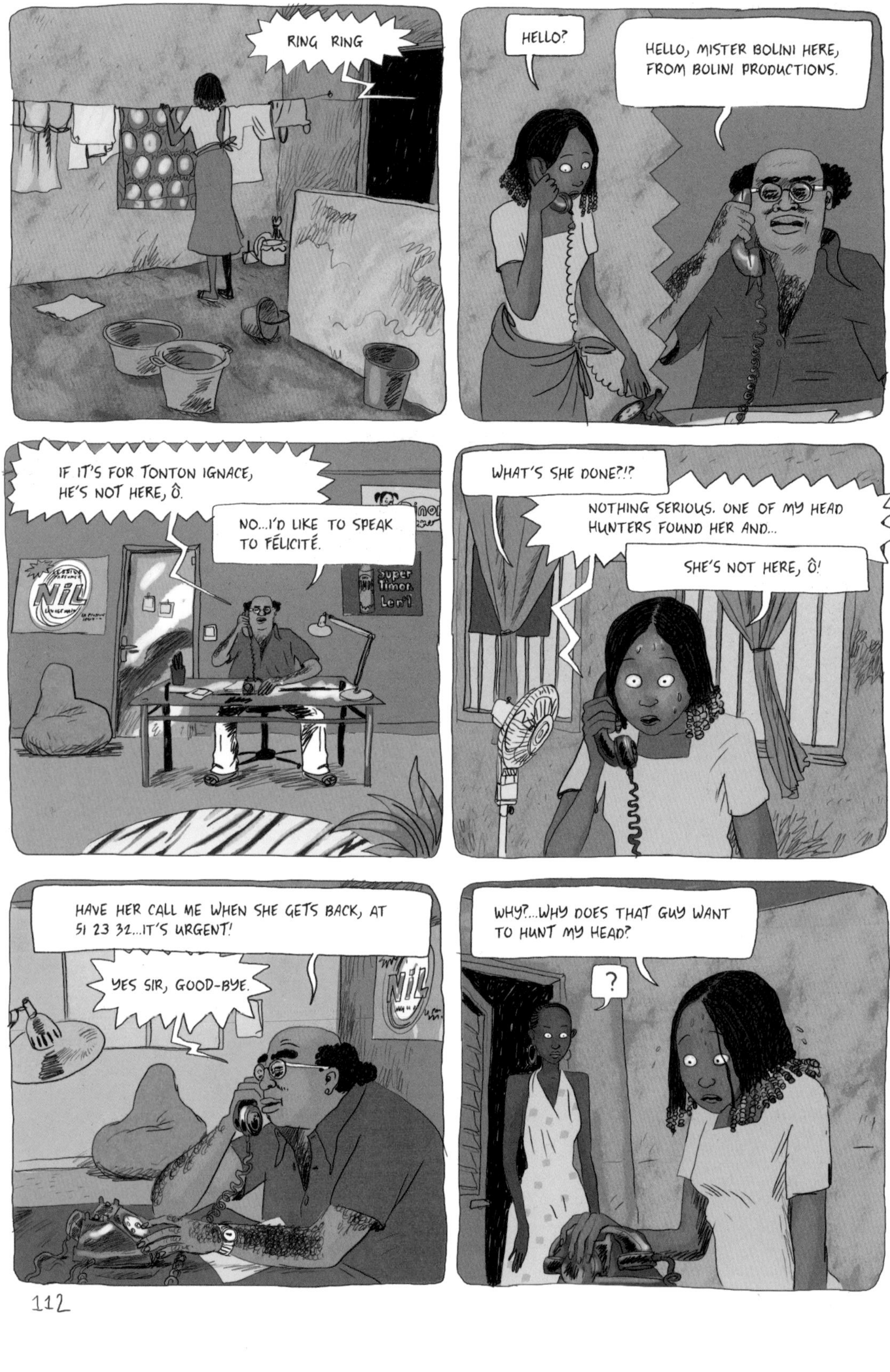
RING RING
HELLO?
HELLO, MISTER BOLINI HERE, FROM BOLINI PRODUCTIONS.
IF IT'S FOR TONTON IGNACE, HE'S NOT HERE, Ô.
NO...I'D LIKE TO SPEAK TO FÉLICITÉ.
NIL
Super Timor Len'l
WHAT'S SHE DONE?!?
NOTHING SERIOUS. ONE OF MY HEAD HUNTERS FOUND HER AND...
SHE'S NOT HERE, Ô!
HAVE HER CALL ME WHEN SHE GETS BACK, AT 51 23 32...IT'S URGENT!
YES SIR, GOOD-BYE.
NIL
WHY?...WHY DOES THAT GUY WANT TO HUNT MY HEAD?
?

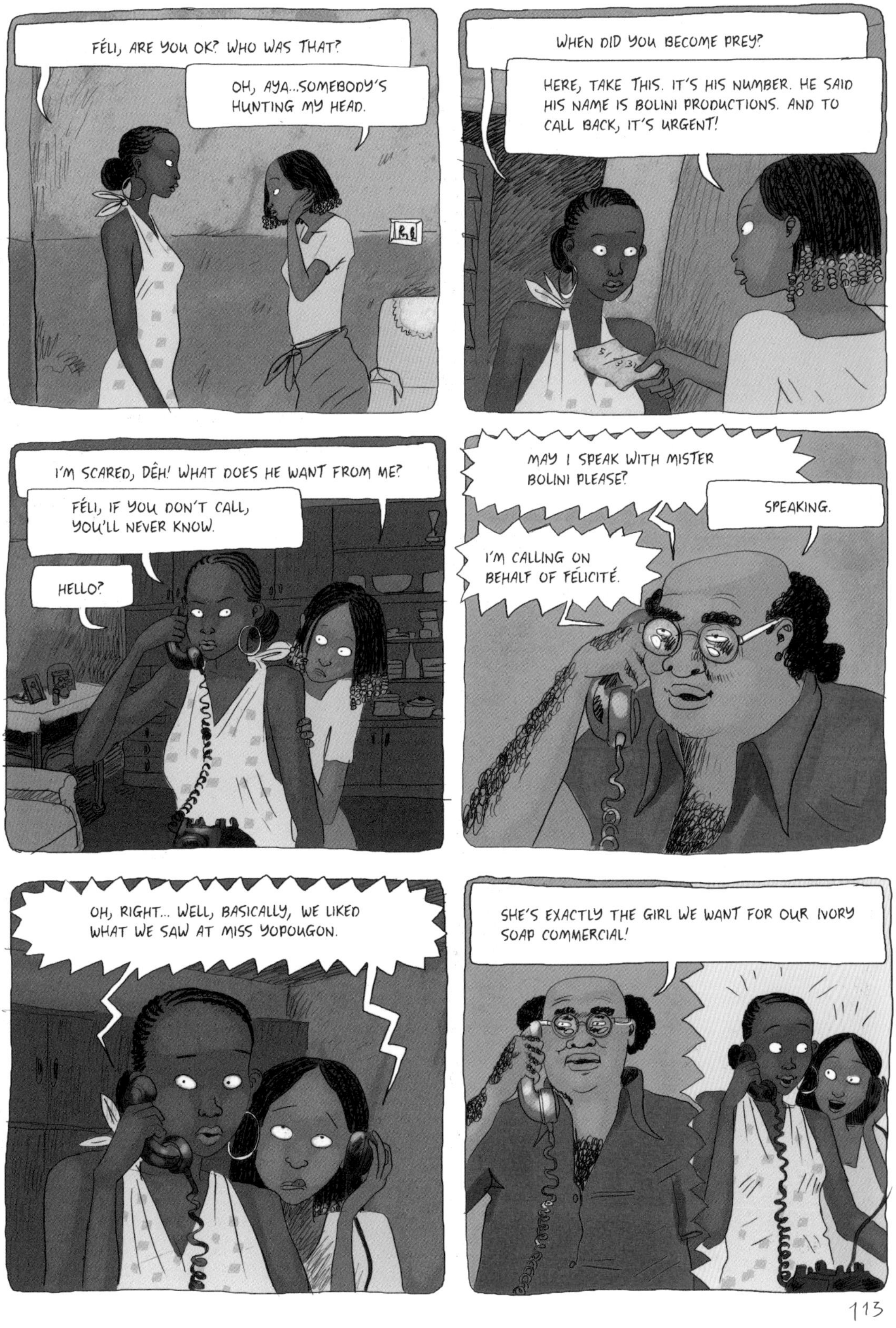
FÉLI, ARE YOU OK? WHO WAS THAT?
OH, AYA...SOMEBODY'S HUNTING MY HEAD.
WHEN DID YOU BECOME PREY?
HERE, TAKE THIS. IT'S HIS NUMBER. HE SAID HIS NAME IS BOLINI PRODUCTIONS. AND TO CALL BACK, IT'S URGENT!
I'M SCARED, DÊH! WHAT DOES HE WANT FROM ME?
FÉLI, IF YOU DON'T CALL, YOU'LL NEVER KNOW.
HELLO?
MAY I SPEAK WITH MISTER BOLINI PLEASE?
SPEAKING.
I'M CALLING ON BEHALF OF FÉLICITÉ.
OH, RIGHT... WELL, BASICALLY, WE LIKED WHAT WE SAW AT MISS YOPOUGON.
SHE'S EXACTLY THE GIRL WE WANT FOR OUR IVORY SOAP COMMERCIAL!

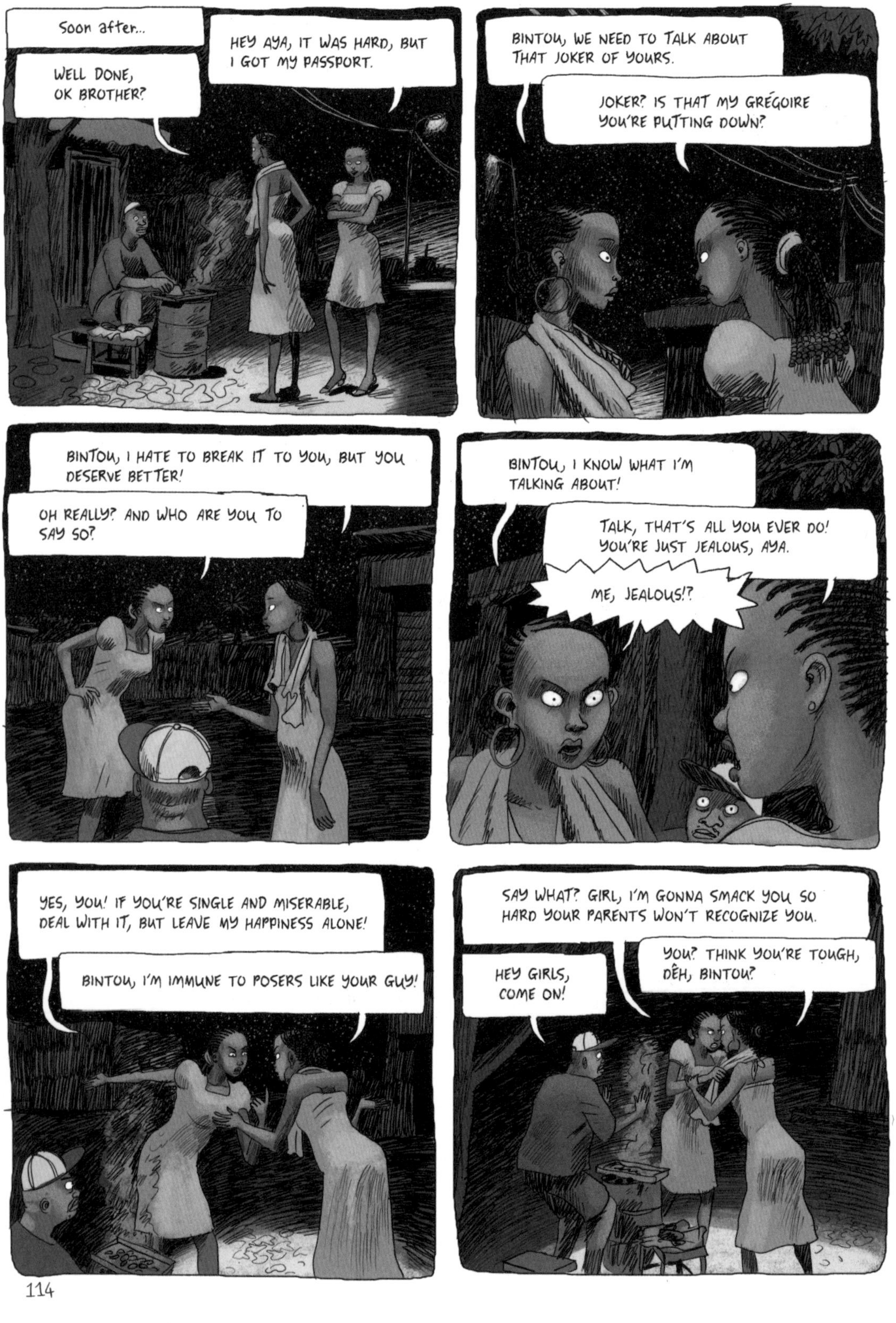
Soon after...
WELL DONE, OK BROTHER?
HEY AYA, IT WAS HARD, BUT I GOT MY PASSPORT.
BINTOU, WE NEED TO TALK ABOUT THAT JOKER OF YOURS.
JOKER? IS THAT MY GRÉGOIRE YOU'RE PUTTING DOWN?
BINTOU, I HATE TO BREAK IT TO YOU, BUT YOU DESERVE BETTER!
OH REALLY? AND WHO ARE YOU TO SAY SO?
BINTOU, I KNOW WHAT I'M TALKING ABOUT!
TALK, THAT'S ALL YOU EVER DO! YOU'RE JUST JEALOUS, AYA.
ME, JEALOUS!?
YES, YOU! IF YOU'RE SINGLE AND MISERABLE, DEAL WITH IT, BUT LEAVE MY HAPPINESS ALONE!
BINTOU, I'M IMMUNE TO POSERS LIKE YOUR GUY!
SAY WHAT? GIRL, I'M GONNA SMACK YOU SO HARD YOUR PARENTS WON'T RECOGNIZE YOU.
HEY GIRLS, COME ON!
YOU? THINK YOU'RE TOUGH, DÊH, BINTOU?

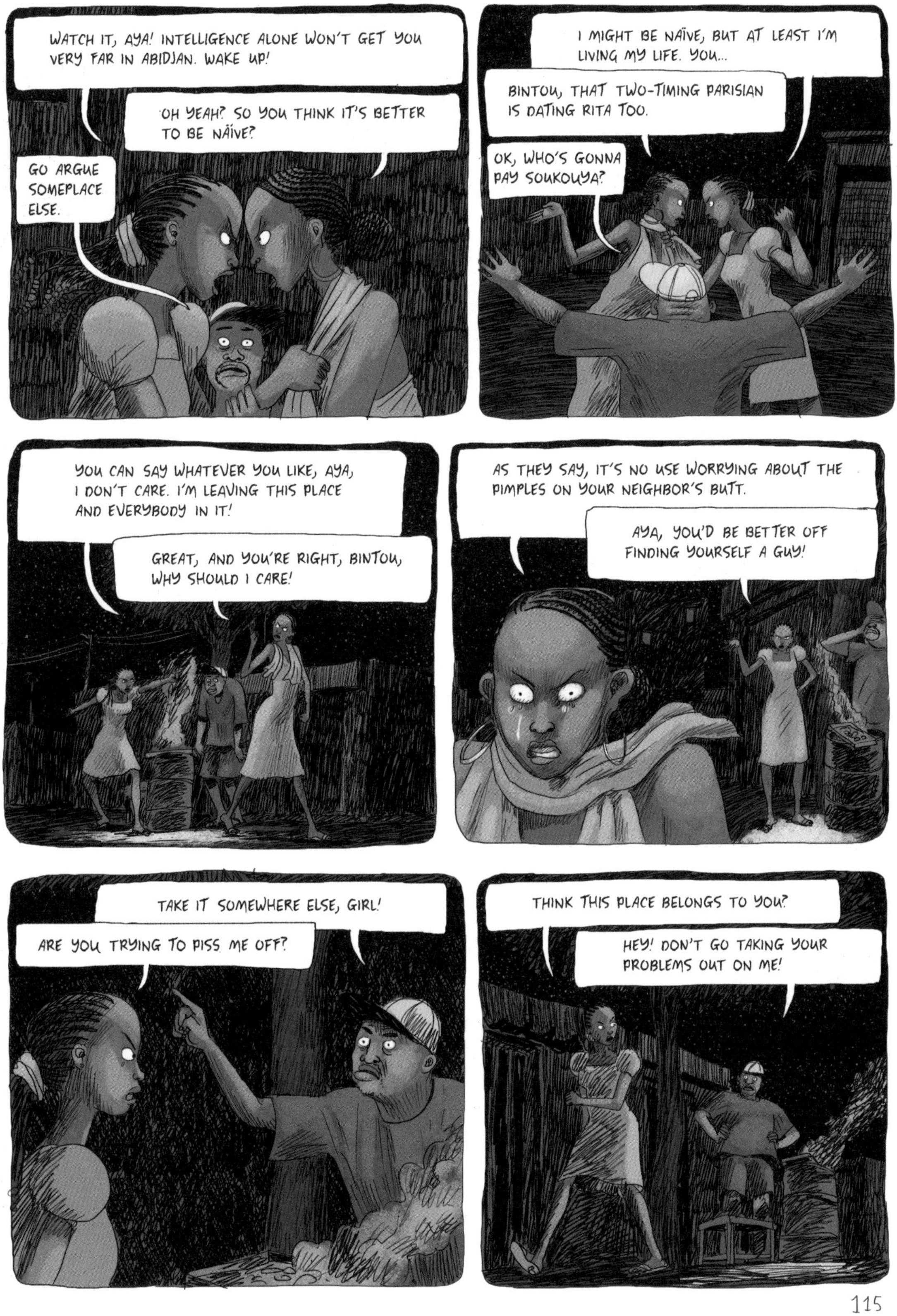
WATCH IT, AYA! INTELLIGENCE ALONE WON'T GET YOU VERY FAR IN ABIDJAN. WAKE UP!
OH YEAH? SO YOU THINK IT'S BETTER TO BE NAÏVE?
GO ARGUE SOMEPLACE ELSE.
I MIGHT BE NAÏVE, BUT AT LEAST I'M LIVING MY LIFE. YOU...
BINTOU, THAT TWO-TIMING PARISIAN IS DATING RITA TOO.
OK, WHO'S GONNA PAY SOUKOUYA?
YOU CAN SAY WHATEVER YOU LIKE, AYA, I DON'T CARE. I'M LEAVING THIS PLACE AND EVERYBODY IN IT!
GREAT, AND YOU'RE RIGHT, BINTOU, WHY SHOULD I CARE!
AS THEY SAY, IT'S NO USE WORRYING ABOUT THE PIMPLES ON YOUR NEIGHBOR'S BUTT.
AYA, YOU'D BE BETTER OFF FINDING YOURSELF A GUY!
TAKE IT SOMEWHERE ELSE, GIRL!
ARE YOU TRYING TO PISS ME OFF?
THINK THIS PLACE BELONGS TO YOU?
HEY! DON'T GO TAKING YOUR PROBLEMS OUT ON ME!

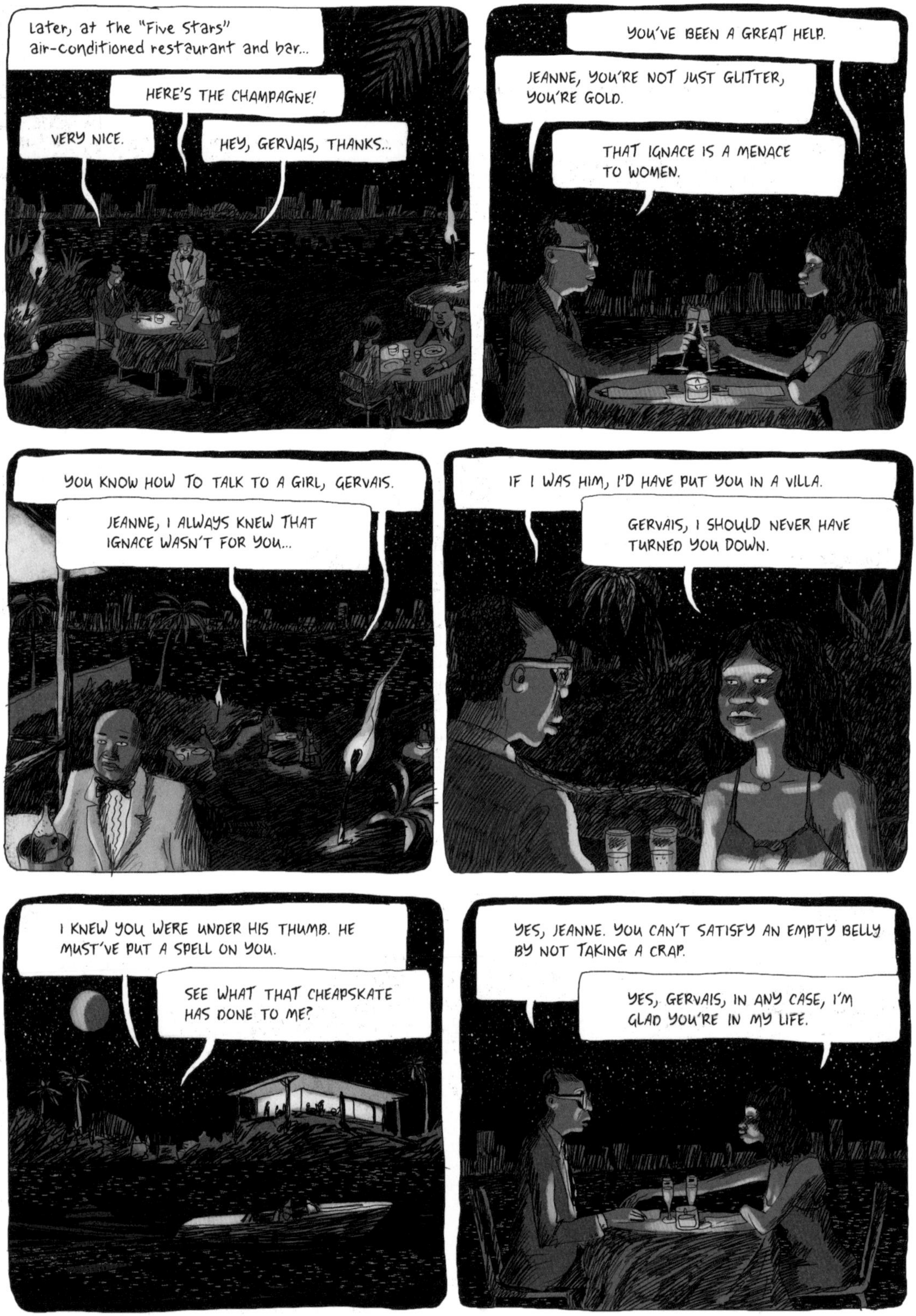
Later, at the "Five Stars" air-conditioned restaurant and bar...
HERE'S THE CHAMPAGNE!
VERY NICE.
HEY, GERVAIS, THANKS...
YOU'VE BEEN A GREAT HELP.
JEANNE, YOU'RE NOT JUST GLITTER, YOU'RE GOLD.
THAT IGNACE IS A MENACE TO WOMEN.
YOU KNOW HOW TO TALK TO A GIRL, GERVAIS.
JEANNE, I ALWAYS KNEW THAT IGNACE WASN'T FOR YOU...
IF I WAS HIM, I'D HAVE PUT YOU IN A VILLA.
GERVAIS, I SHOULD NEVER HAVE TURNED YOU DOWN.
I KNEW YOU WERE UNDER HIS THUMB. HE MUST'VE PUT A SPELL ON YOU.
SEE WHAT THAT CHEAPSKATE HAS DONE TO ME?
YES, JEANNE. YOU CAN'T SATISFY AN EMPTY BELLY BY NOT TAKING A CRAP.
YES, GERVAIS, IN ANY CASE, I'M GLAD YOU'RE IN MY LIFE.

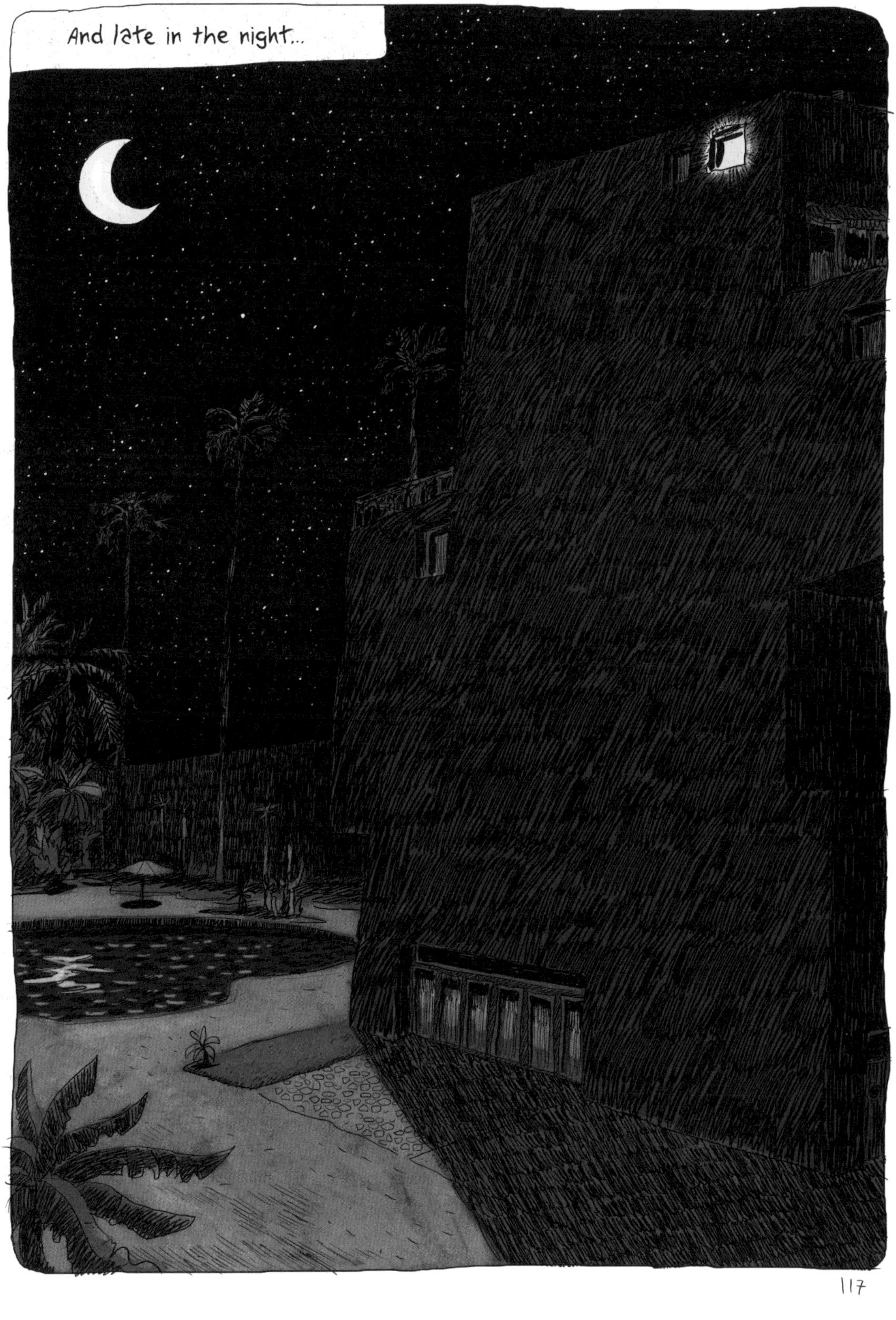
And late in the night...

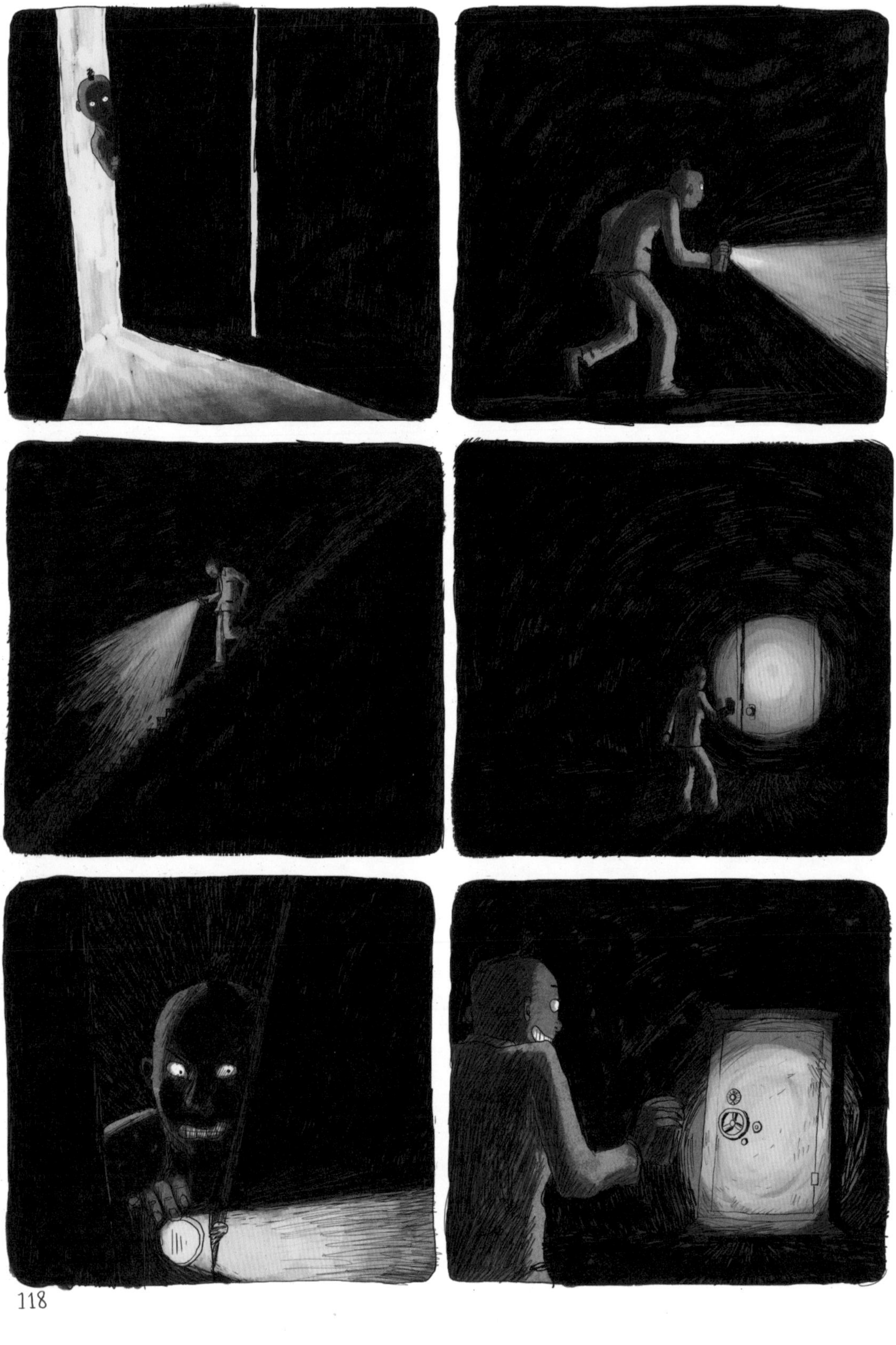

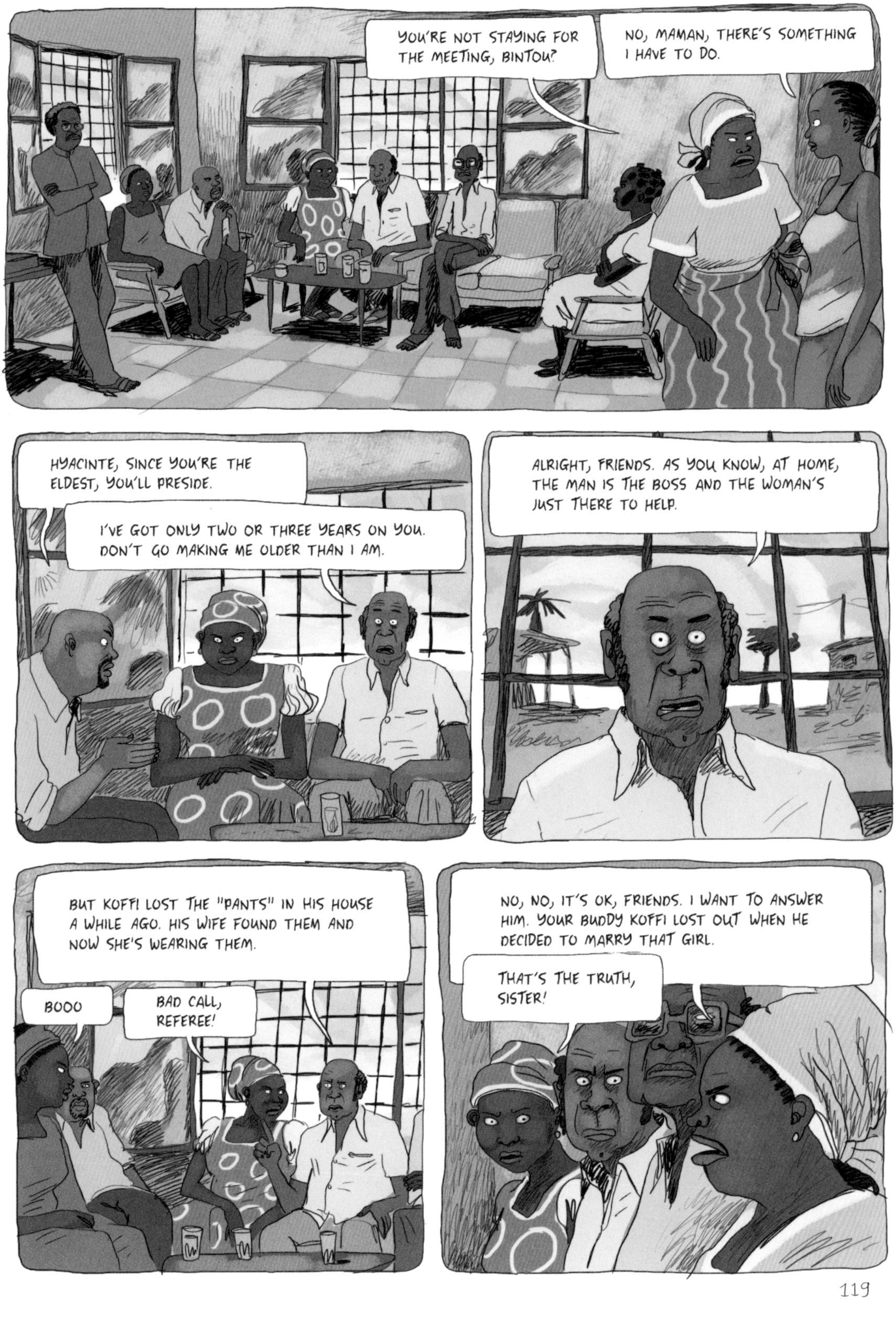

YOU'RE NOT STAYING FOR THE MEETING, BINTOU?
NO, MAMAN, THERE'S SOMETHING I HAVE TO DO.
HYACINTE, SINCE YOU'RE THE ELDEST, YOU'LL PRESIDE.
I'VE GOT ONLY TWO OR THREE YEARS ON YOU. DON'T GO MAKING ME OLDER THAN I AM.
ALRIGHT, FRIENDS. AS YOU KNOW, AT HOME, THE MAN IS THE BOSS AND THE WOMAN'S JUST THERE TO HELP.
BUT KOFFI LOST THE "PANTS" IN HIS HOUSE A WHILE AGO. HIS WIFE FOUND THEM AND NOW SHE'S WEARING THEM.
BOOO
BAD CALL, REFEREE!
NO, NO, IT'S OK, FRIENDS. I WANT TO ANSWER HIM. YOUR BUDDY KOFFI LOST OUT WHEN HE DECIDED TO MARRY THAT GIRL.
THAT'S THE TRUTH, SISTER!

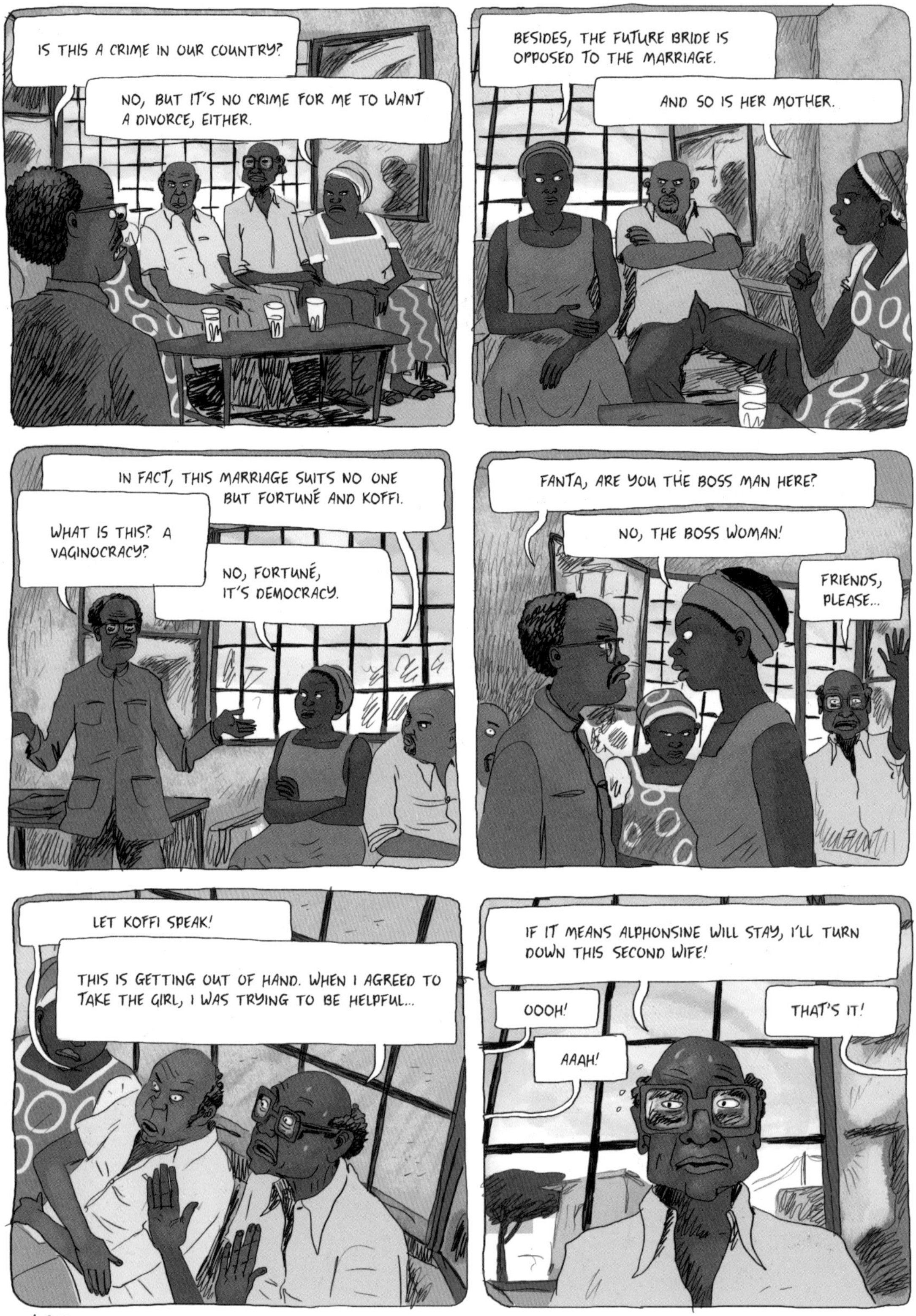
IS THIS A CRIME IN OUR COUNTRY?
NO, BUT IT'S NO CRIME FOR ME TO WANT A DIVORCE, EITHER.
BESIDES, THE FUTURE BRIDE IS OPPOSED TO THE MARRIAGE.
AND SO IS HER MOTHER.
IN FACT, THIS MARRIAGE SUITS NO ONE BUT FORTUNÉ AND KOFFI.
WHAT IS THIS? A VAGINOCRACY?
NO, FORTUNÉ, IT'S DEMOCRACY.
FANTA, ARE YOU THE BOSS MAN HERE?
NO, THE BOSS WOMAN!
FRIENDS, PLEASE...
LET KOFFI SPEAK!
THIS IS GETTING OUT OF HAND. WHEN I AGREED TO TAKE THE GIRL, I WAS TRYING TO BE HELPFUL...
IF IT MEANS ALPHONSINE WILL STAY, I'LL TURN DOWN THIS SECOND WIFE!
OOOH!
AAAH!
THAT'S IT!

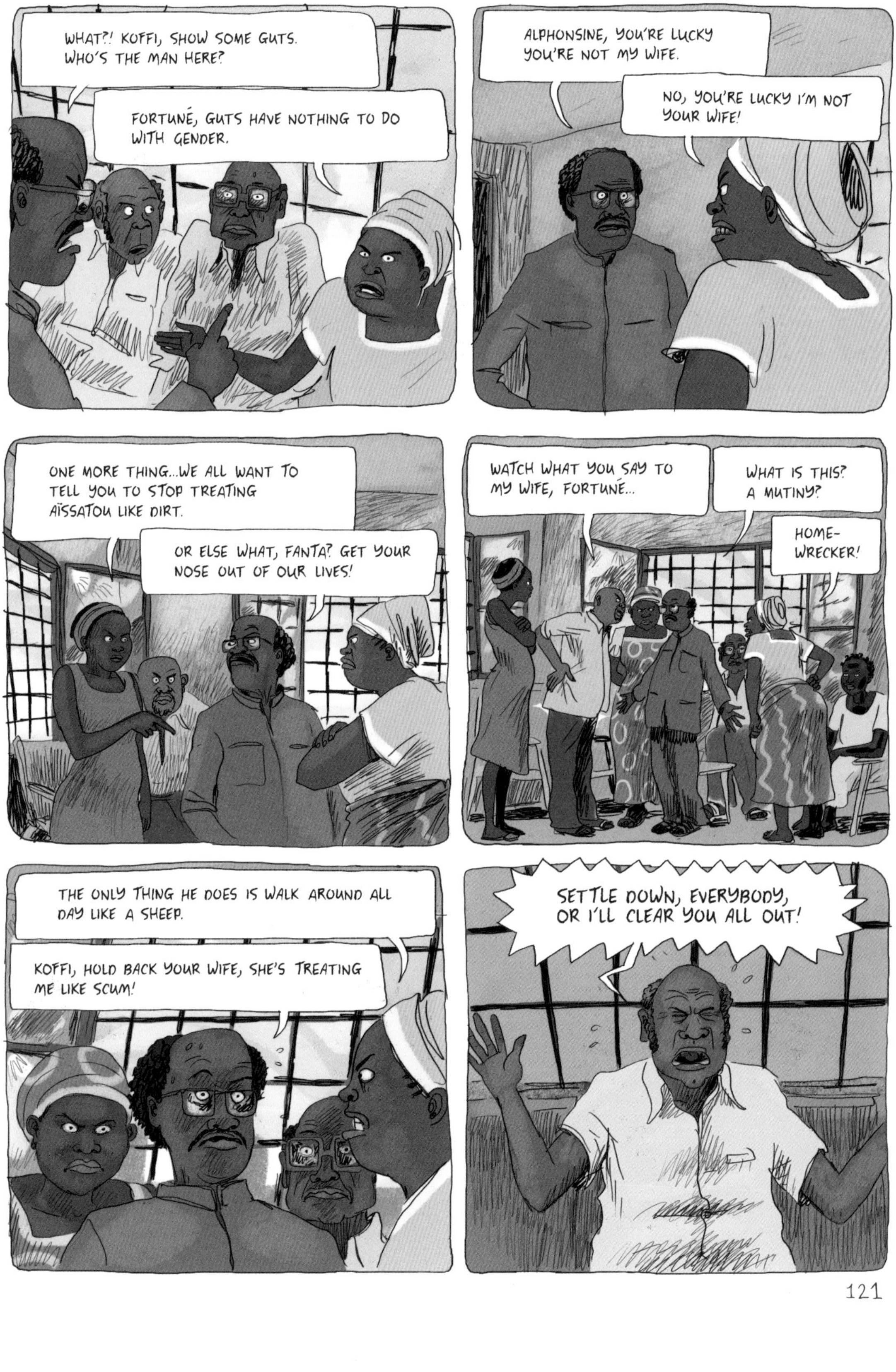
WHAT?! KOFFI, SHOW SOME GUTS. WHO'S THE MAN HERE?
FORTUNÉ, GUTS HAVE NOTHING TO DO WITH GENDER.
ALPHONSINE, YOU'RE LUCKY YOU'RE NOT MY WIFE.
NO, YOU'RE LUCKY I'M NOT YOUR WIFE!
ONE MORE THING...WE ALL WANT TO TELL YOU TO STOP TREATING AÏSSATOU LIKE DIRT.
OR ELSE WHAT, FANTA? GET YOUR NOSE OUT OF OUR LIVES!
WATCH WHAT YOU SAY TO MY WIFE, FORTUNÉ...
WHAT IS THIS? A MUTINY?
HOME-WRECKER!
THE ONLY THING HE DOES IS WALK AROUND ALL DAY LIKE A SHEEP.
KOFFI, HOLD BACK YOUR WIFE, SHE'S TREATING ME LIKE SCUM!
SETTLE DOWN, EVERYBODY, OR I'LL CLEAR YOU ALL OUT!

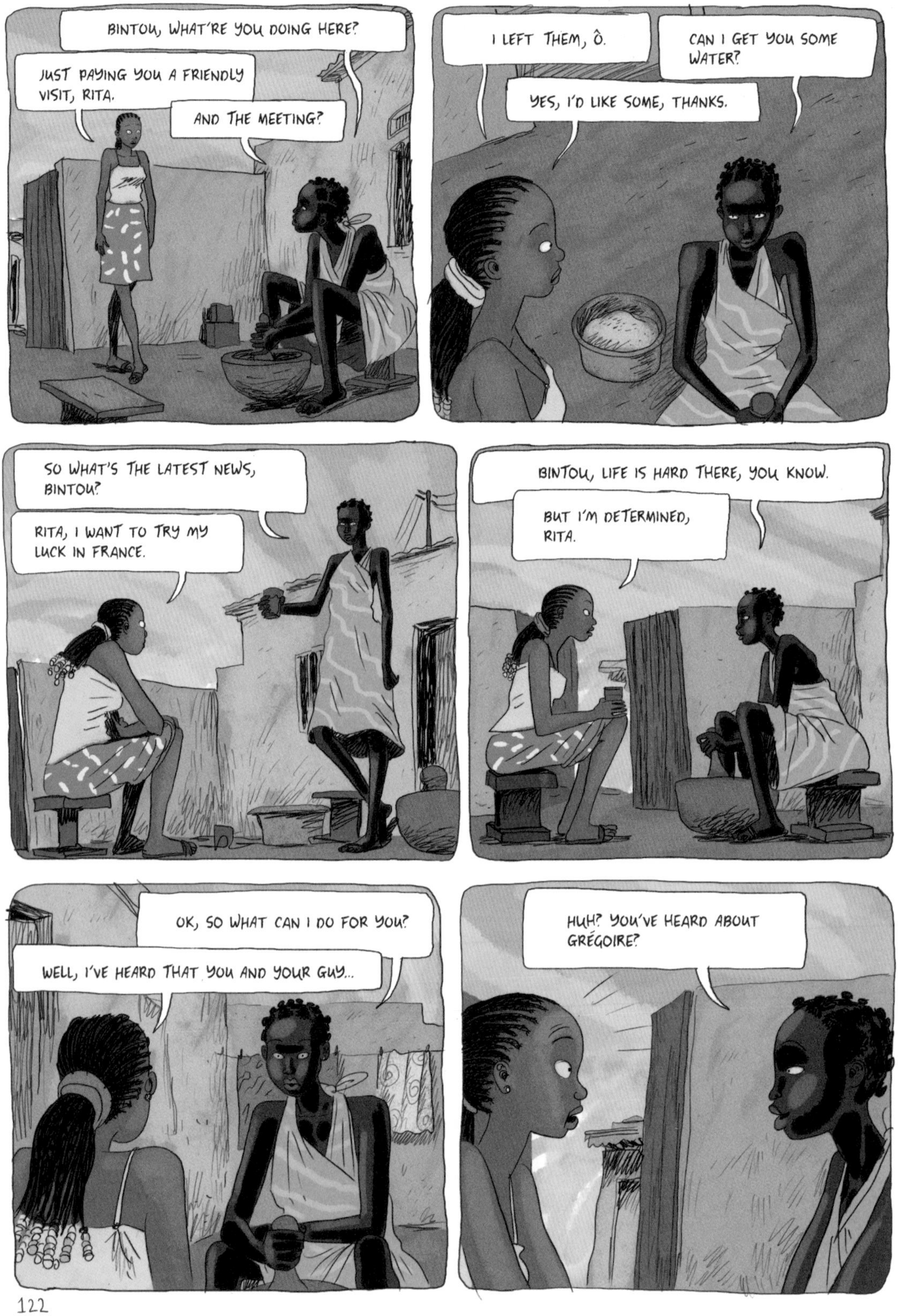
BINTOU, WHAT'RE YOU DOING HERE?
JUST PAYING YOU A FRIENDLY VISIT, RITA.
AND THE MEETING?
I LEFT THEM, Ô.
YES, I'D LIKE SOME, THANKS.
CAN I GET YOU SOME WATER?
SO WHAT'S THE LATEST NEWS, BINTOU?
RITA, I WANT TO TRY MY LUCK IN FRANCE.
BINTOU, LIFE IS HARD THERE, YOU KNOW.
BUT I'M DETERMINED, RITA.
OK, SO WHAT CAN I DO FOR YOU?
WELL, I'VE HEARD THAT YOU AND YOUR GUY...
HUH? YOU'VE HEARD ABOUT GRÉGOIRE?

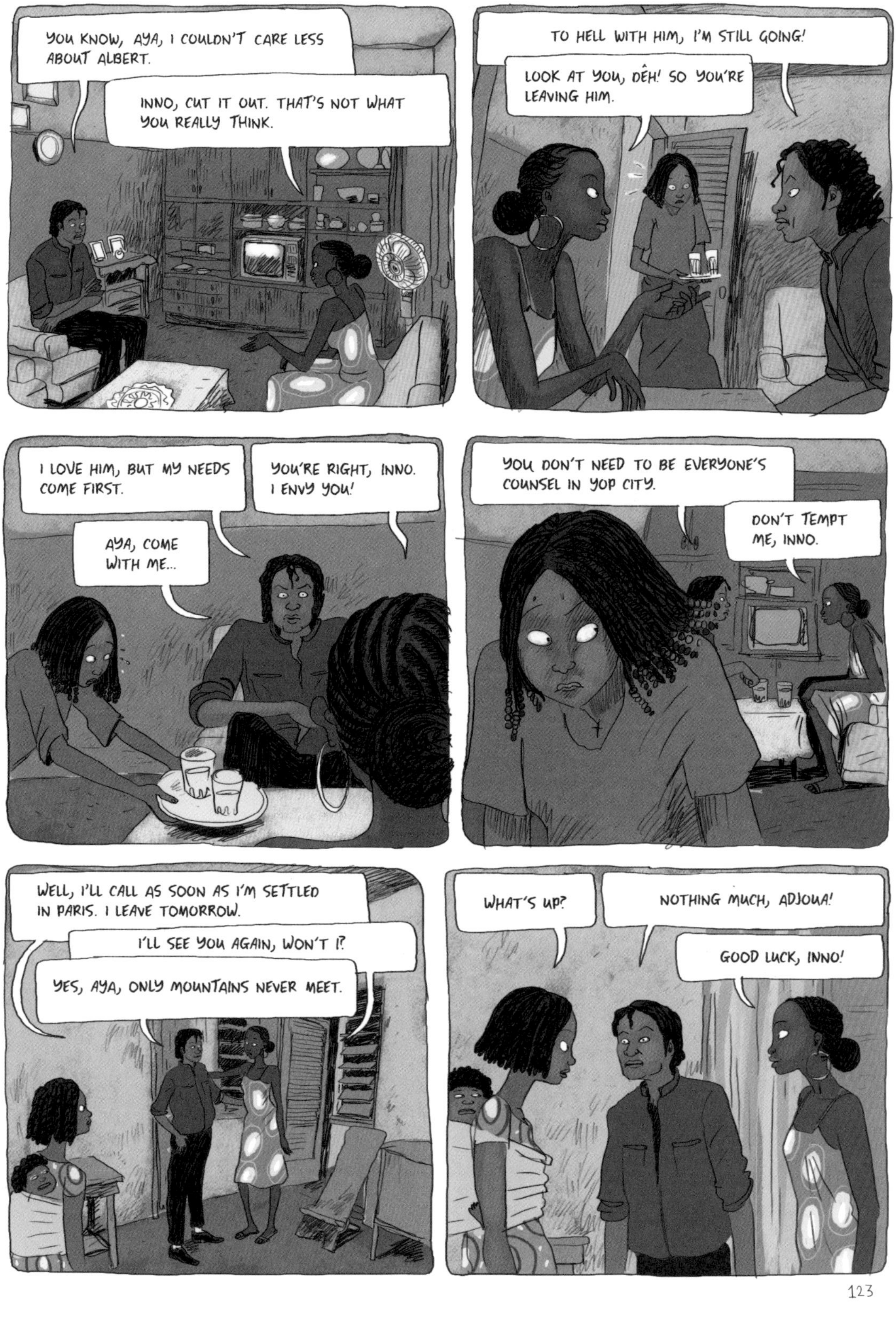

YOU KNOW, AYA, I COULDN'T CARE LESS ABOUT ALBERT.
INNO, CUT IT OUT. THAT'S NOT WHAT YOU REALLY THINK.
TO HELL WITH HIM, I'M STILL GOING!
LOOK AT YOU, DÊH! SO YOU'RE LEAVING HIM.
I LOVE HIM, BUT MY NEEDS COME FIRST.
YOU'RE RIGHT, INNO. I ENVY YOU!
AYA, COME WITH ME...
YOU DON'T NEED TO BE EVERYONE'S COUNSEL IN YOP CITY.
DON'T TEMPT ME, INNO.
WELL, I'LL CALL AS SOON AS I'M SETTLED IN PARIS. I LEAVE TOMORROW.
I'LL SEE YOU AGAIN, WON'T I?
YES, AYA, ONLY MOUNTAINS NEVER MEET.
WHAT'S UP?
NOTHING MUCH, ADJOUA!
GOOD LUCK, INNO!

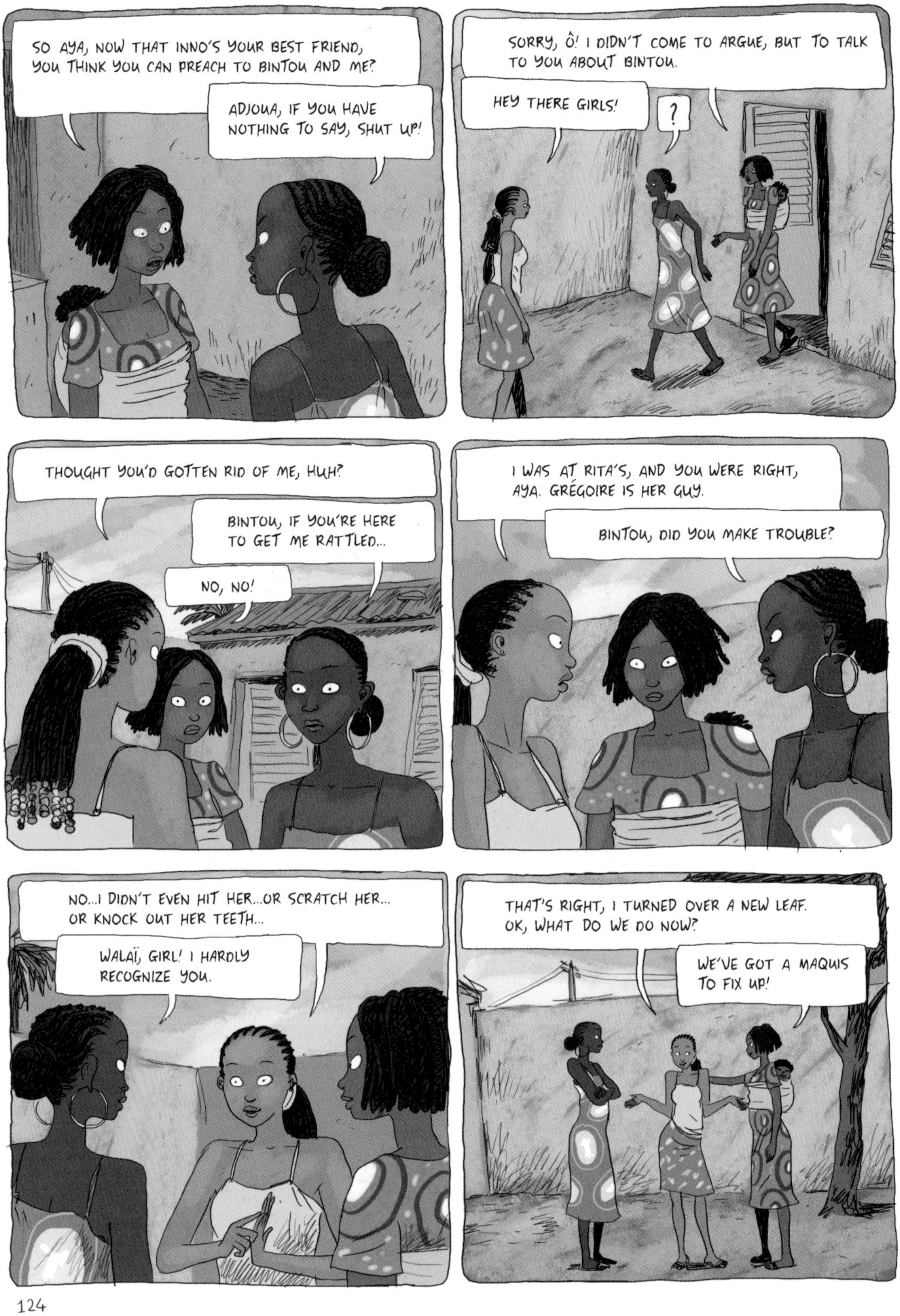
SO AYA, NOW THAT INNO'S YOUR BEST FRIEND, YOU THINK YOU CAN PREACH TO BINTOU AND ME?
ADJOUA, IF YOU HAVE NOTHING TO SAY, SHUT UP!
SORRY, Ô! I DIDN'T COME TO ARGUE, BUT TO TALK TO YOU ABOUT BINTOU.
HEY THERE GIRLS!
?
THOUGHT YOU'D GOTTEN RID OF ME, HUH?
BINTOU, IF YOU'RE HERE TO GET ME RATTLED...
NO, NO!
I WAS AT RITA'S, AND YOU WERE RIGHT, AYA. GRÉGOIRE IS HER GUY.
BINTOU, DID YOU MAKE TROUBLE?
NO...I DIDN'T EVEN HIT HER...OR SCRATCH HER... OR KNOCK OUT HER TEETH...
WALAÏ, GIRL! I HARDLY RECOGNIZE YOU.
THAT'S RIGHT, I TURNED OVER A NEW LEAF. OK, WHAT DO WE DO NOW?
WE'VE GOT A MAQUIS TO FIX UP!

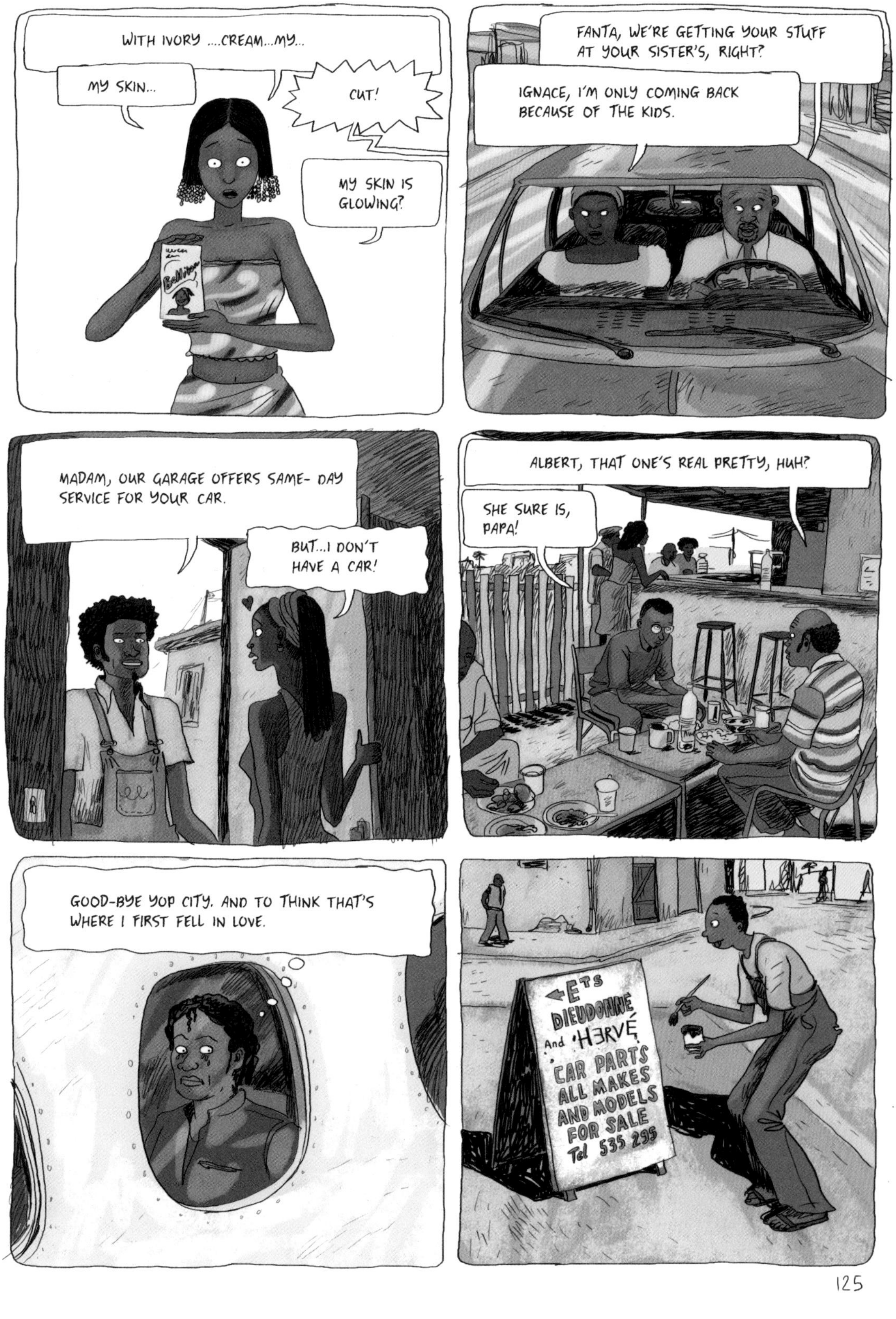
WITH IVORY ....CREAM...MY...
MY SKIN...
CUT!
MY SKIN IS GLOWING?
FANTA, WE'RE GETTING YOUR STUFF AT YOUR SISTER'S, RIGHT?
IGNACE, I'M ONLY COMING BACK BECAUSE OF THE KIDS.
MADAM, OUR GARAGE OFFERS SAME- DAY SERVICE FOR YOUR CAR.
BUT...I DON'T HAVE A CAR!
ALBERT, THAT ONE'S REAL PRETTY, HUH?
SHE SURE IS, PAPA!
GOOD-BYE YOP CITY. AND TO THINK THAT'S WHERE I FIRST FELL IN LOVE.
ETS DIEUDONNÉ And HERVÉ
CAR PARTS ALL MAKES AND MODELS FOR SALE
Tel 535 295

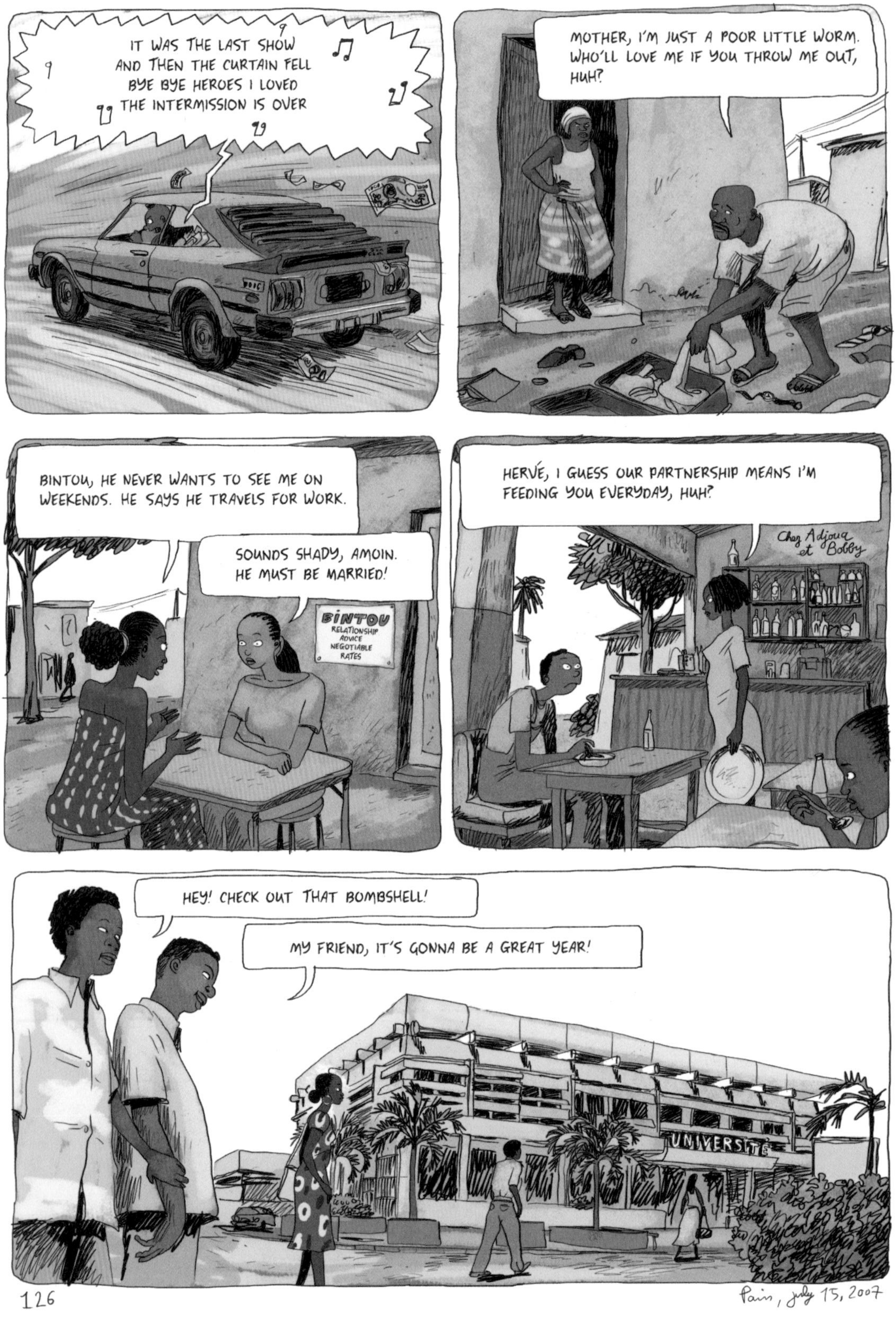
IT WAS THE LAST SHOW AND THEN THE CURTAIN FELL BYE BYE HEROES I LOVED THE INTERMISSION IS OVER
MOTHER, I'M JUST A POOR LITTLE WORM. WHO'LL LOVE ME IF YOU THROW ME OUT, HUH?
BINTOU, HE NEVER WANTS TO SEE ME ON WEEKENDS. HE SAYS HE TRAVELS FOR WORK.
SOUNDS SHADY, AMOIN. HE MUST BE MARRIED!
BINTOU
RELATIONSHIP ADVICE
NEGOTIABLE RATES
HERVÉ, I GUESS OUR PARTNERSHIP MEANS I'M FEEDING YOU EVERYDAY, HUH?
Chez Adjoua et Bobby
HEY! CHECK OUT THAT BOMBSHELL!
MY FRIEND, IT'S GONNA BE A GREAT YEAR!
UNIVERSITÉ

Paris, july 15, 2007

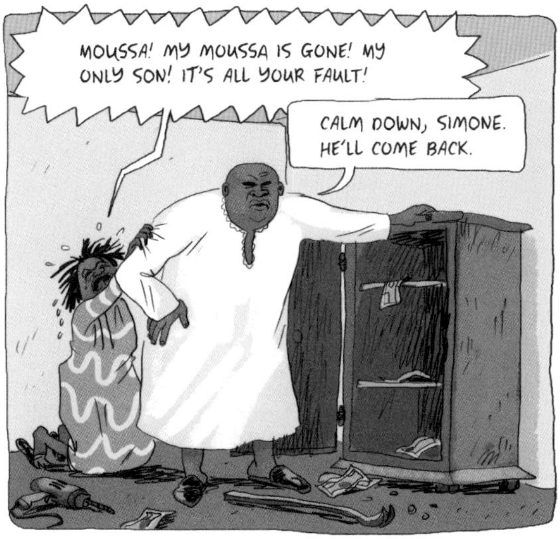
MOUSSA! MY MOUSSA IS GONE! MY ONLY SON! IT'S ALL YOUR FAULT!
CALM DOWN, SIMONE. HE'LL COME BACK.

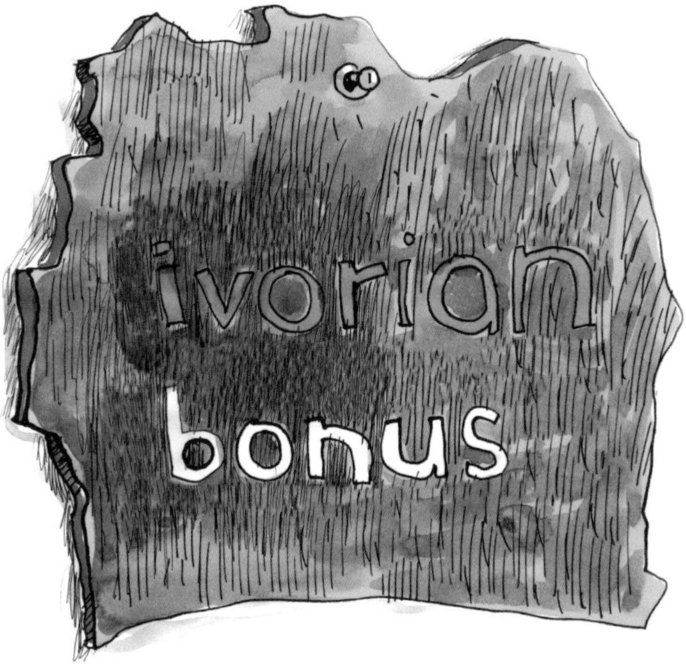
ivorian
bonus

HERE'S A **LITTLE GLOSSARY** TO HELP YOU BETTER UNDERSTAND THE STORY

- BANGALA: SLANG, MALE REPRODUCTIVE ORGAN.
- CLACLOS: SMALL FRIED DUMPLINGS MADE OF RIPE PLANTAINS MIXED WITH FLOUR, ONIONS AND SALT, WITH OR WITHOUT A LITTLE CHILI PEPPER.
- CÔCÔTA: NOOGIE.
- DÈGUÉ: BEVERAGE MADE OF MILLET, CURDLED MILK AND SUGAR.
- FAMILY BOOK: MARRIAGE CERTIFICATE AND OFFICIAL RECORD OF PARENTAGE AND RELATIONSHIPS AMONG FAMILY MEMBERS.
- FOUTOU: DISH OF MASHED PLANTAIN AND CASSAVA.
- GÔ: GIRL.
- IJIOH!: OOH LA LA!
- KOUTOUKOU: A POTENT ALCOHOLIC BEVERAGE DISTILLED FROM PALM WINE.
- MAGGI CUBE: A BRAND OF BOUILLON CUBES COMMONLY USED IN IVORIAN COOKING.
- MAMAN: MOM.
- MAQUIS: OPEN-AIR RESTAURANT WITH CHEAP FOOD, MUSIC AND ROOM TO DANCE.
- PALU: SHORT FORM OF "PALUDISME," THE FRENCH WORD FOR MALARIA. ALSO USED FOR MINOR INFECTIONS, FEVER OR FATIGUE.
- WALAÏ: GOOD LORD!
- WOUBI: GAY.
- YACO: I'M SORRY.

"SO WHERE ARE ALL THE PSYCHOLOGISTS IN AFRICA?"

- "HEY ADJARA, GIRLFRIEND, IT'S BEEN A WHILE, Ô. YOU JUST VANISHED. WHAT WAS THAT ALL ABOUT?"
- "AFFOUÉ, YOU DIDN'T HEAR WHAT HAPPENED TO ME?"
- "WHAT? DID YOU HAVE A DEATH IN THE FAMILY?"
- "EVEN WORSE, GIRLFRIEND, YOU GOTTA HEAR THIS..."
- "GO AHEAD, I'M LISTENING."
- "MY HUSBAND CHEATED ON ME...WITH MY YOUNGER SISTER!!!"
- "WALAÏ, ARE YOU KIDDING ME?"
- "AFFOUÉ, I WAS TRAUMATIZED."
- "I CAN IMAGINE, POOR THING."
- "IT HURT SO MUCH, I EVEN HAD TO GO SEE A PSYCHOLOGIST."
- "A WHAT?"
- "A PSYCHOLOGIST. PEOPLE WHO DEAL WITH MENTAL PROBLEMS..."
- "NO WAY! I CAN SEE HOW IT WAS HARD ON YOU, BUT WHY GO TO A PSYCHOPSY...?"
- "A PSYCHOLOGIST? AFFOUÉ, I WAS IN SUCH PAIN, I THOUGHT OF ENDING IT ALL. SOMEBODY HAD TO HELP ME."
- "SURE, BUT THAT'S YOUR FAMILY'S JOB. AND YOU DIDN'T GO CRAZY. ONLY CRAZY PEOPLE GO TO THE PSYCHOLOCO... OR DID YOU GO NUTS?"
- "AFFOUÉ, HOW CAN YOU SAY THAT?"
- "BECAUSE IF THAT'S THE CASE, GIRLFRIEND, YOU'VE GOT TO TELL ME... THROWING AWAY MONEY WHEN SO MANY PEOPLE NEED IT. NOW THAT'S CRAZY!"

 POOR ADJARA! IF SHE'D KNOWN, SHE NEVER WOULD HAVE TOLD AFFOUÉ THAT SHE HAD GONE TO SEE A PSYCHOLOGIST. THANKS TO AFFOUÉ, THE WHOLE NEIGHBORHOOD'S GOING TO HEAR THAT SHE ALMOST ENDED UP IN THE LOONY BIN. HER NAME WILL BE DIRT IN ALL OF ABIDJAN!

AROUND HERE, IF YOU DECIDE TO STUDY PSYCHOLOGY, PSYCHIATRY, CHILD PSYCHIATRY OR ANYTHING ELSE THAT STARTS WITH "PSY-", IT'S BECAUSE YOU DON'T WANT TO WORK AFTER YOUR STUDIES OR YOU JUST WANT TO WASTE YOUR TIME ON SCHOOL BENCHES, WEARING A HOLE IN THE SEAT OF YOUR PANTS OR SKIRT. BECAUSE ONCE YOU GET YOUR DIPLOMA, YOU WON'T FIND ANY PATIENTS. THAT'S FOR THE GOOD AND SIMPLE REASON THAT AFRICANS THINK YOU MUST BE ON THE VERGE OF LOSING YOUR MIND IF YOU GO SEE THESE DOCTORS. AND FOR AFRICANS, LOSING YOUR MIND IS THE WORST ILLNESS IN THE WORLD, EXCEPT MAYBE NOT BEING ABLE TO EAT CHICKEN KÉDJÉNOU, OR PEANUT SAUCE, OR GRILLED FISH...

SO NOW YOU'RE WONDERING, HOW DO ALL THESE KIDS COPE WHEN THEY FIND OUT THEY HAVE NEW BROTHERS AND SISTERS? HOW DO THESE WOMEN WHO HAVE BEEN CHEATED ON CONTINUE WITH THEIR LIVES? AND HOW DO THE MEN KEEP GOING - MEN WHO LOSE THEIR JOBS OVERNIGHT OR END UP ON THE STREET BECAUSE THEY HAVE NO MONEY TO PAY THE RENT?

AS FAR AS THE KIDS GO, WELL, THEY SIMPLY DEAL WITH IT.

WITH SO MANY NEIGHBORS AND FAMILY MEMBERS GOING THROUGH SIMILAR SITUATIONS, THEY GET USED TO THESE SOAP OPERAS. IT'S ALL PART OF DAILY LIFE.

SO IF THE FATHER NEXT DOOR LIVES WITH THREE WIVES AND ALL THEIR MANY CHILDREN, OR IF THE KIDS' FRIENDS INTRODUCE THEM TO NEW BROTHERS AND SISTERS FROM THE SAME FATHER BUT NOT THE SAME MOTHER, THEY'RE NOT SHOCKED IN THE LEAST. AND IT'S NO BIG DEAL FOR CHILDREN TO COME LIVE WITH THEM WITHOUT THEIR PARENTS AND TO BE INTRODUCED AS COUSINS. THE KIDS ARE TOLD TO CONSIDER THEM AS BROTHERS AND SISTERS, BECAUSE ULTIMATELY, WHAT REALLY MATTERS IS FORMING A REAL FAMILY.

IN AFRICA, CHILDREN ARE THE ONES WHO ARE MOST RESILIENT IN THESE SITUATIONS. THAT'S BECAUSE THEY'RE LUCKY ENOUGH TO BE PART OF A LARGE FAMILY.

THERE'S THE LARGE FAMILY AT HOME, OF COURSE, BUT THE NEIGHBOR-HOOD MAKES UP A LARGE FAMILY AS WELL. SO CHILDREN DON'T HAVE TO BEAR THE BRUNT OF ADULT QUARRELS.

THEY HAVE MORE INTERESTING THINGS TO DO THAN TO FRET ABOUT FAMILY DRAMAS, LIKE PLAYING WITH FRIENDS OR - THIS IS A FAVORITE - SIZING EACH OTHER UP BY COUNTING HOW MANY BROTHERS AND SISTERS THEY HAVE.

OUR PSYCHOLOGISTS ARE THE PEOPLE AROUND US.

IT'S A WHOLE OTHER STORY FOR THE ADULTS, THOUGH. THEY SUFFER SO MUCH THAT SOME GO SEE WITCH DOCTORS. NOT TO HEAL THEIR EMO-TIONAL PAIN; THERE'S NO SENSE IN IT AND THAT'S NOT THE MOST IMPOR-TANT THING. INSTEAD, WITCH DOCTORS ARE ASKED TO BRING BACK LOVED ONES WHO STRAY, HELP A WIFE MAKE HER HUSBAND MORE VIGOROUS IN BED, DISPENSE A MAGIC POTION THAT WILL LET YOU GET A RAISE OUT OF YOUR BOSS OR MAKE SOMEONE LOVE YOU MORE THAN ANOTHER.

BUT DO ANY OF THESE REALLY WORK...ESPECIALLY THE POTION TO IMPROVE SEXUAL PERFORMANCE? I COULDN'T TELL YOU BECAUSE I'VE NEVER TRIED THEM!

- AYA

THE FIRST TIME I WENT TO SEE A PSYCHOLOGIST WAS IN PARIS. I HAD JUST ARRIVED FROM MY HOME COUNTRY OF IVORY COAST. I WAS 12 YEARS OLD AND I WAS GOING INTO 6TH GRADE. THE PRINCIPAL, WHO KNEW THAT I'D LEFT MY PARENTS, TOOK PITY ON ME AND ASKED THAT I BE MONITORED BY A CHILD PSYCHIATRIST. TWICE A WEEK FOR AN HOUR, I FOUND MYSELF SITTING IN FRONT OF A STRANGE MAN WHO DIDN'T TALK MUCH AND ALWAYS START- ED THE CONVERSATION WITH "SO HOW ARE YOU DOING TODAY?"

YOU CAN IMAGINE HOW PROUD I WAS! I HAD SOMEONE ALL TO MYSELF WHO LISTENED WITHOUT SAYING A WORD AND SMILED AT EVERY SEN- TENCE I UTTERED. I HAD BECOME A VERY IMPORTANT PERSON IN FRANCE. BUT THE BEST THING ABOUT OUR MEETINGS WAS THE PASTRIES AND CANDIES ON HIS DESK THAT I WAS ALLOWED TO EAT. THOSE SWEETS HELPED ME A LOT IN TELLING HIM THE WHOLE STORY OF MY SHORT 12-YEAR OLD LIFE (WHICH WAS ALREADY PRETTY FULL OF EXPERIENCE, RIGHT?). I TOLD HIM ABOUT MY FAMILY (IN ALL THE DETAILS), THINGS THE NEIGHBORS HAD DONE (SPICY), AND MY MISFORTUNES (MEMORABLE) WITH MY GIRLFRIENDS (HOW WE'D MEET UP TO HAVE A FIGHT OR HOW WE MADE A LITTLE MONEY BY DANCING, AND SO ON). IN A NUTSHELL, I TOLD HIM ANYTHING AND EVERYTHING. IN FACT, HE GOT TO HEAR WHATEVER WAS PASSING THROUGH MY POOR HEAD, AND WHEN I HAD NOTHING LEFT TO TELL, I'D MAKE UP STORIES. I DIDN'T WANT HIM TO STOP OUR SESSIONS JUST BECAUSE I DIDN'T HAVE ANYTHING LEFT TO SAY. DID HE BELIEVE ME OR NOT? WHAT WAS HE DOING WITH ALL THOSE NOTES AND ALL MY STORIES? WOULD HE MENTION THEM TO THE SCHOOL PRINCIPAL OR THE PRESIDENT OF FRANCE? I NEVER FOUND OUT. BUT MY TEETH GOT TO KNOW WHAT CAVITIES FEEL LIKE. WHEN I TOLD MY MOTHER OVER THE PHONE THAT I WAS SEEING A PSYCHOLOGIST, AND HOW GREAT IT WAS, AND HOW I NEVER WANTED IT TO END, AND THAT HE WAS SO KIND TO ME BECAUSE HE LET ME GO ON FOR HOURS AND GAVE ME TASTY TREATS TO EAT, AND THAT I HAD FINALLY FOUND SOMEONE WHO WAS INTERESTED IN WHAT I HAD TO SAY IN THIS NEW COUNTRY, SHE BURST INTO TEARS. FRANCE HAD DRIVEN HER LITTLE GIRL CRAZY. BUT I THINK SHE WAS CAREFUL TO NOT MENTION ANY OF IT TO PEOPLE IN THE NEIGHBORHOOD.

- MARGUERITE ABOUET

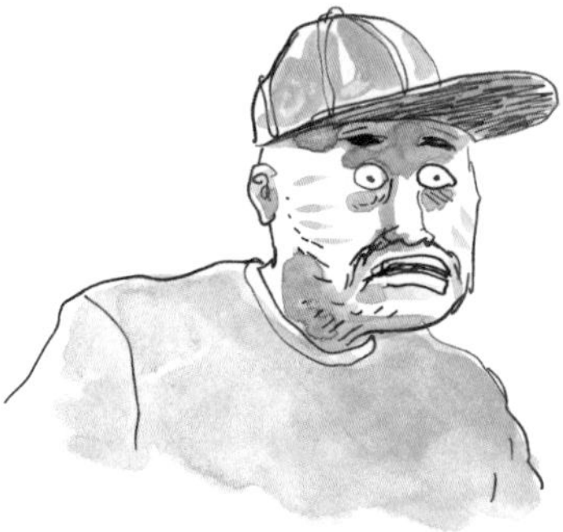

HEY, I'M IN THE BOOK TOO, Y'KNOW. ALRIGHT, I'M GOING TO SHOW YOU HOW TO MAKE "SOUKOUYA." WITH ME BEING A SMALL-TIME SOUKOUYA VENDOR, THIS RECIPE WILL MAKE ME FAMOUS, WHICH WOULD BE GREAT!

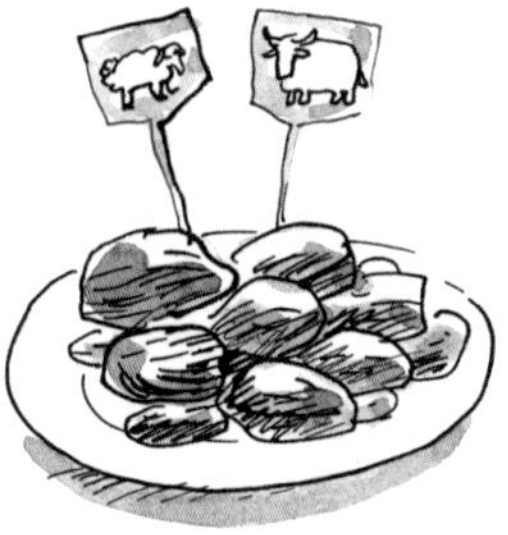

FOR 2 PEOPLE:

- 500 GRAMS OF MUTTON
(OR OTHER MEAT, BUT MUTTON IS THE MOST TENDER, DÊH!)

- 1 LARGE ONION

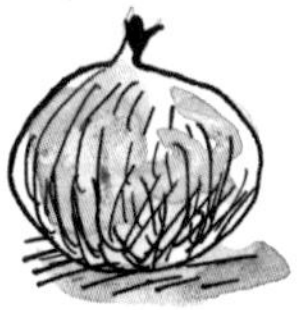

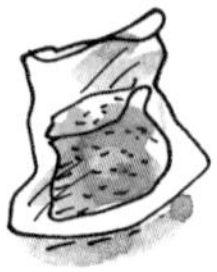

- CHILI PEPPER

(THIS IS FOR YOU TO SEE IF YOU'RE MAN ENOUGH TO HANDLE IT, DÊH!)

- 1 MAGGI CUBE

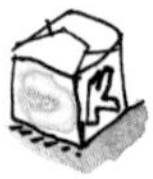

CUT THE MEAT INTO PIECES, PLACE THEM IN A BOWL, ADD THE MAGGI CUBE AND MIX WELL. THEN PLACE THE MEAT IN A GRILL PAN AND TURN IT OVER FROM TIME TO TIME. WHEN THE MEAT IS ALMOST COOKED THROUGH, ADD THE CHOPPED ONION AND THE CHILI PEPPER, STIR AND SERVE HOT, DÊH, AND EAT IT WITH ANYTHING YOU WANT. ENJOY YOUR SOUKOUYA!

GIRLFRIENDS

MY BRAISED CHICKEN IS BETTER THAN TANTIE
AFFOUÉ'S.
I'LL GIVE YOU MY RECIPE SO YOU CAN SEE FOR
YOURSELF HOW DELICIOUS MY COOKING IS.

"ADJOUA'S BRAISED CHICKEN"

SERVES 4:

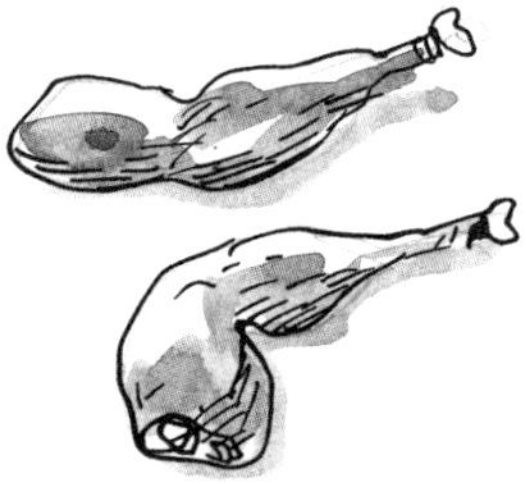

- 4 THIGHS FROM FREE-RANGE CHICKENS

- 1 BUNCH OF PARSLEY

- 2 LARGE ONIONS

- 1 SMALL PIECE OF GINGER

- OIL, SALT, AND PEPPER

- A MAGGI CUBE

- 2 GARLIC CLOVES

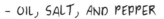

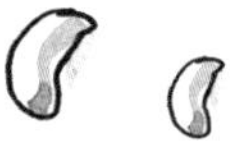

PURÉE GINGER, PARSLEY, GARLIC, AND ONION IN A BLENDER AND PLACE THE
MIXTURE INTO A BOWL. ADD SALT, PEPPER, AND THE MAGGI CUBE. COAT THE
CHICKEN PIECES, PLACE THEM ON THE GRILL AND COOK, TURNING THEM FROM
TIME TO TIME.

MY SPECIAL TOUCH: IN A FRYING PAN, BRAISE THE GRILLED CHICKEN PIECES
AND THE REMAINING SPICE MIX IN A BIT OF OIL FOR 15 MINUTES. SERVE HOT.

YOU CAN ACCOMPANY THIS DISH WITH ATTIÉKÉ (CASSAVA SEMOLINA), RICE,
FRIED OR MASHED YAMS, FRIED OR BOILED POTATOES, OR COUSCOUS. ENJOY!

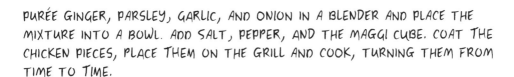

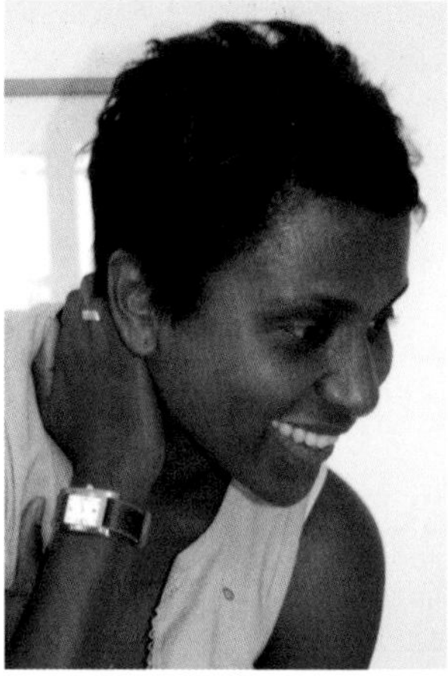
© Antoine Delesvaux

Marguerite Abouet was born in Abidjan in 1971. Her mother was a management secretary at Singer and her father was a salesman at Hitachi. She grew up with her family in the working-class neighborhood of Yopougon. When she was 12, her parents sent her and her older brother to Paris to live with their great-uncle and pursue "extensive studies." Breaking off her studies earlier than expected, she began to write novels that she didn't show to anyone, and was by turns a punk, a super-nanny for triplets, a caregiver for the elderly, a waitress, a data entry clerk and a legal assistant at a law firm. She now lives in Romainville, a suburb of Paris, and spends all of her time writing. *Aya* and *Aya of Yop City* were her first graphic novels. Written in a fresh voice and with a keen sense of humor, it told the story of an Africa far removed from clichés, war and famine. In 2006, Marguerite Abouet and Clément Oubrerie received the prize for best first comic book at the prestigious Angoulême International Comics Festival.

Clément Oubrerie was born in Paris in 1966. After completing high school, he enrolled at the Penninghen School of Graphic Arts, breaking off his studies after four years to visit the United States. He stayed there for two years, holding down various odd jobs and seeing his work published for the first time before landing in a New Mexico jail for working without papers. Back in France, he went on to a prolific career in illustration as the author of more than 40 children's books and as a digital animator. He is the graphic talent behind several television series, including *Moot-Moot*, produced by Eric Judor and Ramzy Bedia. He is also the co-founder of the La Station animation studio and Autochenille Productions, which is working on the screen adaptation of Joann Sfar's *The Rabbi's Cat*. In the *Aya* books, his first graphic novels, his unique talent brings Marguerite Abouet's stories to life with vibrant spirit and authenticity.
http://clementoubrerie.blogspot.com

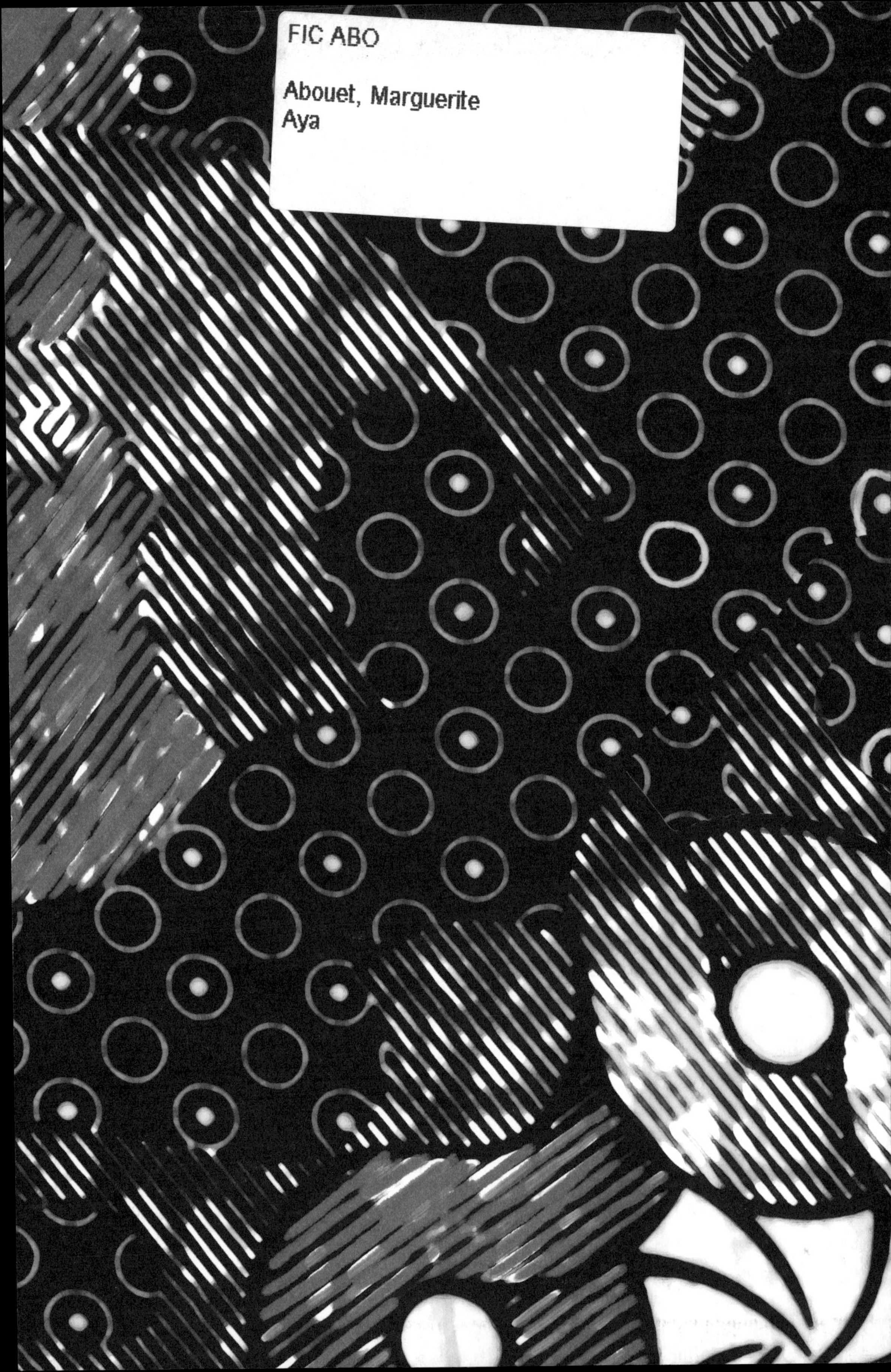